Darwin and Archaeology

Darwin and Archaeology

A Handbook of Key Concepts

EDITED BY John P. Hart
AND John Edward Terrell

Foreword by Gary M. Feinman

BERGIN & GARVEY
Westport, Connecticut • London

Library of Congress Cataloging-in-Publication Data

Darwin and archaeology : a handbook of key concepts / edited by John P. Hart and John
Edward Terrell ; foreword by Gary M. Feinman.
     p.   cm.
   Includes bibliographical references and index.
   ISBN 0–89789–878–8 (alk. paper)—ISBN 0–89789–879–6 (pbk. : alk. paper)
   1. Human evolution.   2. Evolution (Biology)   3. Social evolution.   4. Natural
selection.   5. Anthropology.   6. Archaeology.   7. Ethnoarchaeology.   8. Darwin,
Charles, 1809–1882—Contributions in archaeology.   I. Hart, John P.   II. Terrell, John.
GN281.D39   2002
930.1—dc21   2001043975

British Library Cataloguing in Publication Data is available.

Library of Congress Catalog Card Number: 2001043975
ISBN: 0–89789–878–8
     0–89789–879–6 (pbk.)

First published in 2002

Bergin & Garvey, 88 Post Road West, Westport, CT 06881
An imprint of Greenwood Publishing Group, Inc.
www.greenwood.com

Printed in the United States of America

The paper used in this book complies with the
Permanent Paper Standard issued by the National
Information Standards Organization (Z39.48–1984).

10 9 8 7 6 5 4 3 2 1

Contents

Foreword *by Gary M. Feinman* vii

Table of Key Words xv

1. Introduction 1
   John Edward Terrell and John P. Hart

2. Adaptation 15
   Todd L. VanPool

3. Biological Constraints 29
   James Steele

4. Cause 49
   Michael J. O'Brien and R. Lee Lyman

5. Classification 69
   R. Lee Lyman and Michael J. O'Brien

6. Complexity 89
   John Kantner

7. Culture 107
   Paul Roscoe

8. Descent 125
   Scott MacEachern

9. History 143
   Sibel Barut Kusimba and Chapurukha M. Kusimba

10. Individuals   161
     Dean R. Snow

11. Learning   183
     Stephen J. Shennan

12. Models   201
     Bruce Winterhalder

13. Natural Selection   225
     Robert D. Leonard and George T. Jones

14. Population   243
     Kevin M. Kelly

About the Contributors   257

Foreword

Gary M. Feinman

In the anglophile scholarly world, the intellectual roots of evolutionary studies (including Darwinian approaches), anthropology, and archaeology are closely intertwined, extending back in their academic heritage for roughly a century and a half. Nevertheless, the appropriate and most scientifically productive relationships between these intellectual domains and the future agendas for them remain unresolved and a matter of significant current discussion and debate (e.g., Barton and Clark 1997; Gould 1997a, 1997b; Maschner 1996; Sanderson 1990; Spencer 1997; Wilson 1998). In this encyclopedic volume, key evolutionary constructs and concepts are explored to reflect on and clarify the potential for Darwinian evolutionary perspectives to inform and help chart a more synthetic course for contemporary anthropological archaeology.

In the spirit of full disclosure, I confess that I have never really considered myself a Darwinian archaeologist, nor has a reading of this set of papers caused me to have a midnight conversion. Yet as an anthropological archaeologist working in a natural history museum, who has interests in evolution, history, and change, it is impossible to remain dispassionate in regard to the central issues and questions raised in this text. After all, one day recently, the popular media trumpeted "academic warfare" (Shulevitz 2001) between scientific and humanistic intellectual streams in American anthropology, while practically the next day it speculated on the relationship between a simpler-than-expected human genetic code and the diversity that we recognize in our species (Karow 2001). With such pivotal and contemporary debates at stake, my aim here is to provide a somewhat critical commentary on the diverse range of theoretical perspectives offered in this compendium, while endeavoring to define a productive common ground. At the same time I stress, in voice with the vision of the editors, why a concern with language and effective terminology is so central to framing a more holistic twenty-first century investigation of the human career.

SETTING AN AGENDA

Although evolution and archaeology have had a long and close relationship, they still have not arrived at a satisfactory marriage. For example, the contributors to one recent collection that was aimed at reintroducing Darwinian thought to archaeology open their article by noting: "an unfortunate parallel between evolutionary archaeology and the weather: everyone *talks* about it but no one *does* anything about it" (Bettinger and Eerkens 1997: 177; emphasis in original). In large part, this discrepancy stems from the fact that in archaeology there is precious little current agreement about what an evolutionary approach should constitute, and what its principal theoretical aims should be. This lack of focus and consensus in regard to overarching questions and research goals is unfortunate; for as the renowned biologist Ernst Mayr (1999: 373) opined wisely: "The most memorable lesson I have learned from Darwin is that the most important thing in scientific research is not to add to the accumulation of facts, but to ask challenging questions and to try to answer them."

In this regard, there seems little convincing reason to shrink from or reduce the central scientific mission that anthropological archaeology, particularly in the United States, long has had. In his classic article, "The Aims of Anthropological Research," Franz Boas (1932: 606) wrote,

we may . . . best define our objective as the attempt to understand the steps by which man has come to be what he is biologically, psychologically, and culturally. Thus it appears . . . that our material must necessarily be historical material, historical in the widest sense of the term.

Given its fundamental attributes, especially time depth, contemporary archaeology remains pivotal to the investigation of Boas' still-vital and valid scientific mission, that is, the comparative study of human behavior and diversity, and how cultural and biological diversity has come to be. Archaeology is particularly vital to the investigation of the latter necessarily diachronic agenda, although an approach with just the proper balance between the history, comparison, and the systematics of science has remained elusive (see Feinman 1994; Johnson 1999; Trigger 1989).

Given Boas' unfinished agenda and the centrality that his broad mission gives to the enterprise of most contemporary archaeologists, why has a unified approach and a sense of mission been so difficult to achieve? In part, the problem may stem from changes in the way we are trained as

professionals and the lack of constructive communication and dialogue between the increasingly balkanized subdisciplines of anthropology and even
segmented schools within archaeology (e.g., Givens and Skomal 1993). Yet
the lack of constructive intercourse between different intellectual schools
often has been amplified by the philosophical view that there is only one
truly valid or scientific approach or paradigm to address evolutionary questions in our field. To paraphrase Matthew Johnson (1999: 187; see also
Feinman 1994), the way that our core literature in archaeology has frequently been polarized in this way often has fostered the impression that
"there ain't nothin' in the middle of the road 'cept white lines and dead
armadillos."

CONSTRUCTING A SYNTHESIS

The mission outlined for diachronic investigation by Boas involves a suite
of "big messy" questions regarding the human career. By definition, to
account for the biological and cultural diversity that we see in peoples
today, we must concern ourselves with both the distinct historical pathways
(Terrell 1986) that different members of our species traveled and empirically observable, broader directional trends that are neither unilineal, progressive, nor necessary (Gould 1988). The latter trends, which cross-cut
specific historical contexts, include (among other phenomena) aspects of
demographic growth and expansion, the increasing size of human groups
and groupings, and generally expanded degrees of differential wealth and
power.

As seen in this collection, the investigation of such issues requires the
interlocking consideration of diverse theoretical domains. These conceptual
domains must range from (but are by no means limited to) human biological capacities and the interplay between learned behavior and natural
selection, to different strategies of social reproduction and cultural transmission, and the definition of selective forces that may account for the
emergence of hierarchical forms of human organization.

If our overarching explanatory framework is to be truly evolutionary,
then it also must concern itself with both scientific meanings of that term
(Rambo 1991: 26–28). That is, the term "evolution" generally has been
used to refer to both the succession of forms that have evolved over time
and to the process of evolution, which includes the contextual circumstances and causal mechanisms that lead to such changes in form. This dual
usage applies whether one is speaking of the neo-Darwinian synthesis in
biological evolution or a more colloquial concern with the evolution of
information-processing technologies. In both instances, an understanding
of the historical sequence of forms and a concern with the causal mechanisms and selective forces that account for these changes are requisite.

We see in this collection that a broad agenda has been outlined for evolutionary archaeology, along with a wide array of complex issues that could be encompassed by such an overarching theoretical approach. How do we proceed? I would propose that the current, rather unbridled plurality of approaches and philosophies is not the most productive direction, because it tends to hinder effective communication and interchange across scholarly cells that ascribe to their own distinctive and specialized languages and underpinning assumptions.

In this volume and more broadly in the discipline, two other alternatives are evident. One is to strive for paradigmatic theoretical unity, which in some contributions here is (but does not necessarily have to be) based on Darwinian reductionism. This analytical approach endeavors to construct a single theory that relies largely, if not entirely, on Darwin's central principle of natural selection (O'Brien and Holland 1995: 181). From this atomizing perspective, the

incorporation of archaeological materials into a Darwinian framework rests on the key tenet that those items were parts of previous phenotypes. Without this tenet the application of evolutionary theory to the understanding of how things found in the archaeological record came to be the way they are makes absolutely no sense. (O'Brien and Lyman 2000: 141)

A second approach (ascribed to by the volume's editors in the Introduction, and many other scholars) calls for a more synthetic approach to theory construction (Preucel 1999). Such an approach would require the nesting or bootstrapping of a series of smaller theories, including aspects of Darwinian evolutionary theory, into a potentially much more recursive framework that endeavored to account for the complexity of human history.

In this regard, it is worth considering recent theoretical discussions in two of anthropology's academic neighbors, biology and geography. Historians of the former have charted the failed effort to reduce all of life's diversity and history to the supposedly more scientific constructs of chemistry and physics (Mayr 1982, 1988). At the same time, the recognition of this failure of reductionism has necessitated an expansion of the definition of science to account for the importance of both history and contingency (Gould 1986, 1987; Mayr 1988).

This point has been driven home all the more dramatically with the aforementioned decipherment of the human genome (Pennisi 2001). This long-awaited development has prompted scientific and public surprise both in the relatively small number of human genes (roughly 30,000) and in the degree of genetic similarity that was found between humans and other similarly deciphered species (Wade 2001a, 2001b). Furthermore, these discoveries have led some to suggest that the surrounding context and architecture of specific genes may affect how these genes act under particular circumstances (Reuters 2001). Although still early, clearly these preliminary findings have struck a serious blow against a narrowly reductionist mode of thought within biology itself. As Stephen Jay Gould (2001) has remarked in response to these recent announcements, "the failure of reductionism doesn't mark the failure of science, but only the replacement of an ultimately unworkable set of assumptions by more appropriate styles of explanation that study complexity at its own level."

In geography, a recent presidential address (Gober 2000) focuses on an intellectual dilemma that is painfully parallel to the increasing fragmentation and compartmentalization that we see in contemporary anthropology. Like anthropology and archaeology, modern geography includes disparate intellectual elements that range from the humanistic to the scientific, often with little communication between the cultural and physical segments. Over the last decades, this segmentation (and the subsequently diminished or fractured voice of the field) has been sufficiently serious to allow for the dissolution of a number of prominent departments of geography.

Gober's (2000) address recognizes that geography's central concerns with space and place cannot be reduced to any uniform, narrow analytical program or theory. She further notices that its standing in the academy and beyond is diminished by its disparate sections and fractured message. Following the ecologist Steward Pickett (1999), she calls for the development of new "habits of the mind" or a reconsideration of the practices and training associated with ways of thinking. Training should be more effectively geared to a synthetic set of ideas, concepts, and theories that are appropriate and suitable for the study of large-scale and complex phenomena. In other words, Gober (2000: 8) calls for the continuance of pluralistic perspectives in geography, but ones shaped by a more clearly elucidated and synthetic agenda and fostered by the definition of a common language to facilitate communication between the different segments that make up her field.

LOOKING FORWARD

As evolutionary archaeologists, where do we go from here? Can we learn from these parallel discussions that are taking place in cognate disciplines? To tackle the complex historical agenda that we have long set for ourselves, and in concert with recent developments in biology and geography, a synthetic approach (as opposed to the simple melding of extant approaches) clearly is in order. Perhaps there is no need to join the armadillos in the middle of the road. But I do stand with the editors of this volume in calling for the hard critical work necessary to bridge the diverse perspectives that must be interlocked under a large theoretical umbrella in order to understand human diversity and how it came to be.

As Pickett (1999) and Gober (2000) likewise have surmised for their respective fields, such an approach in anthropology also will require new "habits of the mind" as well as practices that foster communication and tolerance rather than competition and polarization between differing perspectives and "isms" that share our discipline. The necessary bridging efforts and new ways of training required to interdigitate perspectives may sound easy to implement until one realizes that we have grown up in a field whose key ideas and approaches have been repeatedly introduced and then juxtaposed in a rather different manner (e.g., Binford 1972; Dunnell 1980; Harris 1980; Hodder 1985).

Despite the obvious challenges ahead, I remain optimistic about the contemporary archaeological endeavor. Scholars in the discipline and related fields have started to accept and digest new views of science that are more synthetic than analytic. At the same time, the appropriateness of Kuhnian notions of science, which in recent decades has tended to foster an expectation of broad paradigmatic swings and theoretical reversals, has been challenged (e.g., Blanton 1990).

These important changes in our philosophical landscape provide a strong basis for this volume's important, yet still unfinished, effort to establish a plain and workable language that cross-cuts theoretical streams in evolutionary archaeology. The meaningful completion of such efforts along with a concerted willingness to rephrase and reframe our questions in a way that allows them to be informative and interesting to a broader range of archaeologists operating within interlocked but distinct evolutionary perspectives represent key next steps. If we are able to meet these synthetic challenges and forge a more holistic evolutionary approach, then we can reverse the centrifugal and cacophonous tendencies of the past 20 years and finally make long overdue strides necessary to tackle the significant agenda outlined by Boas seven decades ago.

REFERENCES

Barton, C. M., and G. A. Clark (eds.). (1997). *Rediscovering Darwin: Evolutionary Theory and Archeological Explanation.* Archeological Papers No. 7. Arlington, VA: American Anthropological Association.

Bettinger, R., and J. Eerkens. (1997). Evolutionary implications of metrical variation in Great Basin projectile points. In C. M. Barton and G. A. Clark (eds.), *Rediscovering Darwin: Evolutionary Theory and Archeological Explanation.* Archeological Papers No. 7. Arlington, VA: American Anthropological Association, pp. 177–191.

Binford, L. R. (1972). *An Archaeological Perspective.* New York: Seminar Press.

Blanton, R. E. (1990). Theory and practice in Mesoamerican archaeology: A comparison of two modes of scientific inquiry. In J. Marcus and J. F. Zeitlin (eds.), *Caciques and Their People: A Volume in Honor of Ronald Spores.* Anthropological Paper No. 89. Ann Arbor: Museum of Anthropology, University of Michigan, pp. 1–16.

Boas, F. (1932). The aims of anthropological research. *Science* 76: 605–613.

Dunnell, R. C. (1980). Evolutionary theory and archaeology. In M. Schiffer (ed.), *Advances in Archaeological Method and Theory*, vol. 3. New York: Academic Press, pp. 35–99.

Feinman, G. M. (1994). Toward an archaeology without polarization: Comments on contemporary theory. In J. Marcus and J. F. Zeitlin (eds.), *Caciques and Their People: A Volume in Honor of Ronald Spores*. Anthropological Paper No. 89. Ann Arbor: Museum of Anthropology, University of Michigan, pp. 13–43.

Givens, D. B., and S. N. Skomal. (1993). The four fields: Myth and reality. *Anthropology Newsletter* 34(5): 1, 19.

Gober, P. (2000). Presidential address: In search of synthesis. *Annals of the Association of American Geographers* 90: 1–11.

Gould, S. J. (1986). Evolution and the triumph of homology, or why history matters. *American Scientist* 74: 60–69.

Gould, S. J. (1987). Preface. In *An Urchin in the Storm: Essays about Books and Ideas*. New York: Norton, pp. 9–16.

Gould, S. J. (1988). On replacing the idea of progress with an operational notion of directionality. In H. Nitecki (ed.), *Evolutionary Progress*. Berkeley: University of California Press.

Gould, S. J. (1997a). Darwinian fundamentalism. *New York Review of Books* 44(10): 34–37.

Gould, S. J. (1997b). Evolution: The pleasures of pluralism. *New York Review of Books* 44(11): 47–52.

Gould, S. J. (2001). Humbled by the genome's mysteries. *New York Times*, February 19 (http://www.nytimes.com/2001/02/19/opinion/19GOUL.html).

Harris, M. (1980). *Cultural Materialism: The Struggle for a Science of Culture*. New York: Random House.

Hodder, I. (1985). Postprocessual archaeology. In M. B. Schiffer (ed.), *Advances in Archaeological Method and Theory*, vol. 8. New York: Academic Press, pp. 1–26.

Johnson, M. (1999). *Archaeological Theory: An Introduction*. Oxford: Blackwell.

Karow, J. (2001). Reading the book of life. *Scientific American* (February) (http://www.sciam.com/explorations/2001/021201humangenome/).

Maschner, H.D.G. (ed.). (1996). *Darwinian Archaeologies*. New York: Plenum.

Mayr, E. (1982). *The Growth of Biological Thought*. Cambridge, MA: Harvard University Press.

Mayr, E. (1988). *Toward a New Philosophy of Biology: Observations of an Evolutionist*. Cambridge, MA: Harvard University Press.

Mayr, E. (1999). Understanding evolution. *Trends in Ecological Evolution* 14: 372–373.

O'Brien, M. J., and T. D. Holland. (1995). The nature and premise of a selection-based archaeology. In P. Teltser (ed.), *Evolutionary Archaeology: Methodological Principles*. Tucson: University of Arizona Press, pp. 175–200.

O'Brien, M. J., and R. L. Lyman. (2000). Evolutionary archaeology: Reconstructing and explaining historical lineages. In M. B. Schiffer (ed.), *Social Theory in Archaeology*. Salt Lake City: University of Utah Press, pp. 126–142.

Pennisi, E. (2001). The human genome. *Science* 291: 1177–1180.

Pickett, S.T.A. (1999). The culture of synthesis: Habits of mind in novel ecological integration. *Oikos* 87: 479–487.

Preucel, R. W. (1999). Review of *Evolutionary Archaeology: Theory and Application* (ed. M. J. O'Brien). *Journal of Field Archaeology* 26: 93–99.

Rambo, A. T. (1991). The study of cultural evolution. In A. T. Rambo and K. Gillogly (eds.), *Profiles in Cultural Evolution: Papers in Honor of Elman R. Service*. Anthropological Papers No. 85. Ann Arbor: Museum of Anthropology, University of Michigan, pp. 23–109.

Reuters. (2001). Corrected: Junk DNA may not be such junk. *New York Times*, February 13 (http://www.nytimes.com/reuters/science/science-genome-junk-d.html).

Sanderson, S. K. (1990). *Social Evolutionism: A Critical History*. Cambridge: Blackwell.

Shulevitz, J. (2001). Academic warfare. *New York Times*, February 11 (http://www.nytimes.com/books/01/02/11/bookend/bookend.html).

Spencer, C. S. (1997). Evolutionary approaches in archaeology. *Journal of Archaeological Research* 5: 209–264.

Terrell, J. (1986). Causal pathways and causal processes: Studying the evolutionary prehistory of human diversity in language, customs, and biology. *Journal of Anthropological Archaeology* 5: 187–198.

Trigger, B. G. (1989). *A History of Archaeological Thought*. Cambridge: Cambridge University Press.

Wade, N. (2001a). Genome's riddle: Few genes, much complexity. *New York Times*, February 13 (http://www.nytimes.com/2001/02/13/health/13HUMA.html).

Wade, N. (2001b). Genome analysis shows humans survive on low number of genes. *New York Times*, February 11 (http://www.nytimes.com/2001/02/11/health/11GENO.html).

Wilson, E. O. (1998). *Consilience: The Unity of Knowledge*. Cambridge: Cambridge University Press.

Table of Key Words

Acculturation, 163
Adaptation, 15, 52, 226
Affinity, 74
Agency, 119
Analogous/Analogy, 64, 77, 126
Attribute, 71, 100
Biological constraints, 30
Biological reproduction, 144
Cause, 49
Chance, 145
Character, 71
Class, 80
Classification, 70
    paradigmatic, 71
    taxonomic, 71
Complexity, 98
Concept, 10
Conditioning
    classical, 185
    operant, 185
Cultural history, 148
Cultural reproduction, 112
Cultural transformation, 112
Cultural virus, 191
Culture, 55, 75, 107, 164
Darwinian population, 246
Definition
    extensional, 81
    intentional, 80

Descent, 125
Design, 97
Diet breadth, 22
Drift, 17, 75, 226
Empiricism, 51
Environment of Evolutionary Adaptive-
    ness, 36
Essentialism, 74
Evolved predisposition, 31
Evolution, 3, 74, 90
    biological, 4
    cultural, 4, 56
        general, 166
        specific, 165
    Darwinian, 3, 94
    orthogenetic, 57
    progressive, 3
Evolutionary constraints, 30
Evolutionary ecology, 60, 202
Evolutionary psychology, 32
Exaptation, 19
Explanation, 49, 77, 95
Extrasomatic, 64
Fecundity, 191
Fitness, 4
Form, 71
Frequency seriation, 77
Functional, 227

Functional analysis, 20
Genealogical, 125
Goals, 97
Group, 59, 71, 100, 170
Heritable continuity, 75
Hierarchy, 92
Historical sciences, 148
History, 143
Homologous/Homology, 64, 78, 126
Hypothesis, 164, 250
Imitation, 186
Inclusive fitness, 30
Individual, 161
Inheritance, 54, 75
Interactor, 162, 172
Key, 71
Learn/Learning, 4, 183
    associative, 185
    cultural, 31, 144
    individual, 186
    observational, 186
    social, 31, 112, 186
    situational, 112
    symbolic, 112
    trial-and-error, 185
Lineage, 53, 76, 125
Longevity, 191
Materialism, 74
Mechanism, 49
Meme, 5, 166, 184, 191
Meta-narrative, 150
Metaphor, 214
Metapopulation, 246
Model, 201
    analogical, 205
    analytical, 205
    deterministic, 205
    dynamic, 205
    empirical, 205
    heuristic, 204
    mathematical, 205
    scale, 204
    simulation, 202
    static, 205
    stochastic, 205
    theoretical, 204
Narrative, 149, 214
Natural sciences, 148

Natural theology, 51
Optimal foraging theory, 23
Pathway, 144
Pattern, 144
Performance study, 22
Phenotype, 59, 226
Phenotypic change, 17
Population, 99, 161, 243
Population structure, 246
Population thinking, 74
Potential adaptedness, 19
Process, 49, 74, 144
Progress, 54
Reductionism
    constitutive, 215
    explanatory, 215
    tactical, 215
    theoretical, 215
Replicative success, 227
Replicator, 172, 191
Resource, 101
Sampling strategy, 250
Scaffolding, 191
Selection, 3
    artificial, 4, 225
    by consequence, 146
    catastrophic, 229
    cultural, 226
    Darwinian, 4
    directional, 228
    disruptive, 228
    group, 229
    natural, 29, 53, 75, 89, 145, 225, 245
    sexual, 4, 29, 229
    stabilizing, 228
    variability, 41
Society, 110
Somatic, 17
Species, 75
Stasis, 54
Style, 81
Stylistic, 227
Synology, 126
Systematics, 64, 71
Taxonomy, 71
Teleology, 51
Theory, 50, 74, 164
Trait, 90

Transformation, 162
Transmission, 54
  cultural, 227
  horizontal, 188, 248
  oblique, 188
  vertical, 188, 248
Type, 71
Typological essentialism, 244
Typological thinking, 74

Typology, 71, 91
Unit, 70
  descriptional, 80
  empirical, 80
  functional, 82
  ideational, 80
  phenomenological, 80
  stylistic, 81
  theoretical, 80

Darwin and Archaeology

Chapter 1

Introduction

John Edward Terrell and John P. Hart

Dictionaries tell us that *archaeology* is the scientific study of material remains, such as graves, tools, and pottery, of past human life and activities. They also say that *evolution* is about life's unfolding story, a word referring to a gradual process of change in a certain direction during which something changes into a different and usually more complex or better form, an account of continuous change from "a lower, simple, or worse" into "higher, more complex, or better state." The first definition scarcely begins to account for what archaeology today is all about. These several definitions of evolution are not only misleading, but—from a Darwinian point of view—are also fundamentally wrong. The proposition of this book is simple. We think a good way to do archaeology well is to study archaeological evidence—"the material remains of the past"—the way that Charles Darwin studied the origin of species. These various dictionary definitions, however, are disconcerting. If most people would agree with these definitions, then we need to begin this book by saying why we do not.

ARCHAEOLOGY AND EVOLUTION

For archaeologists—and for many who enjoy reading about archaeology—much of the excitement of this science comes from the discovery of relics from bygone times. But make no mistake. Regardless of what dictionaries say, most archaeologists are looking for more than ancient remnants and elusive signs of prehistoric people. Most archaeologists also want to write **HISTORY,**[1] and so they are looking for things that are profound and worth saying about the past. Furthermore, many archaeologists want to discover whether the past has lessons to teach us that can help us better

Figure 1.1. Is this a vase or two faces drawn in profile facing one another?

understand ourselves today—and perhaps better understand what may happen to us in the future, as well.

Saying that archaeologists want to write history leaves too much unsaid. To begin with, as the renowned historian E. H. Carr (1965) once asked, what is history? There is no simple answer to this deceptively simple question. The observation that history is a tale of contradictions may be key. Like the well-known drawings showing either a flower vase or two faces in profile (see Figure 1.1), history shows us two sides of the past simultaneously: how things have changed over time and also how they have remained the same (or so it would seem), sometimes for eons. Anyone writing about history, therefore, must be prepared to write about both *change* and *continuity*—and explain both the *evolution* of new kinds of things and situations and also the *persistence* of old ways and institutions.

But then what is evolution? Although it may sound unconventional to say so, Charles Darwin's theory of evolution is above all else a theory of history. While initially offered as an encompassing theory about the origin of new species by means of **NATURAL SELECTION**, Darwin's insights into the causes of biological evolution and persistence soon proved to be so powerful that many have sought to apply Darwinian theory to human affairs—to use Darwin's ways of thinking about history and evolution to explain not only our own origins as a remarkably clever kind of animal (see **BIOLOGICAL CONSTRAINTS**), but also our human ways and the history of human institutions and social practices (major elements of what many anthropologists and others call **CULTURE**).

These brief observations about history and evolution still leave too much unstated, and unfortunately, confusion about history and evolution often begins right at the beginning. For example, the word **evolution** is commonly used in two different ways. It is frequently used simply to mean the *history of life*—what has actually happened since the beginning of time. Thus we read about "the evolution of the dinosaurs," or "the evolution of Homo sapiens." While it may seem an overly subtle point to make, using this word to mean "what has happened" tells nothing about *why* things have changed—or why some things seemingly have not. Much confusion can be avoided by keeping in mind that the word "evolution" does not imply any specific theory of evolution, Darwinian or otherwise. It often just means history, as in "the history of life on earth," although, as we have seen from the dictionary definitions given at the start of this introduction, this word popularly means not just "the earth's history" but also implies that things have become better or more complex with the passage of time.

When dictionaries say that evolution is a gradual process during which something changes into a different and usually more complex or better form, such a view of how evolution works is called **progressive evolution**. Some archaeologists reason that human societies have evolved to become more complex in more or less the same ways everywhere on earth (e.g., Earle 1991). However, there is little scientific agreement on how to define **COMPLEXITY**. Many insist that human societies cannot be ranked as "higher" or "lower," "better" or "worse," "complex" or "simple," and so on. While Darwin's own ideas about progress and complexity are open to differing interpretations (Richards 1987; Ruse 1992), the authors of this book are mostly skeptical about progressive theories of evolution. In this volume, "evolution" means **Darwinian evolution**; specifically, Darwin's way of explaining why living things change and also why they can persist in more or less the same forms, in both cases as natural consequences of selection.

Selection is the name that can be given to several kinds of feedback processes effecting (and affecting) the behavior and biology of organisms. These processes depend on three critical conditions: (1) there has to be something to select—that is, there must be *variation* of some kind that can be sorted out; (2) there has to be some way of actively sorting through this variation—there must be a *selective mechanism*; (3) there has to be a way of repeating the selection process so that the effects of selection can accumulate and thereby change the pool of variation available for sorting—there must be a *feedback mechanism* (that is, as dictionaries say, a "process whereby the results of action serve continually to modify further action").

TYPE OF SELECTION	source of variation	selective mechanism	feedback mechanism
Darwinian selection	genetic variation	breeding success	gene replication
artificial selection	genetic variation	choice	gene replication
learning	behavioral variation	behavioral conditioning	reinforcement (memory)

Table 1.1. Three kinds of selection.

Given these three conditions, there are three basic kinds of natural selection (see Table 1.1): **Darwinian selection** (measured by **fitness**, that is, by reproductive success); **artificial selection** (measured, for instance, by the *achievement* of some intended genetic outcome); and **LEARNING** (measured, for instance, by behavioral *reinforcement*, by how effectively particular responses are strengthened by events immediately following them). These three kinds of selection are not mutually exclusive. To offer a simple laboratory example, a learned response to an environmental stimulus—say, a fear reaction to loud noises—may interfere with an animal's (or a person's) sexual functioning, thereby lowering that individual's reproductive fitness.

Some would add that there is also a fourth kind of natural selection, called **sexual selection**, during which breeding success is affected by mate choice. In some cases, sexual selection may be dependent on genetic variation and choice, or on behavioral variation and conditioning, or on both sources of variation and selective mechanism. In any case, the result of sexual selection is breeding success and gene replication and/or reinforcement of behaviors. This kind of selection further illustrates why we say that the processes of selection shown in Table 1.1 are not mutually exclusive.

As several of the chapters in this book discuss, it is conventional in biology and the social sciences to distinguish between **biological evolution** (where the focus of selection is on genetically replicated variation) and **cultural evolution** (where the focus of selection is on behavioral variation and the socially established contingencies of learning). Except in tales of wild children raised by animals such as lions, wolves, and apes, a dominating part of every person's selective environment is the presence of other people. Since it needs no arguing that children learn much of what anthropologists call **CULTURE** from those around them, for human beings it is obvious that selection works not just through "nature red in tooth and claw" but also through the give and take of our daily social lives. This is the reason anthropologists often talk about cultural evolution as *cultural transformation*, and cultural persistence as *cultural reproduction*. Others argue strongly that learning—like reproduction—involves the actual transmission of information (in small units of information now popularly called **memes**) from one individual to another. There is no real need, however, to equate learning with genetic reproduction (see **CULTURE** and **LEARNING**). Simply put, it makes sense to see learning and biological reproduction as alternative (and commonly interacting) pathways of selection (see **DESCENT**).

Therefore, we cannot emphasize too strongly (and in disagreement with several of the authors in this book) that while natural selection structures the earth's biological history (that is, biological evolution) and our own species' behavior (and human history), different feedback mechanisms may be involved. As the behavioral psychologist B. F. Skinner (1981: 501) wrote a number of years ago, learning can be a different kind of "selection by consequences" that may not only supplement Darwinian selection but can replace it as the most influential mode of selection governing the evolution of our species.

In summary, selection has alternative pathways by which it shapes biology and behavior. One pathway is mediated by genes and reproduction; the other pathway is mediated by learning—during which an organism's responses to its surroundings and life's demands are selectively reinforced as a natural consequence of its dealings with the world and its other inhabitants. From this perspective, culture is a process, a form of natural selection.

DARWIN'S METHODOLOGY

Charles Darwin is famous for his theory of evolution by natural selection. If this were his only contribution to science, he might be no better known today than others who have proposed similar ideas about evolution and history. What distinguishes Darwin from others is the methodology he used to support his ideas.

Darwin considered theory to be an essential part of science, but he recognized that theorizing alone would not convince his scientific peers and the educated lay public that evolution is a fact and that selection is the most likely mechanism accounting for that fact (Browne 1995; Mayr 1991; Ruse 1999). To win support for his ideas, he knew he needed both supporting data ("facts") and convincing analogies and metaphors (see Ruse [1999] for an extended account of how Darwin's methodology was directly influenced by contemporary philosophers of science). His best-known analogy is that of artificial selection as an analogy for natural selection. Darwin used artificial selection to argue from an observable, experienced manner of changing organisms to an evolutionary mechanism that is otherwise remarkably difficult to grasp (Ruse 1999: 177).

Darwin also used metaphors to provide easily understood pictures of his theories and hypotheses. His most well-known metaphor is that of "a tangled bank" as a way of describing the interconnected story of the earth's countless species of plants and animals. Yet while he was a master of analogies and metaphors, most of the 2 million words he published in 23 books (King-Hele 1999: 363) are about evidence supporting his theories.

It is perhaps not surprising, therefore, that Darwin was also one of the most accomplished experimental scientists of his time (Browne 1995: 512). If he felt he lacked appropriate facts to evaluate an idea, he designed experiments to test them. He also clearly recognized that no single "crucial experiment" (Terrell 2000) would lead to sufficient support or refutation of a hypothesis. His experiments were many and varied, and he was not hesitant to abandon an idea if he failed to find support for it.

LESSONS FOR ARCHAEOLOGY

Except when studying animal, plant, or human remains, archaeologists do not have opportunities to study genetic variation. Although they may sometimes study living people to help them better interpret the past, archaeologists also cannot directly observe human behavior in the past. Therefore, to use Darwinian approaches, archaeologists must devise indirect ways (see CAUSE, CLASSIFICATION, and MODELS) to link the kinds of evidence they discover ("material remains, such as graves, tools, and pottery") with variation in the past that was susceptible to selection.

The fact that archaeologists rarely study selection directly explains why carefully constructed scientific models are so critical to the success of Darwinian archaeology. Good archaeological models are able to suggest plausible ways in which the variation that archaeologists can see firsthand— variation, for example, in pottery designs or settlement patterns—may have been tied to now vanished domains of genetic and behavioral variation. Well-constructed Darwinian models can help archaeologists identify what were the probable contingencies of selection in the past that affected variation in those domains (see ADAPTATION) that could have led to patterned variation still observable today in the archaeological record.

We asked each of the authors who contributed to this book to briefly summarize case studies illustrating the best uses and future potential of Darwinian thinking in archaeology. Fulfilling this request was not easy. Most of the recent literature on Darwinian archaeology deals with theoretical issues (e.g., Boone and Smith 1998; Broughton and O'Connell 1999; Lyman and O'Brien 1998; O'Brien and Lyman 2000; O'Brien et al. 1998; Preucel 1999; Teltser 1995). Good case studies are few and far between, but the situation is improving. Here are three examples.

In a series of publications in the 1980s, David Braun (e.g., 1983, 1987) presented the results of his research on how pottery technology responded to changing selective contexts during the period of 200 B.C. to A.D. 600 in western Illinois. Braun argued that variation in pottery wall thickness reflected the need for thinner or thicker walls to meet changing functional demands. He was able to identify likely sources of selection in the past, including changing subsistence regimes and population structure. For instance, thinner-walled vessels may have been favored because such pots transfer heat more effectively, resulting in more efficient cooking of starchy seeds—which at that time were becoming increasingly important in subsistence. O'Brien and his colleagues (1994) subsequently did a similar analysis of pottery from the same period in eastern Missouri with comparable although not identical results.

Also in the 1980s, David Rindos (1984) argued that "intentionalist models" of agricultural origins are unverifiable. Following Darwin (1859), Rindos suggested that intention is not needed to explain the domestication of plants. Rather, domestication can be the result of the selective consequences of interactions between humans and plants. This co-evolutionary model provided new insights into the processes of plant domestication that led to new ideas in archaeology about the evolution of seed-crop agriculture in the Eastern Woodlands of North America (Rindos and Johannessen 1991).

More recently, John Hart (1999) drew on Darwinian theory to develop a model of the adoption and evolution of maize agriculture in the Eastern Woodlands of North America. To construct this model, Hart took elements from Rindos' (1984) co-evolution model of agricultural evolution, Wright's (1932, 1978) shifting balance theory of evolution, and modern information about maize genetics and reproduction. Delineating cause and effect relationships via modeling brought out that if one wants to address the early history of maize agriculture, additional data are needed that archaeologists previously had not realized are required. These include a different kind of isotope analysis of human bone than is commonly used, and more intensive and extensive sampling of archaeological sites for plant macro- and micro-fossils to obtain data on early maize production and consumption.

As each of these three examples illustrates, archaeological uses of Darwinian thinking are greatly dependent on the specific details and assumptions of the particular models used to link archaeological evidence with what are hypothesized to have been the likely contingencies of selection in the past. In this regard, however, archaeology is no different from any other science. As the biologist Richard Levins (1966: 430) wrote many years ago, "all models leave out a lot and are in that sense, false, incomplete, inadequate. The validation of a model is not that it is 'true' but that it generates good testable hypotheses relevant to important problems."

A corollary of this observation, nonetheless, is equally certain. Archaeologists (and all scientists) are obligated by the basic canons of good science to do all they can to put all their cards on the table. Model-building in science works well *only* when the basic working assumptions, parameters, variables, and rules of operation of every model built are carefully specified

(Terrell 1986: 6–11). It is all too easy in Darwinian archaeology, for example, to manufacture circular arguments of the "because of" variety; that is, arguments (and poorly specified models advanced to support them) where archaeologically observed changes are claimed to have happened because of "breeding success" or "culture." Such arguments do little more than restate the claim being made in more compact form without actually presenting a case for what are believed to have been the contingencies of selection involved.

Even with all the caution and care in the world, model-building is always dependent on the actual details of the models built and the specific arguments used to justify why *those* modeling ingredients—rather than others— have been used. Consider this example. It is probably a safe bet that most archaeologists today recognize that "complexity" is a problematic concept (Earle 1997: 208). Yet many of those who do still conceptualize the study of human social evolution using typological categories such as "bands, tribes, and chiefdoms" (Service 1971); many continue to see "the evolution of complex societies" as one of the central issues of human history, in spite of the fact that there is no consensus on how to decide whether some human societies were (or are) "more hierarchical, differentiated, and stratified" than others (Feinman 1998: 95).

We think the history of science shows the wisdom of saying that when issues such as "the evolution of complex societies" stubbornly resist generations of research work intended to resolve them, the sticking point is sometimes simply that scientists do not have the right tools to work with. As soon as good tools are invented, the problems quickly dissolve—classic examples being the microscope, the telescope, and today the astonishing tools of molecular genetics. Other times, maybe even often, new tools also reveal that the old sticking points, the old resistant research problems, are not so much solved as disappear. The new tools allow us to see that what we thought were good problems were actually just fundamental misunderstandings of what is involved (Terrell 2001).

RETHINKING ARCHAEOLOGY

While we do not see Darwinian thinking as a new kind of tool, we do see it as a neglected set of powerful concepts and research strategies. Consider again the problem of the evolution of complex societies. We think this issue has been repeatedly "mistyped" as an issue about idealized entities (bands, tribes, chiefdoms, archaic states, etc.) and about how history is headed toward an end-state called "complex." This is not an effective way to conceptualize history or human social organization.

A better way to get at the issues involved—and a better way to study them—would be to rephrase the problem entirely. From a Darwinian perspective, "the better way to think" is to ask: *How predictable have changes in human social organization been due to conditions such as overcrowding or resource scarcity?* This rephrasing shifts debate about human social evolution away from terminological arguments about "the right definition" of complexity and refocuses work on issues of *evidence* and *inference*; and since overcrowding and scarcity are merely two of the conditions that have been suggested by researchers as leading to change in social organization, specifying exactly *what causes* will be under investigation is perhaps the very first step that anyone doing research on human social evolution must take.

Equal care must also be given to picking good ways to talk about the research issues being investigated. Using effective concepts to model research problems is critically important. Here, for instance, is how Richard Levins (in the 1960s) said we should rethink studying evolution in changing environments:

Given the essential heterogeneity within and among complex biological systems, our objective is not so much the discovery of universals as the accounting for differences. For example, instead of seeking a proposition of the form "there is a secular evolutionary tendency toward increasing complexity despite some exceptions," we would begin with the fact of different degrees of complexity and different directions of change, and ask what kinds of situations would give positive selective value to increased or decreased complexity. It may, of course, be argued that the result of such an inquiry would be a universal at a higher level. However, we would guess that such a law would also have a limited domain of relevance. (Levins 1968: 6)

Levins' approach still asks us to model what we want **COMPLEXITY** to mean, but—and we think this is important—also directs us to ask what kinds of situations would give selective value to changes in complexity.

A second example of how Darwinian thinking can make a difference is the sometimes neglected question of *whose* history archaeologists write when they are writing history. Who are the human beings behind archaeological "types," "sites," "phases," "cultures," and the like? Like geneticists studying genes rather than "whole organisms," archaeologists study pieces of the past, not the "whole past." As the chapters that follow explore in some detail, it is much harder to put pieces (or genes) together to write about "people," "societies," or **POPULATIONS** than many may realize, and Darwinian theory can help archaeologists navigate the critical issue of agency in history (see **DESCENT, HISTORY,** and Terrell 2001).

THIS BOOK

During the past two decades, there has been a growing resurgence of interest in evolutionary approaches to the archaeological record. Unlike previous discussions of evolution in the context of archaeology, however, many current discussions are founded in Darwinian theory and important theoretical advances in the social and historical sciences generally. Discussions of Darwinian archaeology are currently dominated by debates between various schools of thought (e.g., Boone and Smith 1998; Lyman and O'Brien 1998; Schiffer 1996). While there have been several calls for integration of these schools under a more inclusive paradigm, debate about theory remains a major focus of current writings in Darwinian archaeology.

Part of the divisiveness lies in the different manner in which the various schools of thought define and use words and concepts. A necessary step to integrate Darwinian archaeology is clarification of major concepts and their key words.

This book is designed to meet this strategic goal. Each chapter in this volume is an essay on a key **concept** (that is, words that link data and theories [Dunnell 1971]). Each chapter surveys a major concept in Darwinian archaeology, defining the concept and answering three guiding questions to clarify for the reader its current uses, sources of controversy, and theoretical contexts.

1. *What does the concept mean to archaeologists today?* What is the concept? Does it have more than one meaning? What does the reader need to know about the concept, its different meanings, and their theoretical context(s) to use it effectively and well?

2. *Why is the concept important in archaeology?* Why (and how) do we need to use this concept to explore important issues/concerns in archaeology today? (Each chapter includes examples of research work illustrating the value of the concept in actual archaeological practice.)

3. *Is there some reason to favor a particular meaning and usage over others that are also in vogue?* How do these "real-life" archaeological examples show why we should prefer one usage/meaning of the concept over others? Or should the concept mean different things in different methodological/interpretative contexts?

The answers given in these chapters addressing this last question show some of the flavor of current debate. Readers will note that we have not limited chapter authorship to members of one particular school of thought. Rather, we have drawn from a number of contemporary points of view.

Each chapter includes definitions of related **key words**. Because the same key words may have the same or different meanings in different conceptual contexts, many of these key words are defined in more than one chapter. Each key word is set in **bold type** on its first use in each chapter. In addition to a conventional table of contents listing each concept by chapter, a second table indexes key words and where to find them in the various chapters.

Hence the volume can be used somewhat like a dictionary, and somewhat like an encyclopedia.

In addition to exploring key concepts, collectively these essays show the broad range of ideas and opinions in this intellectual arena today. As such, these chapters collectively reveal its controversies and strong differences of opinion. This volume reflects—and clarifies—debate today on the role of Darwinism in modern archaeology and, by doing so, may help shape the directions that future work in archaeology will take.

NOTE

1. Words capitalized in this Introduction refer to chapters in this book where the particular concepts are discussed.

REFERENCES

Boone, J. L., and E. A. Smith. (1998). Is it evolution yet? A critique of evolutionary archaeology. *Current Anthropology* 39: S141–S173.

Braun, D. P. (1983). Pots as tools. In J. Moore and A. Keene (eds.), *Archaeological Hammers and Theories*. New York: Academic Press, pp. 107–134.

Braun, D. P. (1987). Coevolution of sedentism, pottery technology, and horticulture in the central Midwest, 200 B.C.–A.D. 600. In W. F. Keegan (ed.), *Emergent Horticultural Economies of the Eastern Woodlands*. Occasional Paper No. 7, Center for Archaeological Investigations. Carbondale: Southern Illinois University, pp. 153–181.

Broughton, J. M., and J. F. O'Connell. (1999). On evolutionary ecology, selectionist archaeology, and behavioral archaeology. *American Antiquity* 64: 153–165.

Browne, J. (1995). *Charles Darwin Voyaging*. Princeton, NJ: Princeton University Press.

Carr, E. H. (1965). *What Is History?* New York: Alfred A. Knopf.

Darwin, C. (1859). *On the Origin of Species by Means of Natural Selection, or the Preservation of Favored Races in the Struggle for Life*. London: Murray.

Dunnell, R. C. (1971). *Systematics in Prehistory*. New York: The Free Press.

Earle, T. (ed.). (1991). *Chiefdoms: Power, Economy, and Ideology*. Cambridge: Cambridge University Press.

Earle, T. K. (1997). *How Chiefs Come to Power: The Political Economy in Prehistory*. Stanford, CA: Stanford University Press.

Feinman, G. M. (1998). Scale and social organization: Perspectives on the archaic state. In G. M. Feinman and J. Marcus (eds.), *Archaic States*. Santa Fe, NM: School of American Research Press, pp. 95–133.

Hart, J. P. (1999). Maize agriculture evolution in the Eastern Woodlands of North America: A Darwinian perspective. *Journal of Archaeological Method and Theory* 6: 137–180.

King-Hele, D. (1999). *Erasmus Darwin: A Life of Unequaled Achievement*. London: Giles de la Mare Publishers.

Levins, R. (1966). The strategy of model building in population biology. *American Scientist* 54: 421–431.

Levins, R. (1968). *Evolution in Changing Environments: Some Theoretical Considerations*. Monographs in Population Biology No. 2. Princeton, NJ: Princeton University Press.

Lyman, R. L., and M. J. O'Brien. (1998). The goals of evolutionary archaeology: History and explanation. *Current Anthropology* 39: 615–652.

Mayr, E. (1991). *One Long Argument: Charles Darwin and the Genesis of Modern Evolutionary Thought*. Cambridge, MA: Harvard University Press.

O'Brien, M. J., T. D. Holland, R. J. Hoard, and G. L. Fox. (1994). Evolutionary implications of design and performance characteristics of prehistoric pottery. *Journal of Archaeological Method and Theory* 1: 211–258.

O'Brien, M. J., and R. L. Lyman. (2000). *Applying Evolutionary Archaeology: A Systematic Approach*. New York: Kluwer Academic/Plenum.

O'Brien, M. J., R. L. Lyman, and R. D. Leonard. (1998). Basic incompatibilities between evolutionary and behavioral archaeology. *American Antiquity* 63: 485–498.

Preucel, R. W. (1999). Evolutionary archaeology: Theory and application. *Journal of Field Archaeology* 26: 93–99.

Richards, R. J. (1987). *Darwin and the Emergence of Evolutionary Theories of Mind and Behavior*. Chicago: University of Chicago Press.

Rindos, D. (1984). *The Origins of Agriculture: An Evolutionary Perspective*. New York: Academic Press.

Rindos, D., and S. Johannessen. (1991). Human-plant interactions and cultural change in the American Bottom. In T. E. Emmerson and R. B. Lewis (eds.), *Cahokia and the Hinterlands: Middle Mississippian Cultures of the Midwest*. Urbana: University of Illinois Press, pp. 35–45.

Ruse, M. (1992). Darwinism. In E. F. Keller and E. A. Lloyd (eds.), *Keywords in Evolutionary Biology*. Cambridge, MA: Harvard University Press, pp. 74–80.

Ruse, M. (1999). *The Darwinian Revolution: Science Red in Tooth and Claw*, 2nd ed. Chicago: University of Chicago Press.

Schiffer, M. B. (1996). Some relationships between behavioral and evolutionary archaeologies. *American Antiquity* 61: 643–662.

Service, E. R. (1971). *Primitive Social Organization: An Evolutionary Perspective*, 2nd ed. New York: Random House.

Skinner, B. F. (1981). Selection by consequences. *Science* 213: 501–504.

Teltser, P. (ed.). (1995). *Evolutionary Archaeology: Methodological Issues*. Tucson: University of Arizona Press.

Terrell, J. E. (1986). *Prehistory in the Pacific Islands: A Study of Variation in Language, Customs, and Human Biology*. Cambridge: Cambridge University Press.

Terrell, J. E. (2000). Anthropological knowledge and scientific fact. *American Anthropologist* 102: 808–817.

Terrell, J. E. (2001). The uncommon sense of race, language, and culture. In J. E. Terrell (ed.), *Archaeology, Language, and History: Essays on Culture and Ethnicity*. Westport, CT: Bergin and Garvey, pp. 11–30.

Wright, S. (1932). The roles of mutation, inbreeding, crossbreeding and selection in evolution. *Proceedings of the Sixth International Congress of Genetics* 1: 356–366.

Wright, S. (1978). *Evolution and the Genetics of Populations, vol. 4: Variability Within and Among Populations*. Chicago: University of Chicago Press.

Chapter 2

Adaptation

Todd L. VanPool

INTRODUCTION

The 1996 edition of *Webster's Encyclopedic Unabridged Dictionary of the English Language* provides three general definitions of the term **adaptation** that are of interest here. The first, and arguably most common meaning in the context of the social sciences is "a slow, usually unconscious modification of individual and social activity in adjustment to social surroundings." The other definitions, more particular to Darwinian evolution, are (1) any alteration in the structure or function of an organism or any of its parts that results from natural selection, and (2) the act of adapting.

HISTORY

The importance of the term "adaptation" in archaeology and more generally anthropology is easily recognized, especially in the common definition of culture as "the extrasomatic means of adaptation" (Binford 1962: 22; White 1959: 8) and the use of terms such as "adaptive milieu," "adaptive systems," and "adaptive strategies" (e.g., Binford 1964: 426; Kirch 1980: 108). Despite the extensive use of the term, there is substantive disagreement among archaeologists concerning what the concept of adaptation really is, and by extension, what the term itself should mean (e.g., Dunnell 1980: 77–82; Kantner 1999; Kirch 1980; O'Brien and Holland 1992). All three of the general definitions presented above are used in archaeological approaches that claim to be evolutionary. The unacknowledged nature of these different meanings has even led to contentious debates (e.g., Dunnell and Wenke 1980; Yoffee 1979, 1980). More specifically, two general frameworks based on the concept of adaptation have been utilized and will be discussed: cultural adaptation and Darwinian adaptation. While the differences may appear to be inconsequential semantic differences, they actually reflect very significant differences in the theoretical frameworks employed by various researchers.

Cultural Adaptation

The first use of the term "adaptation," commonly associated with "Processual archaeologists" such as Binford (1989) and Spencer (1997) builds on the evolutionary approaches advocated by Herbert Spencer, Leslie White, and Julian Steward, among others. This use of the term rests on the premise that the archaeological record is the result of "adaptive responses to changing environmental and social contexts" (Binford 1972: 106; Trigger 1989: 295–297; see also Clarke 1968). Adaptation is defined as a modification of behavior that may be conscious or unconscious, caused in response to changes in the social and natural environment (the first definition presented above). For example, Clarke (1968: 660–661) proposed that because cultural systems are primarily information systems, adaptation should be defined as the process of consciously or unconsciously modifying this informational system to better fit the social and environmental surroundings.

While Clarke's use of the term is common, it is fundamentally incompatible with a Darwinian evolutionary framework (see the discussions in Dunnell 1980: 40–51; Leonard and Jones 1987; O'Brien and Holland 1992; Rindos 1984: 72), as is frequently reflected through the use of the term "cultural adaptation" to differentiate it from Darwinian adaptation (e.g., Kirch 1980: 105). The reasons why cultural adaptation and Darwinian adaptation are not synonymous are fairly straightforward and have been presented by O'Brien and Holland (1992) and Dunnell (1980: 40–51; see also White 1959: 106). To summarize briefly, White's and Steward's evolutionary frameworks, which are the foundation of cultural evolutionary perspectives, are inherently progressive, with evolutionary change leading to increased social complexity illustrated by the linear evolutionary sequence of band, tribe, chiefdom, and state. The progressive nature of these schemes is incompatible with a Darwinian perspective of "descent with modification," because Darwin's approach explicitly denies that evolutionary change is a goal-driven process with progress toward some definable stage or form. Second, cultural evolution is generally seen as operating on cultural systems as opposed to individuals, as illustrated in statements such as "cultural adaptation is thus a process of alteration of a cultural system . . . in response to change in its coupled environmental and/or somatic systems" (Kirch 1980: 108). Darwinian evolution does not and cannot operate on "systems," but instead focuses on the differential persistence of traits of reproducing entities, such as humans. Finally, and most importantly, cultural adaptation is viewed as the *cause* of human behavioral change, a position that is at odds with a Darwinian perspective that defines adaptation as an *outcome* of the operation of natural selection.

Adaptation within a Darwinian Evolutionary Perspective

Archaeologists employing Darwinian evolutionary theory follow biologists and philosophers of biology such as Burian (1992: 7), Mayr (1988: 134–136), Sober (1984: 171, 210–211), and West-Eberhard (1992: 13) in defining adaptations as traits of organisms, including their behavior, that have been fashioned by natural selection because they help organisms survive and reproduce. As such, adaptations are only created by the operation of natural selection through time. Regardless of how beneficial an attribute might be, it is by definition not an adaptation unless it is the product of natural selection.

The development of an adaptation must be explained in terms of natural selection, while the explanation of the presence of features that are not adaptations must employ other evolutionary processes such as **drift** (the differential transmission of traits that is independent of natural selection). The concept of adaptation is therefore important because it specifies the explanatory structure required to account for some **phenotypic change**, that is, change in **somatic** (physiological) and behavioral characteristics. Thus, the explanation of the presence of a particular attribute requires the determination of whether or not it is an adaptation.

In evolutionary contexts, though, the term "adaptation" can be used to specify both a general process called adaptation and the specific adaptations, which are products of the process of adaptation. Adaptation as a process is the action of natural selection to create somatic and behavioral features of organisms that make them better suited to survive and reproduce (Futuyama 1979: 308). Adaptation as an outcome is the particular structure/characteristic (including behavior) that is produced by natural selection. Both uses of the term, as reflected in the second and third dictionary definitions previously present, are legitimate within Darwinian evolutionary contexts.

There are several important implications from the definition of adaptation as an outcome. First, adaptations are the products of past selective environments and may not be beneficial in the current environment. Second, adaptations require time to develop. Third, adaptations must be the direct product of natural selection, and not a secondary characteristic associated by accident with other selectively beneficial traits (Hurt et al. 2001; Sober 1984: 97–102).

Understanding adaptation as a process presents two important implications. First, the process of adaptation has to be studied diachronically. Second, explanations for the process of adaptation rest on identifying the specific selective forces that are driving the evolutionary change.

Archaeologists employing Darwinian evolution agree on both the definition of adaptation and the implications of its use as both an outcome and a process. They do use it at two different scales, however. To begin with, human behavior is viewed as an adaptation. Darwinian archaeologists argue that human behavior is the product of natural selection operating on variation through time, favoring both the ability to modify behavior in the face of changing circumstances and the presence of certain relatively consistent behavioral responses to environmental stimuli (Boone and Smith 1998: S154–S156; Jochim 1983). As a result, natural selection has created the adaptations of great behavioral flexibility (including changing technology) and optimization principles and other behavioral tendencies.

In addition to the adaptation of behavioral flexibility, many Darwinian archaeologists argue that natural selection also creates adaptations at the scale of specific artifacts and behavioral patterns (Leonard 2001; O'Brien and Holland 1992: 46–47; Rindos 1984). Artifacts and behaviors therefore can be adaptations, not just the result of adaptations. In other words, these Darwinian archaeologists argue that not only is the behavioral flexibility that allows snowmobile and ceramic technologies an adaptation; the ceramic and snowmobile technologies can be adaptations themselves (Leonard 1998; O'Brien and Holland 1992).

The argument for the operation of natural selection on behavioral traits, and thus the possibility of adaptations at the level of individual artifact technologies, has been outlined by Dunnell (1980), Leonard and Jones (1987), and O'Brien and Lyman (2000), among others. These authors contend that cultural transmission possesses all of the requirements necessary for the operation of natural selection (i.e., heritable variation generated independently of natural selection that results in differences in the rates of survival and reproduction of the associated organisms [Dunnell 1980: 63]). These archaeologists argue that those behavioral traits and artifacts that affect the survival and reproduction of humans will be affected by natural selection and through time will become adaptations. This position leads to the obvious questions of: (1) how much time does natural selection need to operate on a behavioral trait before it becomes an adaptation, and (2) at what scale should adaptations best be understood (e.g., a plow blade, a plow, or the entire agricultural system)? O'Brien and Holland (1992) and Leonard (2001) address these questions.

The answer to the question of how much time natural selection requires to produce adaptation is intentionally non-specific, because there is no single moment in which a trait suddenly becomes an adaptation (Leonard 2001). However, O'Brien and Holland (1992: 43–52) observe that determining exactly when a trait becomes an adaptation is a relatively moot point because archaeologists can evaluate the **potential adaptedness** (defined as the potential effect on the survival and reproduction of individuals) caused by various traits. Those attributes that affect the reproductive success of humans are acted upon by natural selection through time, and are thereby affected by the process of adaptation and will become adaptations. Thus, by demonstrating that a trait affects the survival and reproduction of humans within a particular selective context and by identifying any changes in the trait that further increases the reproductive success of the associated individuals, a particular trait can be identified as an adaptation.

The second question, at what scale should adaptations be understood, is also answered broadly. Adaptations can occur at virtually any level at which human behavior can be understood. For example, it is clear that technologies defined broadly such as ceramics and agriculture do have profound impacts on human reproduction and survival (Rindos 1984), as can changes in components of these larger technologies such as differences in ceramic temper (Buikstra et al. 1986). Variation affecting the reproductive success of humans can be present at either of these levels, and, as a result, natural selection can produce adaptations at all of them (Leonard 2001).

CONTEMPORARY USES

Archaeologists using Darwinian theory have little disagreement concerning the meaning of the term "adaptation," but currently they struggle with the issue of how to identify adaptations. Perhaps archaeologists employing evolutionary perspectives should not feel too badly about this trouble; biology is having the same difficulty (Burian 1992; West-Eberhard 1992). Biologists employing Darwinian approaches have come to realize that recognizing adaptations is very tricky, because they understand that not all aspects of the biological record are the product of natural selection. To the contrary, other evolutionary processes such as drift can lead to differential persistence of traits (Hurt et al. 2001; Sober 1984: 97–102, 110–134; Vrba and Eldridge 1984; Vrba and Gould 1986).

To further complicate the identification of adaptations, not all traits that appear to be selectively beneficial within a given environment are adaptations (Burian 1992: 9–10). For instance, changing environments may obscure the original selective advantages that led to an adaptation, and may thereby make the identification of the original selective pressure that led to the development of an adaptation difficult. This is especially true in the case of **exaptations**, a term coined by Gould and Vrba (1982) to denote traits that were originally adaptations formed by certain selective forces, but then become beneficial in other contexts than those under which they were created. For example, feathers are exaptations that were originally adaptations for regulating body temperature, but that later proved useful for flying. An explanation for the origin and development of feathers that

relied on their usefulness in flight would necessarily be inaccurate. Furthermore, traits that are acquired through mutation/innovation or introduction are not adaptations, regardless of their selective benefit, until
natural selection has acted to preserve and/or modify them. Therefore, identifying an adaptation requires more than simply illustrating that a trait has
an advantage at a single point in time. It requires tying the historical development of an adaptation to specific selective pressures, a task that is
difficult in both archaeological and biological contexts. As difficult as it is
to demonstrate that slight variation in the human thumb, a finch's beak,
or a turtle's shell affects the probability of a human, a finch, or a turtle
surviving and reproducing, it is even more difficult to demonstrate that
slight variation in projectile point technology, agricultural practices, or architecture affects the probability of a human surviving and reproducing.

Still, the concept of adaptation is fundamental to all archaeologists employing a Darwinian evolutionary perspective, because it specifies the explanatory structure necessary to provide evolutionary explanations of some
phenotypic changes. The development of an attribute that is an adaptation
is *only* explainable through the operation of natural selection and the specification of the selective forces operating to create the adaptation. In contrast, changes in a trait that is not an adaptation *cannot* be directly tied to
natural selection, and are only explainable through drift or other evolutionary processes. Thus, differentiating between those traits that are adaptations and those that are not is the first step in creating evolutionary
explanations.

Given that differentiating adaptations from non-adaptations is fundamental in creating evolutionary explanations based on natural selection,
how do archaeologists do so? Recognizing adaptations rests on identifying
the cause-and-effect relationships between the selective environments and
a phenotypic feature using **functional analysis** (the analysis of the effects of
behavioral or physiological traits in the selective context).

At the most basic level, arguments for determining that a particular trait
is an adaptation and explaining its presence begin by proposing a relationship between the presence and form of particular traits and the survival
and reproduction of individuals. For example, a researcher might propose
that projectile points are an adaptation for hunting, which in turn is favored by natural selection because of its beneficial effect on human nutrition. The proposed relationship can then be evaluated, ideally using
multiple lines of evidence, to determine the effects of an adaptation and
demonstrate how the adaptation increased the reproductive success of its
possessors (O'Brien and Holland 1992: 43–44; see also Millikan 1989;
Rottschaefer 1997). For example, design analysis can be used to determine
if the presence and shape of projectile points affect hunting efficiency and
the subsequent effect of differences in hunting efficiency on the nutrition
and reproductive success of humans. Next, the historical development of

the trait is correlated with the selective environment, thereby allowing the creation of explanations of the adaptation. For example, the development of and changes in projectile points used for hunting could be correlated with changes in game type and availability. Thus, the explanations of an adaptation ultimately rests on identifying its function (its proper function in Larry Wright's [1994] terms) in the selective context, and demonstrating how natural selection led to the development of the adaptation to perform this function (Mills and Beatty 1994; Neander 1991; O'Brien and Holland 1992; Pittendrigh 1958; Rottschaefer 1997).

The use of a particular phenotypic attribute can frequently give insight into the evolutionary function that led to its development. For example, the use of metates in the American Southwest to grind maize into flour may provide insight into the selectively important uses that led to the presence and use of particular types of metates. However, such an approach is not foolproof. Several authors warn against the uncritical assumption that a particular use, regardless of how important it is to the survival and reproduction of individuals within a population, is the reason for the presence of an adaptation (e.g., O'Brien and Holland 1992: 38; West-Eberhard 1992: 15–16). Particular traits can be adaptations under a specific environmental context, but can then be affected by different selective pressures or cease to be affected by natural selection after changes in the environment. For example, as important as gunpowder is in modern hunting and warfare, it would be faulty to argue that its initial development and use is tied to natural selection favoring the use in firearms. Quite to the contrary, it was used in fireworks long before it was used in rifles, and any explanation seeking to clarify its initial development without considering its original function would be faulty.

Burian (1992: 10–11) and Gould and Lewontin (1979) in particular argue against an "adaptationist" perspective that views the specific use of a phenotypic feature in a particular context as the reason for its existence. They caution that adaptations must be separated from exaptations, and must be tied clearly to the specific selective forces that explain their developmental history. Of course, new selective pressures caused by environmental changes and innovation can cause adaptations to be modified after their initial development. The use of gunpowder in firearms has created new selective pressures that have caused substantial changes in gunpowder. Still, the explanation of an adaptation must take into account its developmental history, and therefore requires the identification of the adaptation's "proper function," as discussed above (Burian 1992: 10–11).

As a result, archaeologists identifying adaptations using an evolutionary approach must do what good scientists do; propose hypotheses, in this case concerning an attribute's origin and selective advantage, that can be evaluated and discarded if necessary. Two different approaches have been employed extensively by both biologists and archaeologists to evaluate the accuracy of their proposed functions of adaptations: engineering design analysis and "bootstrapping" (Sober 1984: 81–82).

Engineering design analysis, which is frequently referred to as **performance studies** in archaeology (Schiffer and Skibo 1987, 1997), is used frequently in both biological and archaeological studies. This approach can demonstrate the effects of a particular trait on the reproductive success of organisms independently of the observed patterns of phenotypic change (Leonard 2001; O'Brien et al. 1994; Schiffer 1996). Bootstrapping uses deductive logic to evaluate inductively derived hypotheses (Sober 1984: 81–82; West-Eberhard 1992: 13–14). Basically, the researcher tries to inductively identify the relationship between a proposed adaptation and a specific selective force, and then deductively evaluates the proposed relationship by determining if different individuals exposed to similar selective environments possess similar traits. For example, the hypothesis that the webbed feet of ducks is an adaptation resulting from selection for ducks who could swim more efficiently can be evaluated by (1) completing engineering design analysis to determine if webbed feet actually help ducks swim more efficiently, and then (2) using the bootstrapping approach to determine if other waterfowl who are exposed to similar selective pressures also have webbed feet. Likewise, the proposal that trough metates with wide basins in the American Southwest are adaptations for grinding large amounts of maize relatively quickly can be evaluated by (1) completing an engineering design to determine if trough metates with wide basins are better for grinding maize than other types of metates and (2) by determining if individuals in other areas that grind maize use similarly shaped metates. West-Eberhard (1992: 13–14) also notes that differences in related populations that are subject to different selective environments will help to identify the role of natural selection in the formation of an adaptation.

When engineering design analysis and bootstrapping procedures fail to support a hypothesis concerning the functions of an adaptation, other hypotheses can be developed and evaluated. As O'Brien and Holland (1992: 44) note, "there is nothing wrong with the try and try again approach" to determining the function(s) of a particular adaptation that led to its development. However, archaeologists must keep in mind the fact that not every aspect of an organism's phenotype is likely to be an adaptation. It is thus more parsimonious to assume that a feature is not an adaptation until it can be demonstrated that it is, than to assume that all phenotypic features are adaptations until proven otherwise (West-Eberhard 1992: 16).

CASE STUDIES

One of the most common applications of the archaeological use of adaptation deals with explaining changes in **diet breadth**, defined as the number of different species of plants and animals used by a group of people

(Broughton 1994: 501). For example, Broughton seeks to explain the observed shift in diet breadth from an emphasis on large game during the Paleoindian Period occupation of North America to the more varied prey choice evidenced in the Archaic Period (Bayham 1979). Broughton (1994) compares the frequencies of the remains of various animals and determines that there is a significant shift from large/medium-sized mammals such as sea otters and deer to smaller animals such as pocket gophers during the Archaic Period in central California. This trend reflects an increase in diet breadth, that is, the types of species utilized, through time. Using the concept of **optimal foraging theory,** the premise that humans will maximize their caloric return for the energy invested in an activity, he suggests that humans will have the tendency to take higher ranked resources, that is, resources that provide a greater caloric return for the energy investment in hunting and process when compared to other resources. Optimal foraging is an adaptation caused by natural selection favoring those who practiced this behavior in the past, for various reasons tied partly to their genetic makeup, and who therefore passed on the genes for the behavioral tendency at a greater rate than those who did not possess it.

Because larger animals generally provide more caloric return for the energy invested in hunting and processing them, the adaptation of optimal foraging dictates that humans will generally take larger animals when they are encountered. Thus, the reason why the archaeological record reflects an increased diet breadth, according to Broughton (1994), must be attributed to the fact that humans encountered high-ranked resources less frequently than before, and began to take the next highest-ranked resources that they encountered. In other words, the increase in the number of humans, the decrease in the frequency of large game, or both, caused humans during the Archaic Period to rely on lower-ranked resources (those with a lowered calorie return rate) than before. In doing so, though, the prehistoric inhabitants of California continued to use the highest-ranked resources available to them, including deer and elk, when these animals were encountered. The use of lower-ranked resources caused the appearance of greater diet breadth as the prehistoric inhabitants utilized both the high-ranked resources, such as deer, elk, and sea otters that they had previously used, and lower-ranked resources that they had previously ignored (Broughton 1994). The shift in prey choice then is part of the behavioral flexibility resulting from the adaptation of optimal foraging, a behavioral trait created by natural selection.

The next example of the use of the concept of adaptation in an evolutionary archaeological perspective is gleaned from O'Brien and Holland (1992: 49–52). They observe that during the prehistoric occupation of the American Midwest, a variety of different tempering agents were used in ceramics including grit, limestone, and shell. After A.D. 700, however, shell-tempered ceramics became more popular, so much so that they largely replaced ceramics tempered with other aplastics in certain areas.

The drastic increase in shell-tempered ceramics fits the pattern expected for traits favored by natural selection, causing O'Brien and Holland (1992: 50–51) to hypothesize that shell tempering is an adaptation. To evaluate this hypothesis, O'Brien and Holland rely on an analysis provided by Buikstra et al. (1986). Buikstra et al. present engineering analyses of the effects of shell temper, which indicates that shell temper allows the creation of thinner-walled ceramics that can better withstand thermal shock than ceramics made with other temper. The thinner-walled vessels with increased thermal shock resistance allowed food to be boiled, which in turn allowed for the preparation of starchy foods that could be used to wean young children. Buikstra et al. (1986) further argue that earlier weaning resulted in decreased lactation periods as women weaned their children earlier than they had previously. The shortened nursing period resulted in increased fertility rates, because of the decreased duration of postpartum amenorrhea, a condition that tends to prevent ovulation during nursing. The increased fertility subsequently led to a substantial population increase. O'Brien and Holland (1992: 50) therefore conclude that shell temper is an adaptation, which allowed earlier weaning, and thereby improved the reproductive success of those who used it. The presence and spread of shell-tempered ceramics in the American Midwest is therefore explainable by, and only by, the action of natural selection.

Leonard and Reed (1993) present another example of the use of the concept of adaptation in their discussion of population aggregation in the American Southwest. Southwestern archaeologists have long argued over the causes of population aggregation in areas such as Chaco Canyon, the Aztec area, and the Zuni area. Leonard and Reed (1993) address this issue by first asking whether the population aggregation is an adaptation or not. If it is an adaptation, then the explanation of the phenomenon must rest on the concept of natural selection. If it is not, then the explanation cannot be directly tied to selective forces.

Using a model of agricultural production developed by Rhode (1989) from data on historic agricultural field production in the American Southwest, Leonard and Reed (1993: 653) argue that agricultural production in the region is the product of (1) the available moisture in a given year, (2) the size and potential productivity of the land itself, and (3) the amount of labor invested in agricultural production. Because there is a clear relationship between food production, nutrition, and the fitness of humans, Leonard and Reed argue that increased labor investment in agriculturally productive areas would be favored by natural selection if there was (1) a decrease in available moisture, and/or (2) a decrease in the size and potential productivity of agricultural land. Given that one of the easiest ways to increase labor investment in productive areas is to increase the number of individuals involved in agricultural activity, Leonard and Reed propose that population aggregation is an adaptation caused by the selection for increased labor investment in agriculturally productive areas.

To evaluate this possibility, Leonard and Reed (1993: 655–657) examine rainfall data from the Zuni and Chaco Canyon areas. In the Chaco Canyon region, they (pp. 656–657) find that the three major building episodes, which they argue are proxies for population aggregation, are directly correlated with decreases in the effective moisture available in the region. In the Zuni area Leonard and Reed (pp. 653–656) find that fluctuations in the available moisture after A.D. 1300 decreased both the amount of land available for production and the amount of moisture through time. This change corresponds with an increased size of sites in the Zuni area, suggesting that Zuni was a "labor sink" (p. 655) where increased labor investment could raise agricultural production, or at least hold it constant during a period of declining agricultural potential. Accordingly, Leonard and Reed conclude that population aggregation in these areas is in fact an adaptation resulting from the selection for increased labor investment in agriculturally productive areas during periods of decreased moisture and the decreased availability of agricultural productive land.

FUTURE IMPORTANCE

The term "adaptation" has been used extensively in archaeology, and it has a multitude of meanings. Within an evolutionary context, the term is defined in two ways. The first definition is: those attributes of an organism that have been created by natural selection. The second definition is: the process by which natural selection modifies somatic and behavioral traits of an organism (i.e., the process by which adaptations are formed).

The importance of the concept of adaptation to a Darwinian archaeological approach is difficult to overstate. Adaptation is the process by which natural selection creates behavioral and somatic traits, and the presence of adaptations can only be explained through the action of natural selection. As a result, identifying adaptations and understanding the process that led to their development is imperative for any explanation based on natural selection. When seeking to explain the presence and form of artifacts and artifact patterns reflected in the archaeological record, it is therefore necessary to use engineering and bootstrapping analyses to determine whether the trait or pattern is an adaptation. If it is, then the explanation of the characteristic rests on identifying the selective pressures that caused it to develop. If it is not, then the explanation for the trait must employ nonselective evolutionary processes such as drift.

REFERENCES

Bayham, F. E. (1979). Factors influencing the Archaic pattern of animal exploitation. *Kiva* 44: 219–235.

Bettinger, R. L., and P. J. Richerson. (1996). The state of evolutionary archaeology: Evolutionary correctness, or the search for the common ground. In H.D.G Maschner (ed.), *Darwinian Archaeologies*. New York: Plenum, pp. 221–231.

Binford, L. (1962). Archaeology as anthropology. *American Antiquity* 28: 217–225.

Binford, L. (1964). A consideration of archaeological research design. *American Antiquity* 29: 425–441.

Binford, L. (1972). *An Archaeological Perspective*. New York: Seminar Press.

Binford, L. (1989). *Debating Archaeology*. San Diego, CA: Academic Press.

Boone, J. L. (1998). Comment on "The goals of evolutionary archaeology: history and explanation" by R. L. Lyman and M. J. O'Brien. *Current Anthropology* 39: 631–632.

Boone, J. L., and E. A. Smith. (1998). Is it evolution yet? A critique of evolutionary archaeology. *Current Anthropology* 39: S141–S173.

Broughton, J. M. (1994). Late Holocene resource intensification in the Sacramento Valley, California: The vertebrate evidence. *Journal of Archaeological Science* 21: 501–514.

Buikstra, J. E., L. W. Konigsberg, and J. Bullington. (1986). Fertility and the development of agriculture in the prehistoric Midwest. *American Antiquity* 51: 528–546.

Burian, R. M. (1992). Adaptation: Historical perspectives. In E. F. Keller and E. A. Lloyd (eds.), *Keywords in Evolutionary Biology*. Cambridge, MA: Harvard University Press, pp. 7–12.

Clarke, D. L. (1968). *Analytic Archaeology*. London: Methuen.

Dunnell, R. C. (1978). Style and function: A fundamental dichotomy. *American Antiquity* 43: 192–202.

Dunnell, R. C. (1980). Evolutionary theory and archaeology. In M. B. Schiffer (ed.), *Advances in Archaeological Method and Theory*, vol. 3. New York: Academic Press, pp. 35–99.

Dunnell, R. C., and R. J. Wenke. (1980). Cultural and scientific evolution: Some comments on "The Decline and Rise of Mesopotamian Civilization." *American Antiquity* 45: 605–609.

Futuyama, D. J. (1979). *Evolutionary Biology*. Sunderland, MA: Sinauer Press.

Gould, S. J., and R. Lewontin. (1979). The spandrels of San Marco and the Panglossian paradigm: A critique of the adaptationist programme. *Proceedings of the Royal Society of London* B205: 581–598.

Gould, S. J., and E. S. Vrba. (1982). Exaptation—A missing term in the science of form. *Paleobiology* 8: 4–15.

Hurt, T. D., T. L. VanPool, G.F.M. Rakita, and R. D. Leonard. (2001). Explaining the co-occurrence of attributes and artifacts in the archaeological record: A further consideration of replicative success. In T. D. Hurt and G.F.M. Rakita (eds.), *Style and Function: Conceptual Issues in Evolutionary Archaeology*. Westport, CT: Bergin and Garvey, pp. 51–68.

Jochim, M. (1983). Optimization models in context. In J. A. Moore and A. S. Keene (eds.), *Archaeological Hammers and Theories*. New York: Academic Press, pp. 157–172.

Kantner, J. (1999). Biological evolutionary theory and individual decision-making. Paper presented at the 64th Annual Meetings of the Society for American Archaeology, April 5–9, Philadelphia.

Kirch, P. V. (1980). The archaeological study of adaptation: Theoretical and methodological issues. In M. B. Schiffer (ed.), *Advances in Archaeological Method and Theory*, vol. 3. New York: Academic Press, pp. 101–157.

Leonard, R. D. (1998). Comment on "Is it evolution yet? A critique of evolutionary archaeology," by J. L. Boone and E. A. Smith. *Current Anthropology* 39: S162–S163.

Leonard, R. D. (2001). Evolutionary archaeology. In I. Hodder (ed.), *Archaeological Theory Today*. Cambridge: Polity Press, pp. 65–97.

Leonard, R. D., and G. T. Jones. (1987). Elements of an inclusive evolutionary model for archaeology. *Journal of Anthropological Archaeology* 6: 199–219.

Leonard, R. D., and H. E. Reed. (1993). Population aggregation in the prehistoric American Southwest: A selectionist model. *American Antiquity* 58: 648–661.

Lyman, R. L., and M. J. O'Brien. (1998). The goals of evolutionary archaeology: History and explanation. *Current Anthropology* 39: 615–652.

Mayr, E. (1988). *Toward a New Philosophy of Biology: Observations of an Evolutionist*. Cambridge, MA: Harvard University Press.

Millikan, R. G. (1989). In defense of proper functions. *Philosophy of Science* 56: 288–302.

Mills, S. K., and J. H. Beatty. (1994). The propensity interpretation of fitness. In E. Sober (ed.), *Conceptual Issues in Evolutionary Biology*. Cambridge, MA: MIT Press, pp. 3–24.

Mithen, S. (1990). *Thoughtful Foragers: A Study of Human Decision Making*. Cambridge: Cambridge University Press.

Mithen, S. (1998). Comment on "Is it evolution yet? A critique of evolutionary archaeology," by J. L. Boone and E. A. Smith. *Current Anthropology* 39: S163–S164.

Neander, K. (1991). Functions as selected effects: The conceptual analyst's defense. *Philosophy of Science* 58: 168–184.

O'Brien, M. J. (ed.). (1996). *Evolutionary Archaeology: Theory and Application*. Salt Lake City: University of Utah Press.

O'Brien, M. J., and T. D. Holland. (1992). The role of adaptation in archaeological explanation. *American Antiquity* 57: 3–59.

O'Brien, M. J., T. D. Holland, R. J. Hoard, and G. L. Fox. (1994). Evolutionary implications of design and performance characteristics of prehistoric pottery. *Journal of Archaeological Method and Theory* 1: 259–304.

O'Brien, M. J., and R. L. Lyman. (2000). *Applying Evolutionary Archaeology: A Systematic Approach*. New York: Kluwer Academic/Plenum.

Pittendrigh, C. S. (1958). Adaptation, natural selection, and behavior. In A. Roe and G. G. Simpson (eds.), *Behavior and Evolution*. New Haven, CT: Yale University Press, pp. 390–416.

Rhode, D. (1989). Agriculture and water use before the twentieth century on the Zuni Reservation, west-central New Mexico. Document presented for use as expert testimony to the Institute of the North American West, on behalf of the Zuni Indian Tribe in *City of Gallup v. USA*, No. Civ. 84–0164, District Court, McKinley County, NM.

Rindos, D. (1984). *The Origins of Agriculture: An Evolutionary Perspective*. New York: Academic Press.

Rottschaefer, W. A. (1997). Adaptational functional ascriptions in evolutionary biology: A critique of Schaffner's views. *Philosophy of Science* 64: 698–713.

Schiffer, M. B. (1996). Some relationships between behavioral and evolutionary archaeology. *American Antiquity* 61: 643–662.

Schiffer, M. B., and J. M. Skibo. (1987). Theory and experiment in the study of technological change. *Current Anthropology* 28: 595–609.

Schiffer, M. B., and J. M. Skibo. (1997). The explanation of artifact variability. *American Antiquity* 62: 27–51.

Sober, E. (1984). *The Nature of Selection: Evolutionary Thought in Philosophical Focus*. Chicago: University of Chicago Press.

Spencer, C. S. (1997). Evolutionary approaches in archaeology. *Journal of Archaeological Research* 5: 209–264.

Trigger, B. (1989). *A History of Archaeological Thought*. Cambridge: Cambridge University Press.

Vrba, E. S., and N. Eldridge. (1984). Individuals, hierarchies and processes: Towards a more complete evolutionary theory. *Paleobiology* 10: 146–171.

Vrba, E. S., and S. J. Gould. (1986). The hierarchical expansion of sorting and selection: Sorting and selection cannot be equated. *Paleobiology* 12: 217–228.

West-Eberhard, M. J. (1992). Adaptation: Current usage. In E. F. Keller and E. A. Lloyd (eds.), *Keywords in Evolutionary Biology*. Cambridge, MA: Harvard University Press, pp. 13–18.

Wright, L. (1973). Functions. *Philosophical Review* 82: 139–168.

Wright, L. (1994). Functions. In E. Sober (ed.), *Conceptual Issues in Evolutionary Biology*. Cambridge, MA: MIT Press, pp. 27–48.

White, L. A. (1959). *The Evolution of Culture*. New York: McGraw-Hill.

Yoffee, N. (1979). The decline and rise of Mesopotamian civilization: An ethnoarchaeological perspective on the evolution of social complexity. *American Antiquity* 44: 5–35.

Yoffee, N. (1980). Honk if you know Darwin: Brief reply to Dunnell and Wenke. *American Antiquity* 45: 610–612.

Chapter 3

Biological Constraints

James Steele

INTRODUCTION

As biological organisms, we are the products of our evolutionary history. This history involved the interaction of natural or sexual selection (which optimize design features of an organism) with those structural constraints which limit any genetic lineage to the exploration of a small segment of biological "design space." For example, it has occasionally been argued that our hominid ancestors were subject to selection for an endurance-running capacity, which is thought to be advantageous in running down prey animals in tropical grassland environments. However, even an Olympic athlete cannot run faster than a maximum speed, nor sustain that maximum speed for an extended time, due to physiological constraints on muscle activity. Any adaptive design features of the human locomotor system operate within the evolutionary constraints of a system that is far more easily "tinkered with" than fundamentally redesigned by the mechanisms of selection. **Natural selection** is the process by which environmental pressures determine the rates of propagation of genetically controlled traits; **sexual selection** is the process by which such rates of propagation are determined by individuals' choices of mates.

There are many obvious design features of humans, as organisms, that also constrain or channel the cultural evolution of skills, artifacts, and behavior. We can only survive within a limited range of ambient temperatures. We must maintain a fairly constant intake of water and nutrients to enable the growth and maintenance of our body tissues over the life cycle. We are vulnerable to colonization by disease organisms, many of which are life threatening. Our physiology is geared to a diurnal cycle, and we require a minimum level of sleep at a regular point in that cycle in order to sustain normal physiological functioning. The absolute physical dimensions of our bodies and their component parts constrain the force that we can exert in many tasks, and the ways in which we can most efficiently exert it. Our life cycle, including the timetables for attainment of adult physical size, of reproductive maturity, and of successive levels of cognitive and emotional maturation, is constrained by the developmental factors that determine our rates of growth. These very obvious design features of our bodies are part and parcel of being human, and they (in turn) act as constraints on the evolution of cultural traits in "design space."

However, when we talk of **biological constraints** on human behavior, we are often referring to a more specific range of *inbuilt cognitive constraints on learning and decision making* that are seen as secondary and as limiting factors on the primary mechanism that shapes our choices. This primary mechanism is learning, particularly social or cultural learning. Some anthropologists would see these biological constraints as arising from a drive to maximize our **inclusive fitness**, with our genes keeping culture "on a leash" (inclusive fitness is a term that denotes the effect of possessing some genetically heritable trait on the rate of reproductive propagation of the genes that determine it). But the real reason we might consider such a drive as *constraining* cultural evolution is that cultures can evolve far more rapidly than organisms. Biological constraints are those genetically determined traits which cannot evolve to more adaptive configurations in step with the rate at which we are able to change our own environments.

The concept of biological constraints is important for evolutionary studies in archaeology because it refers to the ways in which our genetically controlled physical makeup may have been channelling the evolution of cultural traits in "design space."

HISTORY AND CONTEMPORARY USES

The concept of **evolutionary constraints** in biology is used to explain situations where an observed genetic response to selection pressure differs from that which we expect. The source of our expectation must be some idealized model, perhaps derived from optimization theory. Organisms may not evolve the traits that we expect because of limits on available genetic variation in their populations. This may be due to the genetic covariance of traits, or to features of population structure (such as small size, restricted gene flow, or selection that acts at a different level to that of the individual).

However, the concept of "biological constraints" in learning theory has a rather different meaning, with its roots in comparative psychology (that is, the study of the behavior mechanisms of different animal species). In the behaviorist framework of animal learning theory, where the development of behavior patterns was seen as primarily shaped by selective environmental reinforcement of responses, "constraints on learning" were invoked to explain species differences in learning. The implication was that such constraints defined species-specific behavioral characteristics that were under direct genetic control. It could be hypothesized that they represent adaptive specializations for solving the major problems of survival and reproduction in each species' natural environment. A classic example of this involves the study of spatial memory ability in birds that store food in caches—a strategy that enables them to survive the winter, and to begin reproducing earlier in the breeding season. Birds of species that cache food in the wild perform much better in laboratory tests of spatial memory than do birds of similar brain and body size from species that do not depend on food-caching in the wild. Anatomical investigations have found a correlate of this enhanced spatial ability: food-caching birds have significant enlargement of a brain structure called the hippocampus, which is known to be involved in spatial memory (Sherry 1998). It should be noted that advocates of an ecological approach to learning might not describe such adaptive specializations as constraints. However, it is also clear that to a general learning theorist, they surely would be seen as constraints (since they explain why some species do not perform as expected in "ecologically invalid" laboratory learning tasks).

In the human case, identifying such biological constraints on learning has been particularly difficult and controversial. This is because of all animal species, we are the most obligate social learners; as a consequence, we are extremely diverse in our behavior patterns across cultures. **Social learning** refers to information learned from other individuals, by mechanisms that include imitation and language (in fact, one of the principal biological constraints on human behavior is our dependence on social learning—which explains the perennial interest in folktales about the behavior of "wolf-children"!). It is very hard, when studying behavior in any single culture, to differentiate between widespread biases that are due to "hardwiring," and those that are due to widespread—but socially learned—behavioral habits. One necessary criterion for recognizing such biological constraints must be that the behavior that we believe to be thus constrained can be found in a similar form in all human cultures. But even then, we need to be sure that the similarities are not due to an alternative mechanism, such as a very widespread diffusion of the trait by social learning.

Notwithstanding these difficulties, there are many contemporary theorists of human behavior who are convinced that human **cultural learning** is shaped by **evolved predispositions** which all individuals share (cultural learning is identified by Tomasello et al. [1993] specifically with "instances of social learning in which intersubjectivity or perspective-taking plays a vital role"; evolved predispositions are inbuilt psychological mechanisms, which bias our learning and decision making in favor of strategies that would have been adaptive at the time of their evolution). Typically, the argument would go as follows. The mechanisms of human cultural learning must have evolved as a result of natural or sexual selection, and must therefore have enabled our ancestors to maximize their inclusive fitness (that is, to achieve the greatest positive differentials in reproductive success). As a consequence, neither our ancestors nor we can have acquired our social values, beliefs, and attitudes purely by social conditioning. Rather, we must be endowed with the propensity to selectively filter such values, beliefs, and attitudes, and to acquire those that are most likely to enhance our own reproductive success. Human genetic diversity is very limited, reflecting the late Middle Pleistocene age of our last common ancestor (as estimated by geneticists using the molecular clock). It is therefore reasonable to assume that we all share such a propensity, and that it evolved in some ancestral hominid population prior to the great diaspora of anatomically modern human hunter-gatherers.

Developing this approach has formed part of the agenda of human sociobiology, although more recently it has become identified with the more specialized field of **evolutionary psychology** (evolutionary psychology is the study of our evolved predispositions). A major goal of such an approach is to identify the psychological predispositions that constrain human cultural learning, and channel it adaptively. One of the reasons why we may choose to identify such predispositions as constraints, rather than as adaptive specializations, is that our environment may have changed so much that they predispose us to do things that are no longer optimal.

BIOLOGICAL CONSTRAINTS ON HUMAN REASONING ABILITY: A PLEISTOCENE HUNTER-GATHERER LEGACY?

We will illustrate this approach (and its archaeological relevance) with a very well-known case study of apparent biological constraints on human reasoning abilities, which was the Ph.D. dissertation topic of Leda Cosmides (one of the most active and articulate recent proponents of evolutionary psychology). Analyzing this case study will require us to think like cognitive psychologists rather than archaeologists, but the effort is worthwhile. As we will see, this exercise is actually highly relevant to our understanding of one major objective of Paleolithic archaeology.

Cosmides and her collaborator John Tooby have argued that human reasoning and decision-making processes do not conform to the expectations of abstract logic (e.g., Cosmides 1989; Cosmides and Tooby 1989; Tooby and Cosmides 1989). In particular, they have attempted to explain why we perform unexpectedly poorly in the psychology lab on many conditional reasoning tasks. In their standard form, these tasks require subjects to test whether a proposition of the form "if P, then Q" is true in a set of four instances, for each of which the subjects initially receive only partial information. An example of such a task is given in Figure 3.1: it is normal to find that only 10% of subjects give the correct solution to such an ab-

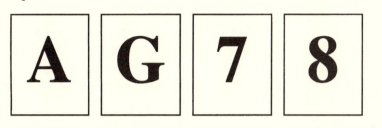

Here are four cards. Each has a letter on one side and a number on the other side. Two of these cards are with the letter side up, and two with the number side up:

Indicate which of these cards you need to turn over in order to judge whether the following rule is true:

If there is an A on one side, there is a 7 on the other side.

Figure 3.1. A standard abstract version of the card selection task (from Sperber et al. 1995). The correct answer is the card with an "A" and the card with an "8."

stract, descriptive version. Cosmides found that subjects performed dramatically better when the task was presented as an exercise in checking whether or not a rule of social exchange had been violated. An example of Cosmides' social exchange version of the task is given in Figure 3.2: she found that 75% of subjects gave the correct solution to such versions.

Cosmides and Tooby (1989) suggest that these differences in performance on versions of the task which share the same logical structure, but which differ in the narrative content of their presentation, must reflect a human psychological specialization for solving adaptive problems relating to cooperation and social exchange. They argue that cooperation can only evolve in situations where individuals will meet many times, and on each occasion will have the opportunity to benefit each other at relatively low cost to themselves. Pleistocene hunter-gatherers met these criteria: individuals were long-lived and lived in small and relatively stable bands, with a high degree of relatedness among their members. Their savannah-woodland adaptation gave them plentiful opportunities for repeated cooperative exchanges, since this involved tool-assisted exploitation of food items too large to be consumed by a single individual (notably, the cooperative hunting of large game animals). According to Cosmides and Tooby,

Successfully conducted social exchange was such an important and recurrent feature of hominid evolution that selection would have favored a reliable, efficient cognitive capacity specialized for reasoning about social exchange. A general-purpose learn-

You are a Kulumae, a member of a Polynesian culture found only on Maku Island in the Pacific. The Kulumae have many strict laws which must be enforced, and the elders have entrusted you with enforcing them. To fail would disgrace you and your family.

Among the Kulumae, when a man marries, he gets a tattoo on his face; only married men have tattoos on their faces. A facial tattoo means that a man is married, an unmarked face means that a man is a bachelor.

Cassava root is a powerful aphrodisiac—it makes the man who eats it irresistible to women. Moreover, it is delicious and nutritious—and very scarce.

Unlike cassava root, molo nuts are very common, but they are poor eating—molo nuts taste bad, they are not very nutritious, and they have no other interesting "medicinal" properties.

Although everyone craves cassava root, eating it is a privilege that your people closely ration. You are a very sensual people, even without the aphrodisiac properties of cassava root, but you have very strict sexual mores. The elders disapprove of sexual relations between unmarried people, and particularly distrust the motives and intentions of bachelors.

Therefore, the elders have made laws governing rationing privileges. The one you have been entrusted to enforce is as follows:

"If a man eats cassava root, then he must have a tattoo on his face."

Cassava root is so powerful an aphrodisiac that many men are tempted to cheat on this law whenever the elders are not looking. The cards below have information about four young Kulumae men sitting in a temporary camp; there are no elders around. A tray filled with cassava root and molo nuts has just been left for them. Each card represents one man. One side of a card tells which food a man is eating, and the other side of the card tells whether or not the man has a tattoo on his face.

Your job is to catch men whose sexual desires might tempt them to break the law—if any get past you, you and your family will be disgraced. Indicate only those card(s) you definitely need to turn over *to see if any of these Kulumae men are breaking the law*.

Eats cassava root	Does not eat cassava root	Has a tattoo	Does not have a tattoo

Figure 3.2. A social contract version of the card selection task (from Cosmides 1989). The correct answer is the card with an "Eats cassava root" and the card with a "Does not have a tattoo."

ing mechanism that operated on all kinds of content indiscriminately is necessarily more inefficient at specialized problems: among other things, being initially "ignorant," it will make costly errors and will continue to do so throughout its learning phase. (Cosmides and Tooby 1989: 86–87)

They contend that the dramatic improvement in performance on conditional reasoning tasks when these are framed as social exchange dilemmas proves that we do have such a specialized cognitive capacity. Furthermore, according to Tooby and Cosmides (1989: 32), we do not need to know what components of the human brain underwrite such cognitive specialization.

The language of cognition provides an economical and powerful language for . . . describing in precise terms what such mechanisms do in solving adaptive problems . . . without becoming entangled in the immensely intricate and largely unknown area of their neurological and physiological basis.

Now arguments of this kind, which postulate evolved propensities for adaptive reasoning that are unique to humans, and that evolved during Pleistocene, have an obvious relevance for archaeologists. But before we rewrite our own narratives of human cognitive evolution and reinterpret the Paleolithic record to fit these postulates, we ought to check their validity. After all, it seems a strange kind of cognitive universal that manifests itself in only 75% of subjects in the psychology lab. Moreover, the subjects of these studies have tended to be undergraduate students in North American and European universities: this hardly constitutes a sufficiently large and unbiased cross-cultural sample.

In fact, other psychological studies have now identified ways of facilitating solution of even the abstract, descriptive versions of the card selection task (Figure 3.1). For instance, Sperber et al. (1995) elicited a nearly 60% success rate from their subjects for the abstract descriptive version given in Figure 3.3 (which has been written specifically to engage the subjects' attention by flagging the relevance of the problem, and by minimizing the effort of arriving at the correct solution). They argue that what motivates us to solve a problem efficiently is not its specific subject matter (social versus non-social), but its perceived relevance. Relevance is achievable in any conceptual domain: it is the product of the effect of new information on an individual's prior beliefs, and of the effort involved in processing it. The most relevant new information is that which is easy to process and which has a large effect on one's beliefs. Sperber et al. (1995) conclude that while it may indeed be the case that we perform best when reasoning about social exchange because of inbuilt adaptive biases, these card selection tasks are certainly not the way to demonstrate it!

This case study illustrates the typical appeal, and also the typical pitfalls,

A machine manufactures cards. It is programmed to print at random, on the front of each card, a 4 or a 6. On the back of each card, it prints a letter:

- when there is a 4, it prints either an A or an E at random
- when there is a 6, it prints an E.

One day, Mr. Bianchi, the person in charge, realizes that the machine has produced some cards it should not have printed. On the back of the cards with a 6, the machine has not always printed an E; sometimes it has printed an A instead of an E. Mr. Bianchi fixes the machine, examines the newly printed cards and says, "don't worry, the machine works fine."

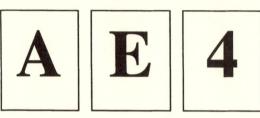 

Indicate which of these cards you need to turn over in order to judge whether the following rule is true:

If a card has a 6 on the front, it has an E on the back.

Figure 3.3. An abstract version of the card selection task, cued for maximum relevance (from Sperber et al. 1995). The correct answer is the card with an "A" and the card with a "6."

of evolutionary psychology. Evidence of human decision-making biases in specific settings is generalized and described as a universal predisposition. It is proposed that this bias would have been adaptive in the Pleistocene **Environment of Evolutionary Adaptedness,** or EEA (the "Environment of Evolutionary Adaptedness" is the term given by evolutionary psychologists to the niche occupied by hominids during the Pleistocene, when—it is proposed—the evolved predispositions that are unique to our species first appeared). It is then proposed that the bias must be under genetic control. However, the universality of the bias has not in fact been adequately demonstrated, while closer scrutiny reveals that the evidence itself is susceptible to alternative explanations in terms of general learning theory. No anatomical or physiological evidence has been adduced to support the proposed scenario, and no tests have been made of the purported context and timetable for the evolution of such a biasing mechanism in ancestral populations of Pleistocene hunter-gatherers. Evolutionary psychology typically postulates that the human brain contains a rich repertoire of such specialized mechanisms for solving problems that were adaptively relevant in the savannah-woodland habitats of Pleistocene Africa. By implication, cultural evolution in the last 10,000 years represents the exploration of a possibility space that is highly constrained by the biases we inherited from our hunter-gatherer ancestors. But on closer inspection, at least on the basis of the case we have just examined, it seems that this approach is simply producing a rather naïve set of "just-so stories."

The main significance of this debate for archaeology is in relation to the interpretation of Paleolithic site formation processes—the processes that brought clusters of lithic artifacts and animal bones into close spatial association. Cosmides and Tooby (1989: 58) cite Isaac's (1978) "home base" model of such processes to support their belief that "Pleistocene hunter-gatherers, like their modern counterparts, engaged in extensive food-sharing." There is an unfortunate circularity to this argument, since Isaac's model was based on the conjecture that modern hunter-gatherer land-use behavior was a suitable analogue for that of early *Homo*. Several other interpretations of late Pliocene and early Pleistocene site formation must also be considered, including the behavioral models of routed foraging and of stone caching, and the taphonomic model of accidental association (Potts 1992). In the extreme, Yellen (1996) has suggested that the earliest clear signs of modern hunter-gatherer camp site structure are at the Middle Stone Age site of Katanda 9 in Zaire, dating to perhaps 90,000 B.P. We certainly cannot use Isaac's model, in itself, to validate conjectures about the EEA.

BIOLOGICAL CONSTRAINTS ON DIET AND HEALTH: ANOTHER PLEISTOCENE HUNTER-GATHERER LEGACY?

A similar style of argument has been adopted recently by some anthropologists, who are concerned at the high prevalence in developed countries of "diseases of civilization" (such as obesity, hypertension, coronary artery disease, and cancer). In this case, their emphasis is not on biological constraints on human reasoning, but on the biological constraints that determine what constitutes a healthy diet. For example, Cordain et al. (2000: 682) argue that "the diets of modern hunter-gatherers may represent a reference standard for modern human nutrition and a model for defense against certain 'diseases of civilization'." They analyze ethnographic data on the contributions of animal and plant foods to hunter-gatherer diets, and conclude that hunter-gatherers typically derive more than half of their energy requirements from animal foods, with less than one in seven ethnographically documented hunter-gatherer societies subsisting mainly on plant foods (Figure 3.4). Breaking down typical hunter-gatherer food intake into its constituent energy sources (proteins, carbohydrates, and fats), they

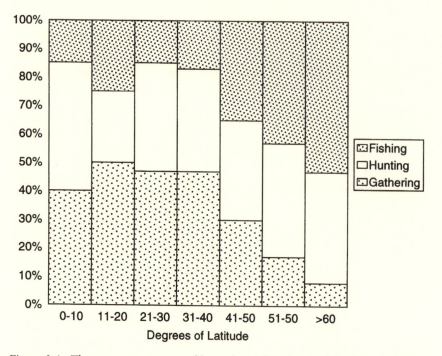

Figure 3.4. The mean percentages of hunted and fished animal foods and of gathered wild plant foods, in the diets of hunter-gatherer societies sampled at different latitudes (after Cordain et al. 2000).

conclude that this reference diet would contain higher levels of protein, comparable or higher levels of fat, and lower levels of carbohydrate than those of a typical modern diet in a Western developed country. Modern food habits in the United States, as documented by the 1987–1988 National Food Consumption Survey, are taken as the model for modern Western diet. In the United States, more than half of an individual's energy intake is typically derived from cereal grains (31%), dairy products (14%), beverages (8%), oils and dressings (4%), and discretionary sugar and candy (4%). These modern food preferences derive from the agricultural revolution, since such foods are obtained from domesticated plants and from the secondary products of domesticated ungulates (notably, dairy cows). According to Cordain et al. (2000), an elevated consumption of carbohydrates may be partly responsible for the elevated modern prevalence rates of diseases of civilization.

This argument has a similar structure to the evolutionary psychologists' explanation of human reasoning deficits. Evidence is adduced of a correlation between modern disease patterns and dietary dependence on processed foods derived from domesticated crops and animals. It is proposed that the typical diet of ethnographically documented hunter-gatherers can serve as a reference standard for the diet to which we are most adapted. By implication, the cultural evolution of subsistence practices in the last 10,000 years represents the exploration of a "possibility space" that is highly constrained by the physiological needs and nutrient absorption mechanisms that we inherited from our hunter-gatherer ancestors. The high prevalence of degenerative diseases in developed Western societies therefore reflects the biological constraints of our physiology, which is adapted to the hunter-gatherer diet of a Pleistocene environment of evolutionary adaptedness.

In fact, this argument is highly contestable. As Milton (2000) points out, the ethnographically documented sample of modern hunter-gatherers encompasses a wide spectrum of dietary strategies, and among them there is little evidence that diseases of civilization occur more frequently in societies such as the !Kung, where gathered wild plant food supplies a high proportion of food energy, or the Yanomamo, where a high proportion of food energy comes from a single, domesticated plant cultivar. In addition, there is no evidence that we have any digestive tract specializations for carnivory. Human digestive physiology is the legacy of a primate ancestry shared with the great apes, and in which plant foods were the main source of food energy. It is true that some components of our gastrointestinal tract are reduced in size, which means that our food intake must be more energy-dense and more highly digestible if we are to maintain basal rates of tissue metabolism. However, this can be achieved by tool-assisted processing of plant foods, and does not mandate an increased dependence on animal carcass resources. Obligate carnivores such as the cat family, in contrast, have metabolic adaptations to an all-flesh diet which act as far stricter biological constraints on dietary flexibility. These include "an unusually high requirement for protein for maintenance and growth, an unusual pattern of gluconeogenesis, and an inability to synthesise vitamin A and niacin from dietary precursors" (Milton 2000: 665). Such specialized adaptations are not present in our own species. Perhaps the reason that hunter-gatherers experience fewer of the diseases of civilization is not that they eat more animal protein and fewer carbohydrates, but that wild foods tend to be less energy-dense than modern processed foods, and take a long time to transit through the gut. This, and the greater levels of physical activity which characterize the hunter-gatherer lifestyle, act as a natural check to obesity and some other diseases of civilization.

This is not to say that the dietary shift from foraging to farming was without costs. Bioarchaeologists have documented skeletal manifestations of health changes across this transition in different regions of the world. Often, but by no means always, we see signs in the farming populations of nutritional deficiency and its consequences. These may include generalized growth retardation; and increased prevalence of iron-deficiency anemia, of dental enamel formation defects, of dental caries, and of bone infections (Larsen 2000). However, we should bear in mind the many possible causes of such health trends. Farmers tend to have a narrower diet, which puts them at greater risk of nutritional deficits. Their economic strategy involves a simplification of their ecosystem, with consequent loss of resilience and vulnerability to periodic collapse (famines). Sedentism and large community sizes promote the spread of diseases, including zoonoses (diseases of other animals that transfer to humans). Of all of these, it is the narrowing of dietary breadth that Larsen (2000) identifies as the main cause of nutritional deficiency and its consequences for prehistoric health. But in this account, it is the breadth of hunter-gatherer diet (and not its focus on animal protein) which explains the typically better health of prehistoric foragers. The moral would seem to be that if we want to stay healthy we should eat a more balanced diet, with enough animal protein or its substitutes, but also with more fresh fruit and vegetables and with more natural fibre.

DYNAMIC APPROACHES TO BIOLOGICAL CONSTRAINTS: VARIABILITY SELECTION AND GENE–CULTURE CO-EVOLUTION

The evolutionary arguments that we have just examined are important because, by their very nature, they assert a common human legacy of social cooperation for mutual aid and a common nutritional reference standard for human health. But while one important dimension of anthropology will always remain the assertion of such characteristics of what Brown (1991) calls "the universal people," there are some fundamental flaws in the ways in which such assertions are currently being made. Typically, the claim is made that human adaptive specializations are the product of intense selection pressures during the five million years or more that separate us from a last common ancestor shared with the chimpanzees. During that period, it is implicitly believed, hominids were adapting to a stable set of challenges in a single niche—the so-called "Environment of Evolutionary Adaptedness." This niche is usually identified as that of large-bodied, tool-assisted bipedal primates in a savannah-woodland habitat, whose subsistence included an important new focus on the hunting of large animals. By comparison with the long time scale of the Plio-Pleistocene, the last 10,000 years (which have seen the most dramatic and rapid phases of human cultural evolution) are considered too short a time for significant genetic changes to have affected the human species and its behavioral repertoire. Seen from this perspective, while people's social and economic lives have changed and diversified enormously during the recent past, they have inevitably remained subject to the biological constraints of a Plio-Pleistocene genetic inheritance.

Despite their obvious appeal, such arguments are flawed. They assume that human evolution during the Plio-Pleistocene involved adaptive responses to a single, stable ecological niche. They also assume that no significant genetic adaptations to novel environmental challenges have occurred during the last 10,000 years. Both of these assumptions can be called into question.

Richard Potts (1998) has proposed a major correction to the assumption that our distinctively human traits evolved as adaptations to a particular ancestral habitat—the open, grassland-dominated habitat of an East and Southern African savannah-woodland mosaic. Climatic evidence adduced in support of that assumption generally includes the observation that during the last five million years (during the geological epochs known as the Pliocene and Pleistocene), global temperature trends have produced a progressively cooler and drier world (Figure 3.5). However, as Potts points out, superimposed on that long-term trend have been a series of shorter time-scale fluctuations in global temperature; and these fluctuations have been getting progressively more and more extreme during that same five-million-year time period (Figure 3.5). Potts suggests that this second trend, toward greater climatic instability, is just as important as the overall long-term global cooling trend.

We should not think of human evolution as a story of increasingly successful adaptation to a savannah-woodland Environment of Evolutionary Adaptedness. Habitat types have fluctuated in their distribution within the geographical ranges of hominids during this period. At successive times, the same low-latitude African localities have been either dry and open, or moist and highly vegetated. We should, rather, think of human evolution as the product of **variability selection**: that is, characterized by the appearance of "complex structures or behaviours that are designed to respond to novel and unpredictable adaptive settings" (Potts 1998: 85). These structures and behavioral mechanisms include a locomotor system that permits a wide range of movements; a dental structure or foraging strategy that enables a wide range of food types to be exploited; a large brain that enables sophisticated processing of environmental data; and social behaviors which permit a wider range of mating systems and grouping strategies. Potts suggests that while such characteristics may not be the most efficient adaptive response to the challenges of any single environment (such as dry, open savannah grasslands), the instability of such environments on the Plio-Pleistocene time scale would ultimately have selected against "habitat specialists" and in favor of behavioral versatility and diversity. "Variability selection" refers to a form of natural selection in which the environmental pressures that affect gene frequencies operate on millennial and higher-order time scales (in which climate and environment are most characterized by cyclical oscillations between extremes, and not by constancy). This is very far from the view that our behavior is biologically constrained by the

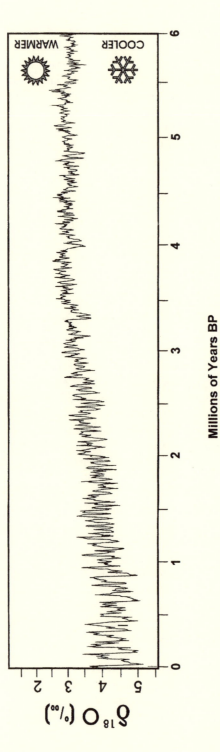

Millions of Years BP

Figure 3.5. Composite oxygen isotope curve for the past 6 million years showing both the overall cooling trend and the increasing amplitude of the oscillations in the later part of that period (from Potts 1998).

adaptive legacy of life in a single, stable Environment of Evolutionary Adaptedness.

The second assumption that characterizes the kinds of arguments about biological constraints that we examined in earlier sections of this chapter is illustrated by this quotation from Tooby and Cosmides (1989: 35):

The evolution of the psychological mechanisms that underlie culture turned out to be so powerful that they created a historical process, cultural change, which (beginning at least as early as the Neolithic) changed conditions far faster than organic evolution could track, given its inherent limitations on rates of successive substitution.

Although Tooby and Cosmides were thinking primarily of the limited scope that exists for novel cognitive adaptations to emerge in response to novel culturally determined conditions during the last 10,000 years, the same assumption underlies claims for the benefits of "Paleolithic nutrition." As we have seen, this would lead us to regard the dependence on agricultural produce as in some way "unnatural," and as an explanation of the high modern levels of "diseases of civilization" which we find in Western developed societies.

In fact, there is a whole branch of theoretical population genetics that is devoted to analyzing the interactions of genetic and cultural inheritance systems. This is known as "gene–culture co-evolutionary theory" (Durham 1991). Gene–culture co-evolutionary theory models the evolution of gene frequencies and of cultural trait frequencies, in populations where information is transmitted in both systems (with interacting effects). An individual's genes may influence what he or she learns, but cultural modifications to the environment in which he or she develops may also change the selective forces acting on genetically controlled traits. Two of the best-known examples of gene–culture co-evolution in human populations relate specifically to genetic adaptations during the last 10,000 years that confer disease resistance and modify digestive physiology as a response to the cultural changes of the agricultural revolution.

As one example, it can be shown that frequencies of the sickle cell gene (that confers resistance to malaria) among West African populations are correlated with maximum monthly rainfall (Durham 1991). This rainfall index is an indirect predictor of malarial severity, since *Anopheles gambiae*, the principal mosquito vector of the malaria parasite *Plasmodium falciparum*, requires warm, sunlit freshwater ponds for its reproduction. But in addition, Durham (1991) has shown that high frequencies of the sickle cell gene only occur in populations of this region that have long histories (on the order of 2,000 years) of slash-and-burn cultivation of the yam. This is because such cultivation practices, in opening up closed-canopy vegetation and creating contexts for freshwater pond formation, dramatically increase the opportunities for reproduction of the disease's mosquito vector. Adjacent populations of yam cultivators from the same language group, living in areas with similar rainfall patterns, do not have the same distributions of the sickle cell gene; but they have only very recently converted from a closed canopy rainforest hunter-gatherer lifestyle to agriculture. Agricultural practices have created new environments, and new patterns of disease prevalence. This has created intense selection pressures for enhanced disease resistance, and gene frequencies of the sickle cell trait have changed (over a millennial time scale) as an adaptive response.

As a second example, it is evident that a long history of dairying in human societies, particularly those inhabiting higher latitudes, is associated with high frequencies of the genes for lactose absorption (Durham 1991). Most humans, in common with other mammals, lose the ability to digest lactose once past the weaning age (lactose is the principal solid and sole sugar in milk). This is evidently the conservative condition, derived from our Pleistocene ancestors. Relatively low prevalence rates of the genes for lactose absorption are also found in societies where milk from domesticated mammals is consumed as a staple, but mostly in a form where the digestion or removal of lactose has taken place before it enters the human gut. This can be achieved by processing milk into soured and fermented products such as yogurt, or by converting it to cheeses by first separating and draining off the lactose-rich whey. However, in societies of the Old World with a long tradition of dairying and in which large quantities of milk are consumed in raw form, we find very high prevalence rates of these genes, which enable lactose to be broken down into simple sugars in the gut and absorbed across the cell wall of the small intestine. Durham (1991) suggests that the adaptive advantage of this cannot just lie in the ability it confers to extract more of the food value from milk (since this can also be achieved by consuming soured and fermented milk, or aged cheese). There is, however, an additional advantage of being a lactose absorber. Lactose has an action in the gut similar to that of vitamin D, in that it facilitates absorption of calcium from the small intestine. People living in higher latitudes have reduced exposure to sunlight (and ultraviolet B radiation is a stimulus for formation of vitamin D in the human epidermis). Durham (1991) describes the close relationship between latitude, dietary dependence on dairying, rates of consumption of unprocessed milk, and rates of prevalence of the lactose absorption genes. He proposes that the very high proportions of "lactose absorbers" found in such societies reflects a history of gene–culture co-evolution. Given an initial exposure to milk consumption as a secondary consequence of the domestication of herbivorous mammals, the health benefits of increased calcium intake by lactose absorbers (and consequent avoidance of growth deficiency diseases such as rickets) would have promoted a feedback cycle favoring both the cultural practices of dairying and milk consumption, and the spread of the lactose absorption genes.

In this account the health of modern descendants of these lactose absorbers, far from being constrained by the inheritance of a Pleistocene digestive physiology, has the potential to be improved by increased use of dietary elements that would never have played a part in the Pleistocene lifestyle! There is an exciting new body of work on the archaeological evidence for prehistoric dairying, which includes studies of lipid residues in archaeological pottery vessels (Dudd and Evershed 1998), and stable isotopic studies of weaning and slaughtering age in young cattle at Neolithic sites (Balasse et al. 1997). If this work were integrated with paleopathological studies of changing prevalences of rickets, then we would have a good archaeological basis for testing Durham's co-evolutionary hypothesis.

FUTURE IMPORTANCE

In the opening section of this chapter, we noted that cultural evolution was very obviously constrained by our functional morphology (when humans are considered as organisms). However, we also identified a narrower sense in which the concept of "biological constraints" is used. This is to denote the ways in which our own adaptive specializations, which are the product of our evolution over the last five million years, limit and channel our present-day choices. We examined the claims made that our reasoning skills, and our health, exemplify the constraints imposed on our lives in this way by our genetic inheritance from an older Environment of Evolutionary Adaptedness.

If such arguments are correct, then there is one important implication for the way we analyze the archaeological record. We should be trying hard to identify in the Paleolithic archaeological record the features that defined that ancestral hominid adaptation, assessing the stability through the Pleistocene of the human social and economic strategies that are recorded in Paleolithic site structure and in land-use patterns. Another implication is that we should be trying to test predictions of the effects of such constraints on human adaptive success during the most recent 10,000 years of cultural evolution. For instance, if we really are constrained in our conditional reasoning ability in the way that Cosmides (1989) proposes, then we should find that people today perform far from optimally in situations requiring them to reason effectively about situations not involving social contracts—even when these are highly charged with contemporary relevance! We should also expect to see the effects of such a constrained reasoning ability on the cultural dynamics of past societies. Similarly, if a dependence on cultivated plant foods leads to poorer health, then we should expect to see this reflected in the comparative palaeopathology of prehistoric hunter-gatherer and agricultural societies in the archaeological record, as well as in the different patterns of disease prevalence in contemporary hunter-gatherers and subsistence farmers.

However, we have also discussed some very different perspectives on biological constraints. The variability selection hypothesis proposes that what distinguishes our species is the adaptation to uncertainty and to environmental novelty. In addition, the theory of gene–culture coevolution addresses situations where even within the past 10,000 years, cultural change has produced new selection pressures on the human genome (and thus, changing gene frequencies). If these approaches are correct, then they have very different implications for the way we analyze the archaeological record. We should be trying to identify a trend toward increasing diversity of cultural adaptations during the Paleolithic. We should also be trying to identify ways in which cultural changes during the past 10,000 years would have altered the contexts for natural selection on gene frequencies, and we should be testing our predictions of consequent changes in the genetic compositions of populations. If our social and cognitive abilities act not as constraints on adaptation, but as buffers that enable us to cope with a large range of environmental variation, then we should not expect to find significant selection pressures for the genetic modification of these abilities. The most intense selection pressures for genetic adaptation should be on aspects of our physiology that cannot easily be buffered against local environmental variables by social or cognitive means. These would certainly include genetic traits influencing mechanisms of disease resistance and of nutrient absorption.

REFERENCES

Balasse, M., H. Bocherens, A. Tresset, A. Mariotti, and J. D. Vigne. (1997). Emergence of dairy production in the Neolithic? Contribution of isotopic analysis of cattle archaeological bones. *Comptes rendus de l'Académie des Sciences Série 2A* 325: 1005–1010.

Brown, D. E. (1991). *Human Universals*. Philadelphia: Temple University Press.

Cordain, L., J. B. Miller, S. B. Eaton, N. Mann, S.H.A. Holt, and J. D. Speth. (2000). Plant-animal subsistence ratios and macronutrient energy estimations in worldwide hunter-gatherer diets. *American Journal of Clinical Nutrition* 71: 682–692.

Cosmides, L. (1989). The logic of social exchange: Has natural selection shaped how humans reason? *Cognition* 31: 187–276.

Cosmides, L., and J. Tooby. (1989). Evolutionary psychology and the generation of culture, Part II. *Ethology and Sociobiology* 10: 51–97.

Dudd, S. N., and R. P. Evershed. (1998). Direct demonstration of milk as an element of archaeological economies. *Science* 282: 1478–1481.

Durham, W. H. (1991). *Coevolution*. Stanford, CA: Stanford University Press.

Isaac, G. L. (1978). The food-sharing behavior of proto-human hominids. *Scientific American* 238: 90–108.

Larsen, C. S. (2000). *Skeletons in Our Closet: Revealing Our Past through Bioarchaeology*. Princeton, NJ: Princeton University Press.

Milton, K. (2000). Hunter-gatherer diets—A different perspective. *American Journal of Clinical Nutrition* 71: 665–667.

Potts, R. (1992). The hominid way of life. In S. Jones, R. Martin, and D. Pilbeam (eds.), *The Cambridge Encyclopedia of Human Evolution*. Cambridge: Cambridge University Press, pp. 325–334.

Potts, R. (1998). Variability selection in hominid evolution. *Evolutionary Anthropology* 7: 81–96.

Sherry, D. F. (1998). The ecology and neurobiology of spatial memory. In R. Dukas (ed.), *Cognitive Ecology*. Chicago: University of Chicago Press, pp. 261–296.

Sperber, D., F. Cara, and V. Girotto. (1995). Relevance theory explains the selection task. *Cognition* 57: 31–95.

Tomasello, M., A. C. Kruger, and H. H. Ratner. (1993). Cultural learning. *Behavioural and Brain Sciences* 16: 495–511.

Tooby, J., and L. Cosmides. (1989). Evolutionary psychology and the generation of culture, Part I. *Ethology and Sociobiology* 10: 29–49.

Yellen, J. E. (1996). Behavioural and taphonomic patterning at Katanda 9: A middle Stone Age site, Kivu province, Zaire. *Journal of Archaeological Science* 23: 915–932.

Chapter 4

Cause

Michael J. O'Brien and R. Lee Lyman

INTRODUCTION

The *American Heritage Dictionary of the English Language* (New College Edition, 1992) provides several definitions of **cause**; the one under consideration in this chapter is, "That which produces an effect, result, or consequence; the person, event, or condition responsible for an action or result." Cause is a central concept in human thinking and probably has been for thousands of years. Why do things happen? Why do they happen the way they do? Why do they happen that way as opposed to another? Why do they happen at a particular time as opposed to another? These kinds of questions are so fundamental that it would be difficult to imagine any sapient organism *not* asking them. Why-type questions, together with the related how-type questions, form the basis of Western scientific inquiry, which is a precise set of procedures designed to ferret out relations between and among natural phenomena and to formulate **explanations**, or reason-giving statements, for how and why those relations come to be expressed at particular times and in particular places.

One problem that occurs in science is a forced reliance on everyday words to refer to highly specific **processes** and **mechanisms**—two terms that themselves are difficult to define. We define "process" as any action or series of actions that produce something, and "mechanism" as a system of parts that function like those of a machine. Perhaps no field of inquiry has been faced with this problem more than Darwinian evolutionism—the study of descent with modification—although a strong case could be made that by extension anthropology and archaeology share many of the same language-based difficulties. When it comes to the word "cause" and all it entails, anthropology and archaeology fare even worse than does evolutionary biology because the subject matter is humans—organisms that seemingly have the capacity to set agendas, to anticipate changing social as well as physical environments, and to create the means by which to change their environments. In short, humans have the appearance of—and testify to—being the causes, or agents, of change. Humans are unique in the scientific world in that no other organism has the luxury of studying itself, let alone studying its behavior and assigning explanations for what caused that behavior. Such luxury comes at a price, however, in terms of potential loss of objectivity.

It could be argued that there is no loss of scientific objectivity because we *know* why we do things and why those things turn out the way they do. Actions and occurrences are the immediate products of intentions emanating from the minds of the doers; human intent—or so the actors tell us—thus becomes the cause of something, and results are explained in terms of that intent. Such a stance, however, lodges explanation within the things to be explained, which renders the explanation circular. Left unanswered is the question of why A occurred as opposed to B, or at a more fundamental level why A and B were available options in the first place. If anything, such explanations deal with proximate, or near-term causes, not ultimate causes. Science, however, is as interested in ultimate cause as it is in proximate cause, and it uses a mix of inductive and deductive reasoning to arrive at causal statements. **Theory,** defined as a set of things and statements about how those things interact that provide explanations, is as important as empirical evidence in such a mix; importantly, it is the key role afforded theory that sets science apart from other sense-making systems.

Lest we be misunderstood, we should point out that there is no single definition of cause that is appropriate for all sciences, nor is there unanimity over the proper role of explanation in the scientific enterprise. Further, we suspect that most scientists are not particularly upset by the existence of multiple definitions of cause or how the concept of explanation is used in different disciplines. In fact, perusal of the literature supports a proposition that philosopher Ernest Nagel (1965: 12) made in the mid-1960s: "It is beyond serious doubt that the term 'cause' rarely if ever appears in the research papers or treatises currently published in the natural sciences, and the odds are heavily against any mention in any book on theoretical physics." Despite this absence, it is clear that scientists today are as interested in causal processes and mechanisms as their predecessors were over two millennia ago.

HISTORY

The English word "cause" is derived ultimately from the Latin *causa*, which means purpose or reason. Both conceptually and etymologically the word can be traced to the Greek philosophers of the fifth century B.C. and the noun *aitia*, from which is derived *aitiologia* (English *etiology*), the study of cause. Until late in the fifth century B.C., causal explanations were based strictly on philosophical ruminations about the natural world. It is in the work of Plato that we see the beginnings of a marriage between philosophical reflection and **empiricism**, or the view that experience and observation are the paths to knowledge. In the *Timaeus* Plato discussed the origin of the cosmos, arguing that it was created by an intelligent, divine hand that kept it moving toward an ultimate end. **Teleology**, from the Greek word *telos* and referring to the study of natural features and occurrences from the standpoint that there is an overall natural design to them, was part of pre-Platonic Greek philosophy, but so far as we know it received its first in-depth treatment at the hands of Plato.

The notion of a purposive development and an ultimate end reached its greatest expression in the fourth-century B.C. works of Aristotle, but instead of depending on the conscious will of an intelligent designer for the origin and development of the cosmos, Aristotle modeled it as being both empirically sufficient and teleological in and of itself. In other words, Aristotle imbued nature with a vitalistic tendency but bypassed the need for a hands-on creator who constantly tinkered with what he had created in order to keep it moving toward its ultimate and predestined end.

The notion of a divine engineer came to play an important role in Western scientific enterprise throughout the second millennium A.D. Gone was the Aristotelian notion of a world of infinite age, and in its place was the biblical notion of a recently created world. The Bible made clear not only who was responsible for creating the world but also what man's role was in it: "[B]e fruitful and multiply, and fill the earth and subdue it; and have dominion over the fish of the sea, and over the birds of the air, and over every living thing that moves upon the earth" (Genesis 1:28). The Old Testament was the basis for a **natural theology**, or God-centered view of nature and its complexity, which reached a level of prominence through the thirteenth-century work of the Dominican monk Thomas Aquinas, who axiomatized teleology in Western thinking. His *Summa Theologiae* was based on the observation that there is so much order in the universe that there must be a divine creator who directs all natural things toward their proper and ultimate end. Empiricism, which had played an ever-widening role in Greek philosophy, played no role at all in the natural theology of Aquinas and his followers; rather, logic and deduction could provide the necessary answers relative to cause and the explanation of natural phenomena.

The Middle Ages brought about a radical shift in thinking, grounded in mechanics and a search for laws that mechanized the universe—that is, that put matter in motion and kept it there. For the first time, experimental measurement became an inseparable component of science, and the search was on for the identification of regularities in nature. The use of induction to identify the laws behind the regularities—for example, in the work of Polish astronomer Nicolaus Copernicus and Italian astronomer Galileo Galilei—reached a level of sophistication not previously seen in Western science, culminating in the major works of Isaac Newton. Philosophically, the mechanistic view was promoted by Francis Bacon and the neo-Platonic René Descartes, who used his invention, analytical geometry, as a means of teasing out structural relations among natural objects.

Slightly later, English philosopher John Locke attempted to show that despite the existence of mechanical laws that governed matter in motion, no amount of clever thinking could lead to the conclusion that the mind and the thoughts it produces arose out of mere matter and motion. Thus, there had to a thoughtful, intelligent being that preceded, and thus created, matter and motion. It was fruitful to search for laws that governed the inner workings of natural phenomena—these were not denied—but the question as to ultimate causality was already answered.

It may appear as if, by the eighteenth century, there was more or less a consensus among scientists and philosophers over the nature of cause, but a problem was emerging over how much control was being exerted by the intelligent designer. If one adhered to the writings of the physical scientists, then one was forced to conclude that although the designer had created the world, he had after that point kept his interference to a minimum, allowing a few basic laws to steer it forward. In contrast, increasing sophistication of observations of the living world made that conclusion untenable. Whereas physical scientists could study the proximate causes that were manifest by divine law, those studying the living world saw a contradiction. As biologist Ernst Mayr (1982: 103–104) put it,

Here such a diversity of individual actions and interactions is observed that it becomes inconceivable to explain it by a limited number of basic laws. Everything in the living world seemed to be so unpredictable, so special, and so unique that the observing naturalist found it necessary to invoke the creator, his thought, and his activity in every detail of the life of every individual of every kind of organism.

The naturalists saw perfection in every aspect of the living world, especially in the many and varied aspects of organisms that came to be referred to as **adaptations**—physical features and behaviors that the designer gave organisms to help guide them through uncertain environments. The features appeared to be so perfect, how could they be explained through reference to mere laws? The wedding of naturalism and theology that took place in the latter half of the seventeenth century was announced through such works as John Ray's *The Wisdom of God Manifested in the Works of Creation* (1691), and profoundly influenced the work of eminent eighteenth-century naturalists such as Georges Louis Buffon, Carolus Linnaeus, and Jean Baptiste Lamarck. It reached perhaps its clearest expression in two works: William Paley's *Natural Theology* (1802), appropriately subtitled *Evidences of the Existence and Attributes of the Deity Collected from the Appearances of Nature*, and Robert Chambers' (written anonymously) *Vestiges of the Natural History of Creation* (1844).

The term "natural theology" can also be applied to most geological texts of the late eighteenth and early nineteenth centuries. Received wisdom is that one of the great debates of the period was between uniformitarianists and catastrophists, but this glosses over the more important point that the debate was really over whether there was directionality in the history of the world. The ultimate cause of change, the divine creator, was rarely at issue in the debate; rather, emphasis was on secondary causes. For Charles Lyell, the foremost of the uniformitarianists, the earth's history was one of a steady state, with some degree of cyclicity. Once the earth had been created and life had been placed on it, the creator allowed the story to unfold in concordance with physical laws established to guide proper unfolding. For catastrophists such as Georges Cuvier, the earth's history was a tumultuous one, filled with faunal extinctions and replacements, which gave that history a directional, and to some a progressional, appearance. As opposed to the uniformitarianists, who saw the same causes operating throughout the earth's history, the catastrophists posited a series of causes for the early history of the earth that somehow had ceased to operate later in its history.

Charles Darwin's contribution to the nature of cause was to remove it from the domain of natural theology and to place it firmly on external grounds. Darwin's notion of "descent with modification," expressed so well in *On the Origin of Species* (1859), laid the groundwork not only for modern evolutionary biology but for the investigation of the natural world in general. As opposed to his predecessors, Darwin provided a process and a mechanism for the history of life that relied neither on urges inherent to organisms nor on the invisible hand of a designer. Cause—why things happened historically the way they did—could be answered in a straightforward manner: some organisms had certain features, or qualities, that allowed them to do better in a particular environment than did organisms without those features. The winnowing process that led to the demise of certain organisms, and hence of their **lineages**, or lines of hereditary descent, was **natural selection**. This was an unfortunate choice of terms because it implies that choices are actively being made about which organisms make it and which do not. This is true, however, only in the broadest terms. What really happens is that certain organisms living in particular environments do not have certain features that *allow* them to survive and leave offspring. It is this absence of features in the face of environmental (social or physical) problems that is the selective process.

Darwin had little knowledge of particulate **inheritance**, or what gets passed on intergenerationally through **transmission** (the movement of information—cultural or genetic—from one organism to another), and what he did know was for the most part incorrect, but this was of little significance; his theory of cause worked without his knowing the intricacies. After Gregor Mendel's work was discovered in 1900, geneticists could speak of rules of inheritance, but these were the proximate causes of why an organism had a particular genetic composition. They did nothing to explain why certain genes were there to be inherited and why others were not. Darwin's theory of descent with modification by means of natural selection explained that, and yet Darwin himself did not deny the existence of a divine creator, nor did he always apply his theory to humans, which the Bible states were created in the image of God. Thus, his theory tells us nothing about the "ultimate" ultimate cause—why and how life itself began. It has been only in the closing decades of the twentieth century that we have rudimentary insights into those issues (e.g., Cairns-Smith 1982).

With respect to why and how humans and their behaviors evolve, it is difficult to find a single thread emerging from the time of Plato and Aristotle onward. If there *is* a thread, it is cultural idealism, which might best be summarized by the phrase "mind over matter." The assignment of cause here is simple: man simply has willed himself to a continually higher state of being—a notion widespread in Enlightenment thought and manifest in the works of Locke, Diderot, Rousseau, Voltaire, Montesquieu, and others. Implied in some, but certainly not all Enlightenment works on the history of mankind was the notion of **progress**—rendered in terms of "betterment" or increased "complexity"—and usually subdivided for analytical purposes into stages or phases. Thus, Auguste Comte proposed a three-phase system of human development—theological, metaphysical, and positivist; Montesquieu divided early mankind into savages and barbarians; and Anne Robert Jacques Turgot proposed a three-phase system of hunting, pastoralism, and agriculture. In some cases technological advancement was identified as the proximate cause of mankind, or a portion thereof, progressing from one phase or stage to the next higher plateau. Similarly, the environment, both physical and social, often was invoked as the proximate cause of developmental **stasis**, or a period of no change.

The notion of progress was nowhere stated so clearly as in the writings of Herbert Spencer, who wrote in *Social Statics* (1851: 80) that

Progress, therefore, is not an accident, but a necessity. Instead of civilization being artifact, it is part of nature; all of a piece with the development of the embryo or the unfolding of a flower. The modifications mankind have undergone, and are still undergoing, result from a law underlying the whole organic creation; and provided the human race continues, and the constitution of things remains the same, those modifications must end in completeness. . . . [S]o surely must man become perfect.

For Spencer, perfection was the result of mankind's long struggle out of a series of lower stages, propelled along its way by underlying laws—with the caveat that not all peoples were equally imbued with the capacity to raise themselves to higher levels. This racial determinism is manifest throughout the late nineteenth century in the writings of numerous social scientists, perhaps most evident in the works of Edward B. Tylor and Lewis Henry Morgan.

For Tylor, it was inescapable that there

seems to be in mankind inbred temperament and inbred capacity of mind. History points the great lesson that some races have marched on in civilization while others have stood still or fallen back, and we should partly look for an explanation of this in differences of intellectual and moral powers between such tribes as the native Americans and Africans, and the Old World nations who overmatch and subdue them. (Tylor 1881: 74)

Morgan thought likewise, noting, for example, that "The Indian and European are at opposite poles in their physiological conditions. In the former there is very little animal passion, while with the latter it is super-abundant" (Morgan 1870: 207). Morgan went further, using comparative data to conclude, in his lengthy treatise *Ancient Society*, that "the experience of mankind has run in nearly uniform channels; that human necessities in similar conditions have been substantially the same" (Morgan 1877: 8).

Morgan's tripartite evolutionary scheme, consisting of savagery, barbarism, and civilization, was an attempt to pigeonhole ethnic groups, often referred to as "tribes," on the basis of the presence or absence of specified cultural traits; and although the scheme appears naive and racially deterministic, it called attention to cultural differences. More important to our discussion here, "in spite of the disfavor into which Morgan's work fell, his general sequence of stages has been written into our understanding of prehistory and interpretation of archaeological remains, as a glance at any introductory anthropology text will indicate" (Leacock 1963: xi).

CONTEMPORARY USES

Leacock is correct in her assertion that the evolutionary schemes of nineteenth-century researchers such as Morgan have been carried over into modern anthropology and archaeology. What has not been carried over is the racially deterministic component of the schemes, primarily because the twentieth century has witnessed an analytical decoupling of biology from **culture** (Gould 1996)—a complex term that can be defined minimally as socially transmitted behavior. Anthropologists on the whole are quite willing to accept that the evolution described by Darwin is the cause of organismic change over time, but they see an entirely different kind of evolution when it comes to human behavior. This brand of evolution is termed **cultural evolution,** and it became a topic of considerable debate in the 1940s and 1950s, primarily through the work of Leslie White (e.g., 1949, 1959a, 1959b) and Julian Steward (e.g., 1953, 1955). To Steward, White's brand of evolution was "unilinear" and traced its roots directly back to the nineteenth-century notions of Tylor and Morgan; but in reality, Steward, despite his use of the term "multilinear" for his own evolutionism, was as much or more a unilinear evolutionist than White was.

Steward (1953: 15) suggested that the use of cultural evolution as an explanatory model demanded two "vitally important assumptions. First, it [assumes] that genuine parallels of form and function develop in historically independent sequences or cultural traditions. Second, it explains those parallels by independent operation of identical causality in each case." White expressed a similar outlook, noting that the cultural evolutionary process was lawlike (1949, 1959b) and that the sequences of stages was inevitable in the sense that all societies would eventually represent civilizations, whether they all were at one time something else (1947, 1959b). Despite White's (1943: 339) disclaimer that he was not saying that "man deliberately set about to improve his culture," close reading of what he said indicates that he strongly believed all organisms, including humans, had an "urge" to improve and that this was the "motive force as well as the means of cultural evolution." White (1947: 177) also regularly indicated that he and other cultural evolutionists "did not identify evolution with progress [and that they] did not believe progress was inevitable."

However, by default White's cultural evolution *is* synonymous with progress: "[B]y and large, in the history of human culture, progress and evolution have gone hand in hand" (White 1943: 339). In White's view the key evolutionary mechanism—urge or necessity as a motive force—demands absolutely no reference either to a source of variation or to natural selection. Humans thus invent new tools as necessary, and the tools are always better than the preceding ones because they allow the procurement or exploitation of additional energy:

The best single index [of progress] by which all cultures can be measured, is amount of energy harnessed per capita per year. This is the common denominator of all cultures. . . . Culture advances as the amount of energy harnessed per capita increases. The criterion for the evaluation of cultures is thus an objective one. The measurements can be expressed in mathematical terms. The goal—security and survival—is likewise objective; it is the one that all species, man included, live by. Thus we are able to speak of cultural progress objectively and in a manner which enriches our understanding of the culture history of mankind tremendously. And finally, we can evaluate cultures and arrange them in a series from lower to higher. (White 1947: 187)

What gave White's evolution its distinctive form was his belief that change could occur in only two ways: either humans improve the efficiency of old tools or they invent new tools. Evolution via the former is restricted, however, as exemplified in White's (1943: 343) statement that the "extent to which man may harness natural forces [energy] in animal husbandry is limited" and his later statement (White 1959b: 369) that "some progress can of course be made by increasing the efficiency of the technological means of putting energy to work, but there is a limit to the extent of cultural advance on this basis." This is merely an expression of **orthogenetic evolution**—that is, evolution governed by laws and passing through a predetermined sequence of stages.

Cultural evolutionism, then, is concerned with generalities of process and change—cross-cultural regularities, or "laws"; this feature made it scientific in the minds of White and Steward. It also made it scientific in the minds of archaeologists in the 1960s and early 1970s—a time during which a so-called "new" archaeology—*processualism*—was born. The leading architect of a scientific archaeology based on anthropological concepts, most of which center around the notion of culture, was Lewis Binford. He was clear on his objectives:

Specific "historical" explanations . . . simply explicate the mechanisms of cultural process. They add nothing to the explanation of the processes of cultural change and evolution. If migrations can be shown to have taken place, then this explication presents an explanatory problem: what adaptive circumstances, evolutionary processes, induced the migration. . . . We must seek the explanation in systemic terms for classes of historical events. (Binford 1962: 218)

Binford was influenced by the cultural evolutionists of the mid-twentieth century, especially White, whose arguments

became clear, logical vignettes. Culture was not some ethereal force, it was a material system of interrelated parts understandable as an organization that could be recovered from the past. . . . We were searching for laws. Laws are timeless and spaceless; they must be equally valid for the ethnographic data as well as the archaeological data. (Binford 1972: 8)

For the new archaeologists, laws were regularities, confirmed hypotheses, or at the very least, things to be discovered. Hence, Patty Jo Watson, Steven LeBlanc, and Charles Redman (1984: 5–6) made the following claim:

science *is* based on the working assumption or belief by scientists that past and present regularities *are* pertinent to future events and that under similar circumstances similar phenomena will behave in the future as they have in the past and do in the present. This practical assumption of the regularity or conformity of nature is the necessary foundation for all scientific work. Scientific descriptions, explanations, and predictions all utilize lawlike generalizations hypothesized on the presumption that natural phenomena are orderly.

Thus, by understanding something about the present, one could access the past—a stance that fit neatly with Whitean evolution, as it had with the earlier formulations of Tylor (1871) and Morgan (1877). With a few exceptions, the processualists were never clear on how or from where the laws were supposed to be derived, and the general result was a conflation of laws with empirical generalizations; hence cause was rendered in commonsense terms.

Processualists (e.g., Spencer 1997) have pointed out that whereas Darwinian evolutionary theory is capable of explaining the genetically dictated behaviors of non-human organisms, it is not applicable to the study of humans because it does not take into account the role of intention or motivation in causing human behavior. Such a statement immediately sets humans apart from other animals in terms of what is and is not subject to selection. Our answer is that whereas human intent might play a *proximal* role in deciding which among several variants actually gets selected (in the sense of being "chosen"), it plays no ultimate role. As David Rindos (1984: 4) argued, "Man may indeed select, but he cannot direct the variation from which he must select." Alexander Alland (1972: 228) made a similar argument: "Individuals do not have to know why a certain act is adaptive for it to be adaptive. They don't even have to know that they are performing certain repetitive acts for those acts to alter [their] survival capacity."

Perusal of the archaeological and anthropological literature makes it clear that most researchers believe that when it comes to humans there are indeed two kinds of evolution—one biological and one cultural—and that different theory is needed for each. For the biological side of the house, Darwinian evolutionism is appropriate for deriving causal statements; for the cultural side, a decidedly Spencerian, or Whitean, approach is appropriate.

That Spencerian and Darwinian evolution are dissimilar is clear. Americanist archaeologists and cultural anthropologists of the early twentieth century appear to have recognized at least some of the differences between the two, but they were insufficiently knowledgeable about Darwinism to figure out how to use it. Darwinism simply had little to offer anthropology and archaeology because cultural evolution is reticulate—its branches grow back on themselves—whereas biological evolution branches outward continuously. Cultural evolution does not involve the transmission of genes, whereas biological evolution does; and people are not subject to the forces of natural selection and can intentionally direct the evolution of their cultures, whereas biological evolution depends on the natural selection of non-directed mutations.

Discomfort with the removal of human behavior—at least those aspects

deemed to be under the control of culture—from the Darwinian evolutionary process was evident as early as the 1930s, although those voicing discomfort were in a minority:

Archaeologists, noting that modern biology has mounted above the plane of pure
taxonomy [that is, classification], have attempted to follow that science into the
more alluring fields of philosophic interpretation, forgetting that the conclusions of
the biologist are based on the sound foundation of scientifically marshalled facts
gathered during the past century by an army of painstaking observers. This groundwork we utterly fail to possess. Nor will it be easy for us to lay, because the
products of human hands, being unregulated by the more rigid genetic laws which
control the development of animals and plants, are infinitely variable. But that is
no reason for evading the attempt. It has got eventually to be done, and the sooner
we roll up our sleeves and begin comparative studies of axes and arrowheads and
bone tools, make classifications, prepare accurate descriptions, draw distribution
maps and, in general, persuade ourselves to do a vast deal of painstaking, unspec-
tacular work, the sooner shall we be in position to approach the problems of cultural evolution, the solving of which is, I take it, our ultimate goal. (Kidder 1932:
8)

A. V. Kidder correctly indicated that archaeology lacked both the basic
data and a theory consisting of cultural processes parallel to the biological
ones of genetic inheritance and natural selection to help explain a culture's
lineage in evolutionary terms. It was this lack of a basic theory that led to
Robert Dunnell's (1978, 1980) seminal articles on how to apply Darwinian
principles to an examination of the archaeological record. The premise underlying Darwinian evolutionary archaeology is that objects occurring in
the archaeological record were parts of human **phenotypes**—the physical
expressions of organisms—in the same way that bones and skin are. Thus
those objects were shaped by the same evolutionary processes as were the
bodily features of their makers and users. This is a shorthand way of saying
that the possessors of the objects were acted on by evolutionary processes.
Under this perspective, evolution is viewed as the differential persistence of
discrete variants, regardless of the scale of "variant" being defined.

Evolutionary archaeology involves measuring variation—that is, dividing
it into discrete sets of specimens (**groups**) using **ideational units** (conceptual
entities, or classes) derived from whatever theory one is working under;
tracking variants through time and across space to produce a historical
narrative about lineages of particular variants; and explaining the differential persistence of individual variants comprising lineages in particular
time-space contexts (Lyman and O'Brien 1998, 2000; O'Brien and Lyman
2000). Evolutionary archaeology has numerous parallels to modern paleobiology. It is geared toward providing Darwinian-like explanations of the
archaeological record, just as paleobiologists explain the paleontological
record. There are two steps: the construction of cultural lineages and the

construction of explanations for those lineages being the way they are (Sza-lay and Bock 1991). Both steps employ concepts embedded within Dar-winian evolutionary theory, such as natural selection (a process of change), a transmission mechanism (which itself is a source of new variants), inven-tion and innovation (other sources of new variants), and heritability (O'Brien and Lyman 2000).

We point out that despite our view of what evolutionary archaeology is and how it provides explanations, there is considerable debate in the dis-cipline over the applicability of Darwinian evolutionism to an examination of the archaeological record. There are those who view it as reductionistic (e.g., Maschner 1998) or as narrow empiricism (e.g., Watson 1986), as well as those who argue that the proper role of Darwinian evolutionism in an archaeological context is as a framework for the study of function (e.g., Boone and Smith 1998). This perspective, referred to as **evolutionary ecol-ogy**, views evolution in terms of how it engineers a better product—a per-spective that actually is complementary to our characterization of evolutionary archaeology and not a polar opposite (O'Brien et al. 1998; O'Brien and Lyman 2000). The difference between evolutionary archae-ology and evolutionary ecology is where each views ultimate cause as being lodged. Evolutionary ecology leads to the identification of near-term, or proximate, causes, whereas evolutionary archaeology addresses long-term, or ultimate, cause. Evolutionary ecology seeks to know how things work now; evolutionary archaeology seeks to know why things came to work the way they did in particular time-space frameworks (Lyman and O'Brien 1998).

CASE STUDIES

It would be difficult to find another topic in Americanist archaeology that has spawned more discussion, speculation, and models than the ques-tion of where, when, how, and particularly, *why* agricultural systems arose. Agriculture, together with its attendant features and processes, has been viewed as a result of both deliberate human action and the impetus for various human responses to a changing environment. By focusing briefly on the work of Kent Flannery and David Rindos we can examine two contrasting positions—Flannery's cultural ecology and Rindos' Darwinian evolutionism—on the issue of agricultural origins. By emphasizing the sys-temic nature of human–plant interactions, Flannery bypassed many of the contentious issues that have long characterized discussions of agricultural origins, especially the role of population growth in effecting new patterns of subsistence. Important to Flannery's models is the proposition that for long periods of time humans and nature were in harmonic balance main-tained by negative feedbacks that damped change. When the environment (cultural and/or physical) changed, even if those changes were minor, humans made appropriate adjustments to keep up with the changes.

Flannery recognized a long preagricultural phase of human–plant interaction that preadapted humans for the more intensive interactions that followed, although in the background of his models are two important inputs—environmental change and population growth—that cause the initial kick to the system; that is, they cause the "minor deviations" (Flannery 1968: 65) that eventually cause wholesale change in the cultural system. Adaptation thus becomes the inevitable result of environmental change, with human intent lurking in the background: "It is possible . . . that cultivation began as an attempt to produce artificially" stands of plants in the same densities as those produced naturally (Flannery 1968: 89). Why, we might ask, would human groups intentionally modify their environment? The answer, according to Flannery, is because of environmental perturbations that had upset the previous balance humans had established with nature—perturbations in the form of climatic change, population growth, or a host of other factors. All of those can be identified as potential "causes" of agriculture.

There is a way of looking at the origins of agriculture that does not lodge cause in human intent and need, and it was offered by Rindos (1984), who noted that domestication occurs *before* the origin and development of agricultural systems; it is not the *reason* agricultural systems develop. In other words, in a domesticatory environment human behaviors evolve in concert with those of the plants. Agricultural systems actually "evolve" as a result of this mutualism, which is mediated by environmental manipulation. Why, Rindos asked, when there are so many examples in nature of non-human, mutualistic domesticatory systems—ants and acacias, squirrels and oak trees, for example—do we afford human–plant agriculture a special place conceptually and methodologically? Why should we view the co-evolutionary relations that humans and plants have developed over thousands of years any differently than we do the mutualistically reinforced behaviors of other animals and their plants? We suspect that we do it for the simple reason that human informants can tell anthropologists why they did (or might do) something. Ants and squirrels, however, cannot tell us.

Rindos emphasized that there are modes of domestication that occur throughout the domesticatory process, each of which is mediated by different kinds of human behavior and occurs in different environments. The first of these is *incidental domestication*, which is the product of non-purposeful dispersal and protection of wild plants by humans. Over time the developing relationship selects for morphological changes in plants, thus preadapting them for further domestication. There is nothing "agricultural" about the environment in which this relationship takes place, and hence the niche breadth of the incidental domesticate is determined by the environment and the exploitive techniques of the human groups. The human–plant relationship is conservative and reinforces negative feedbacks that maintain the existing exploitive strategies rather than creating positive feedbacks that change the system, as in Flannery's scenario. Yields rarely change, which places limits on the size of the groups that the plant population can support.

Specialized domestication involves an intensification of tendencies present under incidental domestication. Humans, instead of being simply opportunistic agents, now become obligate agents for the plants, which enhances the success of the plants while simultaneously changing the basis of human subsistence strategies. The origin of these behaviors can be found in selective pressures on both humans and plants as incidental relationships intensify. If these co-evolutionary relationships are successful, they may lead to increasingly specialized relationships. Rindos saw several effects of this ever-increasing interaction. First, human dependence on plants may increase to the point that human success is dependent on the success of the plants, which in turn may depend on humans for their survival at higher densities in new locales. Second, the plants no longer are limited by previous environmental restrictions as their realized niche expands through such mechanisms as weeding, watering, and burning. Third, as the co-evolving plants increase their productivity, the potential for human population growth increases.

Agricultural domestication is the culmination of these increasingly obligate relationships and is mediated by specific human behaviors—seed selection and storage, along with all the behaviors at work previously—as well as by evolutionary tendencies embedded in the developing agroecology. Hence, agricultural domestication is closest in concept to what typically is thought of in anthropology simply as "domestication," although it differs substantially in that it is actually a culmination of a long process of plant–human mutualism as opposed to being a "thing" that arose to replace previous food-getting behaviors.

Rindos' model of domestication does not rely on human intent, need, or any other orthogenetic "cause." Rather, cause is found in the increasing mutualism between humans and plants and the selective advantages it brings about; thus it is external to the system under investigation. If one invokes intent and/or need as the cause of domestication, one could pose the question, "Why haven't *all* societies adopted agriculture?" (Pryor 1986: 889). Economist Frederick Pryor, noting that "the origins of agriculture have been left too long to the archeologists" (p. 892), scanned the standard cross-cultural sample of 186 precapitalist societies (Murdock and White 1969) to determine which groups were agricultural and which were not. He then scaled each group in terms of the importance of agriculture, using values from 0 (agriculture absent) to 4 (agriculture very important). Pryor could "explain" away the absence of agriculture among 35 of the 38 groups who scored lowest on the scale, but he had problems with three North

American groups—the Pomo, the Micmac, and the Northern Paiute. After reviewing the technological and economic basis of those groups, he noted that "by all conventional reasons, the Pomo and Paiute (and, with less certainty, the Micmac) *should* have adopted some type of agriculture" (Pryor 1986: 891). The answer, according to Pryor, to why the Paiute should have adopted agriculture is that although they lived in regions of low rainfall, they had easy access to irrigation water in the form of streams and lakes.

As O'Brien and Wilson (1988) pointed out in rebuttal to Pryor, the Northern Paiute (specifically, the Wadadika "band" of the Northern Paiute) *did* develop a highly specialized agroecology—one that involved intensive interaction with a variety of plants. The Wadadika burned tobacco fields and seed fields and stored seeds for planting, but Pryor is correct; the Wadadika did not irrigate their fields. But is this evidence that they were not plant domesticators? No, they *were* plant domesticators, but they had not developed the intensive relationships that Rindos terms "agricultural domestication." To declare that they therefore were not agricultural ignores the evolutionary nature of the domesticatory process and forces the investigator to decide that the "cause" for the lack of agriculture was because the "need" for it was not great enough.

FUTURE IMPORTANCE

It is our impression that the majority of Americanist archaeologists working today would consider themselves, if loosely, processual archaeologists. Thus, much of the effort to identify cause in the archaeological record will, we suspect, follow the tenets of this paradigm. It is worthwhile, then, to briefly review those tenets and where we suspect they will lead the discipline.

Binford (1962: 224) noted in the early 1960s that

Archaeologists should be among the best qualified to study and directly test hypotheses concerning the process of evolutionary change, particularly processes of change that are relatively slow, or hypotheses that postulate temporal-processual priorities as regards total cultural systems. The lack of theoretical concern and rather naïve attempts at explanation which archaeologists currently advance must be modified.

Prior to the time Binford's article was published, there had been little more than occasional grumbling among rank-and-file archaeologists about the lack of "explanation" of the archaeological record. We suspect this was because practitioners were unsure of how to build explanations. Binford's 1962 paper and several more he published over the next five years provided an algorithm.

The algorithm was attractive in its simplicity and it comprised three steps. First, discard the notion of a cultural lineage as a flowing stream of ideas that changed through time and varied over space and replace it with the notion that culture is humankind's **extrasomatic**—non-biological—means of adaptation. This required the second step—new classifications of archaeological materials—because the study of *culture* processes comprised the study of cause-and-effect relations among *cultural*—not archaeological—variables. The culture historian's artifact styles denoted group identity or ethnicity (Binford 1962: 220), and thus a different style might denote a different time period; here the focus was on **homologous** similarity—similarity that is the result of historical relationship. Artifact function was what was critical to the new **systematics** (study and sorting of the diversity of phenomena such that like goes with like), and here the focus was on **analogous** similarity—similarity that is the result of two or more organisms (or groups of organisms) finding similar solutions to similar problems confronting them. Artifact function could be *technomic*—the function of an object in technological situations; *sociotechnic*—the function of an object in social situations; and *ideotechnic*—the function of an object in ideological situations (Binford 1962). Focusing on the function of artifacts was in line with the definition of culture as humankind's extrasomatic means of adaptation. This focus was possible because in Binford's (1962: 219) view the "formal structure of artifact assemblages together with the between element contextual relationships should and do present a systematic and understandable picture of the *total extinct* cultural system."

Potential catalysts for processual change were sought "in systemic terms for classes of historical events such as migrations, establishment of 'contact' between areas previously isolated, etc." (Binford 1962: 218). The problem was one of answering the "why" questions. As we noted earlier, to answer such questions required, it was thought, the establishment of a set of general laws regarding how cultures changed, and which connected *causes* with their *effects*. Establishing the laws comprised the third step of the processual-archaeology protocol (see O'Brien and Lyman [2000] for more details).

The search for laws evident in the literature of the 1970s and early 1980s has slowed in the last fifteen years as processual archaeologists have adopted White's cultural evolutionism, albeit sometimes with bits and pieces borrowed from Darwin's theory of evolution. The net result has been the retention of human intent—often expressed as "directed variation"—thereby keeping cause lodged in the "conscious, purposive strategies that individuals and groups pursue in order to further their own interests" (Spencer 1997: 211). While not denying a role for human intent in the evolutionary history of cultural lineages, we perceive weaknesses in such a focus, the most serious one, as we noted earlier, being that cause is lodged within the phenomena to be explained (Lyman and O'Brien 1998).

The search for cause will continue to be the ultimate goal in science, no less in archaeology than in any other discipline that seeks explanations for the natural world being the way it is. Despite the fact that we often believe we can offer, through experience and common sense, explanations for why and how past humans did the things they did, there is no reason to believe that these explanations should be taken seriously from a scientific point of view. If, as we maintain, objects in the archaeological record are parts of previous phenotypes, then it is reasonable that those phenotypes were acted on by Darwinian evolutionary processes. Reliance on Darwinian evolutionism as a source of causal explanations precludes searching for ultimate cause among the phenomena being studied and places archaeology outside the reach of tautology.

REFERENCES

Alland, A., Jr. (1972). Cultural evolution: The Darwinian model. *Social Biology* 19: 227–239.

Binford, L. R. (1962). Archaeology as anthropology. *American Antiquity* 28: 217–225.

Binford, L. R. (1972). Introduction. In L. R. Binford (ed.), *An Archeological Perspective*. New York: Seminar Press, pp. 1–14.

Boone, J. L., and E. A. Smith. (1998). Is it evolution yet? A critique of evolutionary archaeology. *Current Anthropology* 39: S141–S173.

Cairns-Smith, G. (1982). *Genetic Takeover*. Cambridge: Cambridge University Press.

Chambers, R. (1844). *Vestiges of the Natural History of Creation*. London: Churchill.

Darwin, C. (1859). *On the Origin of Species by Means of Natural Selection; or the Preservation of Favoured Races in the Struggle for Life*. London: Murray.

Dunnell, R. C. (1978). Style and function: A fundamental dichotomy. *American Antiquity* 43: 192–202.

Dunnell, R. C. (1980). Evolutionary theory and archaeology. In M. B. Schiffer (ed.), *Advances in Archaeological Method and Theory*, vol. 3. New York: Academic Press, pp. 35–99.

Flannery, K. V. (1968). Archaeological systems theory and early Mesoamerica. In B. J. Meggers (ed.), *Anthropological Archeology in the Americas*. Washington, DC: Anthropological Society of Washington, pp. 132–177.

Gould, S. J. (1996). *The Mismeasure of Man*, rev. ed. New York: Norton.

Kidder, A. V. (1932). *The Artifacts of Pecos*. Papers of the Southwestern Expedition, Phillips Academy No. 6. New Haven, CT: Yale University Press.

Leacock, E. B. (1963). Introduction to Part I. In L. H. Morgan, *Ancient Society*. New York: Meridian, pp. i–xx.

Lyman, R. L., and M. J. O'Brien. (1998). The goals of evolutionary archaeology: History and explanation. *Current Anthropology* 39: 615–652.

Lyman, R. L., and M. J. O'Brien. (2000). Measuring and explaining change in artifact variation with clade-diversity diagrams. *Journal of Anthropological Archaeology* 19: 39–74.

Maschner, H.D.G. (1998). Review of *Evolutionary Archaeology: Theory and Application* (ed. M. J. O'Brien). *Journal of the Royal Anthropological Institute* 4: 354–355.

Mayr, E. (1982). *The Growth of Biological Thought: Diversity, Evolution, and Inheritance.* Cambridge, MA: Belknap Press.

Morgan, L. H. (1870). *Systems of Consanguinity and Affinity of the Human Family.* Washington, DC: Smithsonian Institution.

Morgan, L. H. (1877). *Ancient Society.* New York: Holt.

Murdock, G. P., and D. R. White. (1969). Standard cross-cultural sample. *Ethnology* 3: 329–369.

Nagel, E. (1965). Types of causal explanation in science. In D. Lerner (ed.), *Cause and Effect: The Hayden Colloquium on Scientific Method and Concept.* New York: Free Press, pp. 11–26.

O'Brien, M. J., and R. L. Lyman. (2000). *Applying Evolutionary Archaeology: A Systematic Approach.* New York: Kluwer Academic/Plenum.

O'Brien, M. J., R. L. Lyman, and R. D. Leonard. (1998). Basic incompatibilities between evolutionary and behavioral archaeology. *American Antiquity* 63: 485–498.

O'Brien, M. J., and H. C. Wilson. (1988). A paradigmatic shift in the search for the origin of agriculture. *American Anthropologist* 90: 958–965.

Paley, W. (1802). *Natural Theology, or, Evidences of the Existence and Attributes of the Deity Collected from the Appearances of Nature.* London: Faulder.

Pryor, F. L. (1986). The adoption of agriculture: Some theoretical and empirical evidence. *American Anthropologist* 88: 879–897.

Ray, J. (1691). *The Wisdom of God Manifested in the Works of Creation.* London: Smith.

Rindos, D. (1984). *The Origins of Agriculture: An Evolutionary Perspective.* New York: Academic Press.

Spencer, C. S. (1997). Evolutionary approaches in archaeology. *Journal of Archaeological Research* 5: 209–264.

Spencer, H. (1851). *Social Statics.* London: Chapman.

Steward, J. H. (1953). Evolution and process. In A. L. Kroeber, *Anthropology Today: An Encyclopedic Inventory.* Chicago: University of Chicago Press, pp. 313–326.

Steward, J. H. (1955). *Theory of Culture Change: The Methodology of Multilinear Evolution.* Urbana: University of Illinois Press.

Szalay, F. S., and W. J. Bock. (1991). Evolutionary theory and systematics: Relationships between process and pattern. *Zeitschrift für Zoologische Systematik und Evolutionsforschung* 29: 1–39.

Tylor, E. B. (1871). *Primitive Culture.* London: Murray.

Tylor, E. B. (1881). *Anthropology: An Introduction to the Study of Man and Civilization.* New York: Appleton.

Watson, P. J. (1986). Archaeological interpretation (1985). In D. J. Meltzer, D. D. Fowler, and J. A. Sabloff (eds.), *American Archaeology Past and Future: A Celebration of the Society for American Archaeology, 1935–1985.* Washington, DC: Smithsonian Institution Press, pp. 439–457.

Watson, P. J., S. A. LeBlanc, and C. Redman. (1984). *Archeological Explanation: The Scientific Method in Archeology.* New York: Columbia University Press.

White, L. A. (1943). Energy and the evolution of culture. *American Anthropologist* 45: 335–356.

White, L. A. (1947). Evolutionary stages, progress, and the evolution of cultures. *Southwestern Journal of Anthropology* 3: 165–192.

White, L. A. (1949). *The Science of Culture: A Study of Man and Civilization.* New York: Farrar, Straus and Giroux.

White, L. A. (1959a). The concept of evolution in cultural anthropology. In B. J. Meggers (ed.), *Evolution and Anthropology: A Centennial Appraisal.* Washington, DC: Anthropological Society of Washington, pp. 106–125.

White, L. A. (1959b). *The Evolution of Culture: The Development of Civilization to the Fall of Rome.* New York: McGraw-Hill.

Chapter 5

Classification

R. Lee Lyman and Michael J. O'Brien

INTRODUCTION

Categorization of individual phenomena has several purposes: the categories provide an information storage and retrieval system; they simplify variation into a small, manageable number of kinds more easily discussed than each individual specimen; and they provide a means of recording variation for purposes of analysis. Given these purposes, categorization occurs in virtually all endeavors. A librarian must decide if a newly published book is a work of fiction, a work of history, or a work of historical fiction. Astronomers must decide if a newly discovered celestial body is a star, a planet, a moon, an asteroid, or something else entirely. Pedologists must decide which category of soil occurs in a particular area. When you buy a new car, you must decide if you want to drive a Ford, a Chevrolet, or a Toyota.

Anthropologists have used a host of sorting systems to simplify, organize, and analyze the materials they study. Nineteenth-century philologists categorized languages in a manner still used to assess the evolutionary development and relations of modern languages. Late in the nineteenth century, Americanist anthropologists applied the notion of culture areas to sort collections of artifacts for museum displays. Nineteenth-century anthropometrists sorted people in various ways, one of the better-known ones using the length–width ratio of the skull—the "cephalic index" developed by Anders Retzius in 1842. A person is brachycephalic (short, broad head) if his skull is 82% as wide as it is long, dolichocephalic (long, narrow head) if his skull is 77% as wide as it is long, and mesocephalic if the length–width ratio falls between those values. These categories were sometimes used by archaeologists between 1900 and 1950 to distinguish among pre-historic groups of people. As we enter the third millennium, many of these sorting schemes have been discarded as unrealistic, invalid, or unusable.

Given the ubiquity of categorization in everyday life, it might be surprising that it took many years, often many decades, to develop the categorization systems used in various everyday, scientific, and humanistic endeavors. The categories earth, air, fire, and water were once adequate for sorting phenomena by material type, but these were replaced when the first periodic table was produced by Russian chemist Dmitri Mendeleev in 1869. He arranged elements by increasing atomic weight, whereas the modern periodic table arranges elements by increasing atomic number. The original system of categorizing soils—phenomena more familiar to archaeologists—went through numerous modifications and revisions as pedologists attempted to develop a system that served some useful purpose. Similarly, the system for categorizing the strata of the geological record has undergone regular revision and has on occasion been modified for archaeological purposes (Gasche and Tunca 1983). Scientific categorizations are always susceptible, and in fact should be amenable, to change.

The systems, processes, and results of categorization are referred to by a plethora of terms that are not always synonymous, even within any given discipline, because they typically have no commonly agreed-on meaning. Standard dictionaries do not always help clarify things because their included definitions may present ideals rather than the meaning of the terms as they are used in particular real-world situations. *Webster's Seventh New Collegiate Dictionary* (1967) defines "classification" not only as "the act or process of classifying," where classifying comprises "assigning to a category," but also as "a systematic arrangement in groups or categories according to established criteria; *specif*: taxonomy." Note that the process of the first definition demands the categories of the second definition. This same dictionary defines "taxonomy" as "the study of the general principles of scientific classification: systematics"; "systematics" in turn is defined as "of, relating to, or concerned with classification; *specif*: taxonomic."

We define **classification** as the creation of new units and the modification and revision of old units by stipulating the necessary and sufficient conditions for membership within a unit (Dunnell 1971). The term **unit** denotes a conceptual entity that serves as a standard of measurement (Ramenofsky and Steffen 1998). A centimeter is a unit constructed explicitly to measure linear distance; the degrees on a compass are units constructed explicitly to measure geographic direction or orientation. As conceptual entities, units must be explicitly defined if they are to be usable for measuring (characterizing, describing, classifying) phenomena. Units can be specified at any scale. Phenomena to be classified may comprise discrete objects such as projectile points or organisms; they may comprise attributes of discrete objects such as the bits of temper in ceramics or the genes in organisms; or they may comprise sets of discrete objects such as aggregates of tools variously termed assemblages or tool kits, or populations of organisms variously termed faunas, floras, or communities. Phenomena are classified on the basis of their **form**, using properties such as size, shape, color, frequency, and material. We use the term "form" and its derivatives throughout to denote **attributes,** or **characters,** of phenomena. Attributes used to classify phenomena occur at a finer, less inclusive scale than the phenomena themselves; attributes are formal properties of the phenomena being classified.

Systematics is the study of diversity of the phenomena of interest, irrespective of the scale or kind of phenomena, and the sorting of that diversity into sets such that like goes with like. The goal of systematics in all disciplines, including anthropology and archaeology, is to sort phenomena into sets of individuals that are in some sense similar; each set should be internally homogeneous such that within-group variation is analytically meaningless and between-group variation meaningful, where a **group** is an empirical unit comprising one or more specimens. Similar phenomena are conceived of as being not only formally similar but as being similar in other ways as well. **Affinity** refers to the relation between formally similar specimens within a group or between groups of formally dissimilar specimens (Simpson 1945). The relation specified when one states that every specimen of kind A has an affinity with every other specimen of that kind, and that specimens of kind A have a different affinity with those of kind B, often is of a particular sort. Multiple kinds of things may be affines because they are close in time, in function or purpose, in symbolism, in ancestry, or in terms of several of these or something else. Specifying and measuring a particular kind of affinity is the ultimate goal of classification, irrespective of discipline.

Typology and **type** are most often found in the archaeological literature, where the former is used as a synonym for systematics and classification and the latter as a synonym for unit (Dunnell 1986). **Taxonomy** concerns the study of theories of classification, their bases, principles, procedures, and rules (Simpson 1961). A **taxonomic classification** is a hierarchical arrangement in which characters are weighted and considered in order of their suspected importance such that units at one rank include parts that are units at lower ranks (Valentine and May 1996). Figure 5.1 shows an example of a four-level taxonomic classification. The particular weighting of attributes reflected by the order in which they are considered influences the nature of the resulting units, and thus a taxonomic classification can be difficult to use (Allen 1996). A **key** is a set of particular attributes arranged such that individual specimens may be identified as belonging to one category or another. A **paradigmatic classification** is a multidimensional arrangement in which each dimension comprises a particular category of attribute (e.g., color, length, material) and its various states (e.g.,

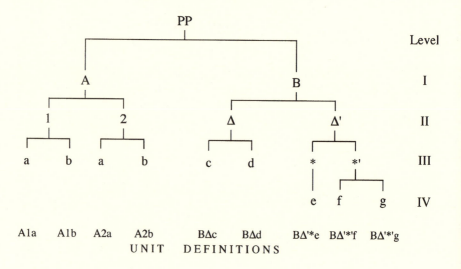

PP = projectile point

A = notches present; B = notches absent, stemmed

1 = side notch; 2 = basal notch

a = shallow notch; b = deep notch

Δ = constricted stem; Δ' = straight stem

c = curved based; d = pointed base

* = short stem; *' = long stem

e = straight base; f = straight base; g = convex base

Figure 5.1. A hypothetical four-level taxonomic classification for projectile points. The four units on the left and the two in the center are each defined by three attributes; the three units on the right are each defined by four attributes. The exclusion of a fourth definitive attribute for the six units on the left indicates either that base shape does not vary or is analytically insignificant, but it is unclear which applies or if both apply. Identifying specimens as members of a particular unit must consider attribute levels I–IV in that order, as reversing the order of levels I and IV would significantly alter unit definitions.

for length, 0.1–1.0 cm; 1.1–2.0 cm; 2.1–3.0 cm; etc.). No dimension or attribute state is given more weight than any other, and all dimensions play a role in the identification of a specimen as belonging to a particular unit (Dunnell 1971). Figure 5.2 shows a hypothetical, two-dimensional paradigmatic classification of projectile points, where dimension 1 is the location of notches and dimension 2 is base shape. All dimensions and attributes are considered of equal weight and thus the order in which they are considered does not influence the nature of the units.

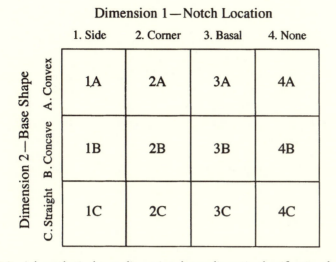

Figure 5.2. A hypothetical two-dimensional paradigmatic classification for projectile points. Dimension 1, base shape, has three attribute states; dimension 2, location of notching, has four attribute states. Twelve units result from intersection of the dimensions (three-by-four); definitions of each unit are shown in each cell. In contrast to taxonomic classification (Figure 5.1), no dimension or attribute is weighted as more or less important than any other, and specimens are readily identified as members of a particular unit because there is no requisite order to consideration of dimensions and attributes.

To be useful, a classification must allow one to do some analytical work. One implication is that traditional archaeological types such as "Clovis points" and "Dalton points" may not satisfactorily perform the analytical work we ask of them today. A second implication is that a set of phenomena can be classified in a virtually infinite number of ways, although we are aware of very few examples of a collection of artifacts being classified in more than one way even when the collection is used to answer disparate analytical questions. A third implication is that the analytical validity of the units produced by classification must be testable. Do they measure the kind of affinity sought? Recent innovative work has involved testing the reliability of identifying specimens as members of a particular unit (Whittaker et al. 1998). Increased technological sophistication in the laboratory has produced insights into attributes of artifacts of finer scale and greater resolution and sometimes of previously unknown attributes. These important advances beg two questions. Of what utility is a classification that is reliably applied from classifier to classifier if it fails to measure the kind(s) of affinity within and between units that the analyst seeks? And, of what use is the fact that we can measure something to the nearest tenth of a millimeter rather than to the nearest millimeter if such instances of finer resolution are not geared toward detecting variation that is of analytical importance?

These questions highlight a final implication of the fact that a classification must allow one to do some analytical work. How do we know in the first place which attributes we should measure, and how do we know we should be measuring, say, a variable to the nearest tenth of a millimeter, the presumption being that measurement to the nearest millimeter is insufficient? There must be some **theory**—a set of things and statements about how those things interact that provide explanations—that guides analysis, because it is theory and its derivative propositions that suggest which attributes are relevant and at what scale they should be measured.

HISTORY

In the fourth century B.C., Aristotle—himself classified as "the first great classifier" (Mayr 1968: 595)—sought to classify biological organisms along a single graded scale known as the *scala naturae*, or "Great Chain of Being," according to their degree of perfection. To accomplish this, Aristotle sought the underlying essence—the essential characteristics—of each kind of organism. In the twentieth century his metaphysic came to be known as **essentialism**, or **typological thinking** (Mayr 1959). This ontology heavily influenced all classifications until Charles Darwin proposed an alternative, today termed **materialism**, or **population thinking**. Darwin focused on the uniqueness of phenomena and thus, although the basic form of individuals within a set of similar phenomena can be captured by, say, a statistical average, such measures of central tendency are abstractions and in no sense real. Alternatively, typological thinking holds that types are real and fixed—a statistical average comprises an essence—and variability between individuals within a kind has no analytical importance.

Either the ontology of essentialism or that of materialism underpins all classifications. This leads to a misunderstanding of the meaning of particular classifications, but it does not mean that one ontology is always preferred over the other. Essentialism is advantageous when prediction and laws are desired about how kinds of things interact. The things and their interactions will always, regardless of their positions in time and space, be the same because the essential properties of the things are the same. The periodic table of chemistry is founded in essentialism. When history is the focus of study, materialism is preferred because although international conflicts, plagues, droughts, and other historical events recur, each particular event is unique in potentially critical attributes, despite the fact that we can construct a classification of them.

The definition of **evolution** as change in the frequencies of phylogenetically related variants demands a materialist ontology because the **processes** (actions that produce a result) of Darwinian evolution—transmission, replication, drift, and natural selection—concern variants. Transmission of information, whether genetic or conceptual, as in teaching an individual how to decorate ceramics, is what results in **heritable continuity** because attributes are replicated. **Drift** comprises differential replication as a result of transmission error or lack of fidelity in **inheritance** (the movement of information—cultural or genetic—from one organism to another), and **natural selection** comprises differential replication of more-adapted and less-adapted forms.

Within paleobiological classification we find problems parallel to those in archaeology and also some possible solutions. Biology and sociocultural anthropology are sister disciplines; both study their subject phenomena when those phenomena are operating. Paleobiology and archaeology are also sister disciplines; both study the prehistory and evolutionary development of organisms, and both grew out of similar disciplinary antecedents (O'Brien and Lyman 2000). All four disciplines have some common goals—to explain the diversity of phenomena of interest and to write and explain a history of the development of that diversity in evolutionary terms. But biologists study organisms and species, and anthropologists study people and **culture** (socially transmitted behavior) or cultures; paleobiologists study fossils, and archaeologists study artifacts. Differences in the materials studied and the desire of paleobiologists and archaeologists to emulate biologists and anthropologists, respectively, is where problems in classification originate.

Biological Systematics

During the middle years of the twentieth century, biologists regularly lamented that systematics, given its central role in biological inquiry (e.g., Huxley 1940; Mayr 1968; Simpson 1945), had not received the recognition that it should have. These laments marked a shift in the focus of biological systematics after the 1940s neo-Darwinian Synthesis from the notion of a species as a morphological unit—what Simpson (1945: 3) referred to as "archetypal" classification—to the biological concept of a **species** as a reproductively isolated population of interbreeding organisms (Mayr 1942). Despite the fact that there are nearly two dozen distinct species concepts presently under discussion (Mayden 1997), many biologists and philosophers of biology recognize that a species is a unit constructed for some analytical or applied biological purpose (Hull 1997; Mayr 1968). Those purposes might be for managing biodiversity or for studying the phylogenetic history of a group of organisms. One's analytical goal dictates which one of the several available species concepts, and thus which set of units, is the most appropriate. Given an interest in evolutionary history, some argue that conceiving of a species as a reproductively isolated set of organ-

isms fulfills the requirement of being an evolutionary unit. What did paleobiologists do in light of the new biological conception of species?

In the nineteenth and early twentieth centuries, paleontologists were
much like their contemporaries, whom modern archaeologists term "anti-
quarians," in terms of their archetypal classifications. Subsequent to the
neo-Darwinian Synthesis, initial efforts were made to rewrite Darwinian
evolutionary theory so that it would explain the data derived from the
paleontological record (e.g., Simpson 1943, 1944; see Eldredge [1985,
1989] for historical overviews). These efforts eventually resulted in the initiation of a new journal in 1975—*Paleobiology*—devoted to studying and
explaining the fossil record in Darwinian terms and to rewriting, fine-
tuning, and expanding that theory in terms of paleontological data (e.g.,
Eldredge 1999). To reach this point required a concomitant change in paleontological systematics and in the language of evolutionary theory. And
here is where archaeologists can learn a valuable lesson.

In the 1940s and 1950s paleontologists worried about how they were
going to operationalize and thus incorporate the biological-species concept
into paleontology (Sylvester-Bradley 1956). Fossils comprising a population
of organisms, after all, did not variously interbreed. Yet paleontologists
wanted to study species because, based on the biological-species concept,
they were thought to have biological meaning and thus to be the units of
evolution. Further, **lineages**—evolutionary continua or lines of heritable
continuity—had to be divided more or less arbitrarily into chunks. Those
chunks were termed either "chronospecies," signifying that the temporal
boundaries of the chunks were arbitrary, or "morphospecies," signifying
that the units were arbitrarily delimited formal ones that may not comprise
a reproductively isolated set of organisms. This awkward state of affairs
resulted because paleontologists were attempting to rewrite the paleontological record in biological terms. In words more familiar to archaeologists,
they were trying to reconstruct the static paleontological record into a dynamic biological system.

These difficulties were resolved, not without debate, after traditional evolutionary theory was rewritten in paleontological terms and the biological
species concept was rendered applicable to the paleontological record. The
rewriting comprised the punctuated-equilibrium version of Darwinian evolutionary theory (Eldredge and Gould 1972; Gould and Eldredge 1977,
1986), produced by paleontologists who viewed (1) fossil-species units as
equivalent to extant biological species because of the formal stasis of each
and (2) formal variation in fossils as a result of genetic variation (Eldredge
1999). Traditional evolutionary theory, written by biologists, viewed evolution as a seamless, continuous, gradual process necessitating "arbitrary"
delimitation of fossil species. But formal stasis over long time periods was
empirically evident to some paleontologists. Granting that these static units
were equivalent to extant biological species, the implications were signifi-

cant for evolutionary theory. Hence, that theory and its attendant units were rewritten in paleontological terms, which is not to say that biological concepts were discarded (Gould and Eldredge [1993] and references therein). Indeed, they form a major part of paleobiology.

Archaeological Systematics

Hallmark events in archaeological systematics include the debate between James Ford (1954a, 1954b) and Albert Spaulding (1953, 1954) in the 1950s (see O'Brien and Lyman [1998] for detailed discussion) and the debate between Lewis and Sally Binford (Binford and Binford 1966) and Francois Bordes (1961) in the 1960s. Both debates focus in part on what kind of affinity an archaeological "type" signifies. The term "type" in archaeology is in many ways parallel to the term "species" in biology and paleobiology. Archaeologists have long desired types that not only allow analytical work to be performed but also are culturally meaningful. That is, they want types (1) that monitor adaptive or functional variation; (2) that serve as index fossils for purposes of stratigraphic correlation; and (3) that signify a particular ethnic, linguistic, or cultural group or some form of social organization or political structure.

During the last third of the nineteenth century and the first fifteen or so years of the twentieth century, anthropologists and archaeologists sought classifications that were universally applicable and which resulted in specimens being placed in their "proper" types. Many of these units can loosely be categorized as functional—weapons of war, items of adornment—but they were informed by common sense and typically only by accident had any useful archaeological meaning. Discussions of the hows and whys of classification were noticeably rare (Dunnell 1986). This situation changed somewhat after 1910 when it was discovered that if types were constructed in particular ways, they had a particular kind of distribution in time and space. The pursuit of what were later termed "styles," or "historical types," became the focus of classification efforts and resulted in and underpinned the emergence of what came to be known as the culture-history paradigm (Lyman and O'Brien 1999; Lyman et al. 1997, 1998).

From the 1930s into the 1960s, archaeological types that allowed analytical work to be performed were warranted by Americanist archaeologists with ethnographic observations, which resulted in such explanatory axioms as the popularity principle that underpins **frequency seriation** (Lyman et al. 1997; frequency seriation involves arranging multiple assemblages of artifacts based on the similarities of the relative frequencies of the included types). Derivation of these kinds of **explanations** (reason-giving statements) became axiomatized with explicit use of ethnographic **analogy** beginning in the 1950s and 1960s (e.g., Ascher 1961; Binford 1967). Simply put, analogy comprises the reasoning that if two phenomena visibly share some

attributes, then they share other attributes as well; typically the latter attributes are invisible in the archaeological specimen but visible in the ethnographic analog. This is thought to provide types with the desired
anthropological, cultural, and human-behavioral significance; the reasoning
is that if two units share some visible formal characters, then they share
other characters that generally are visible in the modern analog and invisible in the archaeological material. However, the modern analog, whether
at the scale of a discrete object or at the scale of sociopolitical organization,
typically comprises an empirical generalization founded on a sample of
ethnographic observations rendered as a type rather than on explicit specification of the necessary and sufficient conditions for membership in a unit
derived from theory. Thus, we have units such as "tribes" and "foragers."
In marked contrast, the biological-species concept was constructed on the
basis of evolutionary theory; the concept was applicable to the paleontological record only after the theory was reworded in terms relevant to the
fossil record.

The historical types constructed by A. L. Kroeber, Nels Nelson, A. V.
Kidder, and Leslie Spier in the second decade of the twentieth century were
of a kind that allowed them to measure time and were founded on a materialist ontology (Lyman et al. 1997; O'Brien and Lyman 1999). These
types had to pass the historical-significance test (Krieger 1944). That is,
they had to occur during only one span of time (length of duration was
unspecified) and in a geographically limited area, the latter to ensure that
temporal variation in form was being measured rather than geographic
variation in form (Lyman and O'Brien 2000; O'Brien and Lyman 1999).
In short, the analytical utility of historical types had to be tested—they had
to have demonstrable temporal affinity. That the types were analytical units
built by trial and error without the benefit of theory escaped notice. As a
result, that some types occasionally overlapped in time—occurred in multiple assemblages—and thus signified heritable continuity (because unit
similarity was **homologous**, or the result of shared ancestry) was noted,
and such phenomena soon became known as traditions. This was largely
ignored, however, in favor of studying temporally discrete and discontinuous units termed phases, cultures, and the like.

Most practitioners agreed that the analytical utility of the types for measuring time had to be tested, but the test was narrowly focused on whether
types measured the passage of time. If they did, it was inferred—in the
absence of theory—that they also measured the heritable continuity demanded by an evolutionary lineage. One could speak of the "historical
relatedness" of archaeological units (Willey 1953), by which was meant
that if two or more units were formally, temporally, and geographically
similar, they were phylogenetically related. One kind of affinity—evolutionary—was inferred from three others—formal, temporal, and spatial. In
the absence of independent chronological data, phylogenetic affinity was

the implicit assumption underpinning the temporal ordering of artifacts, imparting a degree of circularity to the reasoning. This is why stratigraphic excavation quickly became favored over chronological techniques such as seriation (Lyman and O'Brien 1999).

The early twentieth-century explanation given by archaeologists for historical types having the spatio-temporal distributions they did was that the types reflected the passage of time because they represented ethnographically observable changes in taste, fashion, or popularity. Therefore, it was suspected that those types had emic meaning and also some sort of empirical reality—they were more or less accurate reflections of past peoples' mental templates. The validity of such emic units, however, could not be tested empirically. Part of the problem resided in the often murky procedure by which historical types were constructed. Procedural murkiness was attacked explicitly by Spaulding (1953), who advocated statistical tests of the significance of attribute combinations. But such tests only show statistically significant attribute combinations and rest on an essentialist ontology. In the absence of units constructed on the basis of explanatory theory, what those attribute combinations signify—the kind of affinity they measure— is a matter of inference.

CONTEMPORARY USES

Despite the importance of classification to any scientific undertaking and the desire of archaeologists to be scientific, the archaeological literature contains few detailed studies of theories of classification, their bases, principles, procedures, and rules. This is so for two reasons. First, the analytical goals of archaeology today are virtually as diverse as the genotypes of professional archaeologists. Second, Americanist archaeologists, at least, are trained as anthropologists and are steeped in ethnological and cultural theory. In part because of these two facts, archaeologists use the theories they know—anthropological theories—to explain the archaeological record. Because that record is not anthropological it must somehow be made anthropological—meaning it must be turned into a *cultural* record. Further, if archaeological units are to be explained with anthropological theory, they must have anthropological meaning and relevance (e.g., Phillips and Willey 1953). This is precisely the problem that paleontologists struggled with in the middle decades of the twentieth century (1940–1970) as they tried to use the neo-Darwinian version of evolutionary theory written in biological terms such as the biological-species concept. Paleontologists eventually found a way out of this difficulty by rewriting the theory in paleontological terms; some archaeologists are attempting to implement this kind of solution (O'Brien and Lyman 2000), whereas others continue to try to make the original solution work (Spencer [1997] and references therein).

We believe that a version of Darwinian evolutionary theory rewritten in archaeological terms would resolve many of the problems archaeologists face today as well as provide theoretically informed answers to many of their questions (Lyman and O'Brien 1998). Just as the paleontologically applicable version of evolutionary theory known as punctuated equilibrium incorporates elements of the biological version of that theory, so too must an archaeological version of evolutionary theory incorporate various elements of anthropological theory. Concepts such as artifact and processes such as diffusion are examples; the former are treated as parts of the human phenotype and the latter as transmission (the movement of information from one organism to another). Because theory demands classifications of various sorts, part of that rewriting of the theory must attend taxonomy. The methods of classification must be explicitly clear, and why certain methods were used must be equally clear. We prefer paradigmatic classification for reasons mentioned above and elaborated elsewhere (O'Brien and Lyman 2000).

Because theory is the source of our ideas on causes of affinity, it has to be the final arbiter of which units are applicable for which kinds of analytical jobs. Theory dictates which variables out of the almost infinite number that could be selected are actually chosen by the analyst for measurement, and it may specify the values (attributes) those variables should take in our classifications. The variables and values chosen are the units used to construct types, and as such they are conceptual, or **ideational, units** (Dunnell 1971, 1986). The specimens we classify are **empirical**, or **phenomenological, units**. In our view, one major problem in archaeological systematics is the confusion between ideational and empirical units. Perhaps this is because ideational units—**classes**—can be **descriptional units**, used merely to characterize or describe a property or a thing, or they can be **theoretical units**, which are created for specific analytical purposes. For example, in light of a proposed causal relation between function and edge angles of stone tools, edge-angle units such as 1–30°, 31–60°, and 61–90° could be constructed as theoretical units. A theoretical unit is an ideational unit that has explanatory significance specifically because of its theoretical relevance.

Conflation of ideational and empirical units leads to the erroneous conclusion that types have emic-like significance. This conclusion also results from how ideational units are defined. An **intensional definition** comprises the necessary and sufficient conditions for membership in a unit; it explicitly lists the definitive features that a phenomenon must display to be identified as a member of the unit. The significant characteristics of the unit are derived from theory; there is no necessary reference to real, empirical specimens when the unit is constructed other than to specify that, say, projectile points rather than ceramic sherds comprise the phenomena to be classified. Thus the three classes of edge angle mentioned above—1–30°, 31–60°, and 61–90°—derive from our understanding of the mechanics of (stone) tools;

mechanics indicate some edge angles are necessary for efficient performance of some functions, whereas other edge angles are necessary for other functions.

An **extensional definition** also comprises the necessary and sufficient conditions for membership in a unit, but it is derived by enumerating selected attributes shared by the unit's members. That is, the definition is based on observed attributes of the existing members of a unit. The significant characteristics of extensionally defined units are not theoretically informed in an explicit manner because the group of specimens was formed by some murky process prior to the specification of the (extensional) definition. Most types traditionally employed in archaeology are extensionally defined units formed when an analyst subdivides a collection of artifacts into smaller piles based on perceived similarities and differences. (The procedure is murky because what one analyst chooses to perceive may be different from the choices of another analyst.) A summary of the central tendencies of the members of each pile, or a statement on the normal appearance of specimens in each pile, comprises the definitive criteria of a type. Unit definitions depend entirely on the specimens examined. Thus, we cannot know if such extensionally defined units are comparable in terms of the kind of affinity we hope they measure.

An example of the troublesome results of this procedure concerns the early history of the systematics of Paleoindian-period projectile points in the American Southwest. What we would now term "Clovis" points were first referred to by the term "Folsomoid" and the like (LeTourneau 1998). The problem was, there were no definitive criteria for distinguishing between Clovis and Folsom points until sufficient specimens had been examined to detect, by trial and error, which attributes allowed their consistent discrimination in form (and time).

The goals of evolutionary archaeology comprise writing the histories of cultural lineages and explaining why those histories have the forms they do (Lyman and O'Brien 1998). To do this, we need to measure two distinct kinds of affinity, and thus our units need to be of two kinds. We need units that monitor heritable continuity, or what have been termed **styles** or less commonly, **stylistic units**. This kind of unit ensures that we are documenting lineages rather than merely temporal sequences, given that stylistic similarity is by definition the result of transmission (Lipo et al. 1997). Change can occur within a lineage as the result of a lack of perfect fidelity in replication, which explains why various seriation techniques and percentage stratigraphy work as chronometers (Lyman and O'Brien 2000; O'Brien and Lyman 1999, 2000). Such units can be used to track the transmission pathways requisite to answering evolutionary questions, but they also allow the identification of prehistoric interaction over geographic space (Lipo et al. 1997). These units allow identification of prehistoric transmission and thus the writing of phylogenetic history. The analytical utility of styles was recognized early on in anthropology by E. A. Hooton, who noted that "non-adaptive bodily characters" are those that "have been derived from their common descent" and that only these characters are the "result of the same ancestry" (Hooton 1926: 76, 77). Hooton was accounting for the fact that adaptive characters may result from convergence—the derivation of similar solutions to a problem—rather than from shared ancestry.

Evolutionary archaeology also requires units that measure functional variation in artifacts, because this kind of unit allows us to call on natural selection as another process of change (e.g., O'Brien et al. 1994). This is not to say that functional units will not measure transmission; like stylistic units, **functional units** can produce the lenticular curves expected of frequency seriation. However, the transmission and replication of functional units is mediated by selection, often to such an extent that lenticular frequency distributions do not result. Further, because the transmission of functional units is mediated by selection, they are expected to have rather different distributions in time and space than stylistic units (see below). Finally, adaptive convergence may produce units that are similar, and together these may have spatio-temporal distributions that resemble those produced by heritable continuity. Functional properties are those that influence the efficiency with which a task is performed; a projectile point must be pointed to penetrate a prey animal, and it must also be sharp enough to cut sufficient tissue that the animal bleeds to death. Attributes of hafting may also be functional, and although they influence the pierce–cut function, they appear to relate more to the weapon-delivery system (Hughes 1998).

CASE STUDIES

Because they measure different evolutionary processes, both stylistic and functional units are required of any attempt to explain the archaeological record in Darwinian terms. This means that traditional archaeological types often do not comprise units appropriate to the questions evolutionary archaeologists ask. This plus the fact that the theory is still being rewritten in archaeological terms means that a great deal of basic work must go into producing a substantive result. Such results are beginning to appear with some regularity (e.g., Hughes 1998; the papers introduced by Kornbacher and Madsen [1999]; and references therein). Here, we summarize a study that illustrates the innovative insights that can be gained using evolutionary theory and traditional archaeological units. We also describe a study that indicates how a general category of artifact might be classified more than one way, and the different kinds of results that can be produced from each when the classifications are constructed on the basis of evolutionary theory.

Tracking an evolutionary lineage—writing evolutionary history—was the goal of the culture historians (Lyman et al. 1997). Contributing to that end, frequency seriation was used as a chronological tool. This technique works as a chronological tool precisely because it monitors heritable continuity (O'Brien and Lyman 1999), and thus it can be used for purposes other than chronology building. Transmission has both a temporal and a spatial aspect. That is, it takes place over time, and it involves a sender and a receiver who occupy different spatial loci and who may be able to move after sending or receiving information. Frequency seriation requires that the included historical types are relatively limited in their spatial distribution but are relatively less limited in their temporal distribution (O'Brien and Lyman [1999] and references therein). Carl Lipo and his colleagues (1997) explored this aspect of historical types with computer simulations, explicitly basing their simulations on notions of heritable continuity and lineages of artifacts. The simulations matched expectations drawn from evolutionary theory that adaptively neutral units—styles—would produce the familiar battleship-shaped frequency distributions not only over time but within limited spatial units as well.

Lipo et al. (1997) used a set of historical types that had been constructed in the 1940s to seriate collections from numerous sites in an area of the southeastern United States approximately 75 kilometers by 140 kilometers. Because the 50-year-old seriations were successful and later confirmed by independent chronological evidence, this suggested that the types were in fact styles; that is, they were adaptively neutral, or nonfunctional. Lipo et al. used frequency seriation to group collections based on their similarities in terms of the relative abundances of included types, and identified sets of sites that seemed to have been occupied by human groups that interacted with one another. Although such a result may seem trivial in some respects, it most definitely is not for several reasons. First, theory dictated which kinds of units—styles—should be used. Second, archaeology, not anthropology, provided an analytical technique—frequency seriation—that was implicitly yet strongly founded in evolutionary theory. Third, the simulations were based on evolutionary theory and indicated the sort of archaeologically visible signature that would result from interaction of—transmission between—people occupying different positions on the landscape.

Previous efforts to measure such interaction rested on concepts such as horizon styles, and so depended solely on how items were classified. If two artifacts from spatially distinct sites were categorized as members of the same horizon style, then the implication was that people at one site had "influenced" people at the other site (Phillips and Willey 1953). The inference was based on common sense and founded in ethnographic observations of diffusion rather than in theory, and there was no way to test such inferences. Lipo et al.'s (1997) contribution comprises a major step toward rewriting evolutionary theory in archaeological terms while simultaneously incorporating what is known ethnologically also in archaeological terms, particularly with respect to artifact units.

Earlier we indicated that particular sets of artifacts are seldom classified in more than one way. We also indicated that to be successful, evolutionary archaeology required two kinds of units—what we termed styles and functional variants. Melinda Allen (1996) classified a set of fish hooks from East Polynesian sites in terms of what she argued were stylistic attributes, and she also classified the same set of hooks in terms of what she argued were functional attributes. Stylistic attributes are those found on the proximal end—the "head"—of the hook where the fishing line is attached. In general, functional attributes are those influencing hook performance when the line is pulled and involve the curvature of the hook. Specifically, they are the relation between the alignment of the hook shank and the hook point. Based on the general evolutionary model of how adaptively neutral traits and adaptively significant (functional) traits should alter over time, Allen (1996) argued that the relative frequencies of stylistic features captured by intensionally defined classes should fluctuate gradually and unimodally through time, whereas functional classes should vary predictably with environment. The classes she defined do so. Further, the stylistic classes vary independently of environmental setting and independently of functional features, lending support to the notion that these classes are in fact stylistic. In contrast, the functional classes do not vary consistently in their frequencies over time.

Like Lipo et al.'s (1997) study of pottery, Allen's (1996) study of fish hooks may seem trivial. But also like Lipo et al.'s study, it most decidedly is not. The attributes used for both classifications were selected on the basis of expectations derived from the theory of evolutionary descent with modification written in archaeological terms. These expectations were tested by assessing if the hypothesized stylistic classes and the hypothesized functional classes behaved—had temporo-spatial distributions—the way the theory suggests each kind of unit should. Finding that they did behave as they should allowed Allen to then detect evidence of interaction between peoples occupying different islands using the stylistic classes, and to measure adaptive change using the functional classes. Allen did not attempt to reconstitute the archaeological record into something an ethnographer would recognize and then explain that record in anthropological terms. Rather, she used Darwinian evolutionary theory to inform the nature of her classification units and to aid her explanations of the archaeological record in terms an evolutionist, an archaeologist, and an anthropologist would recognize.

FUTURE IMPORTANCE

In 1964, Supreme Court Justice Potter Stewart made the following statement: "I shall not today attempt further to define the kinds of material I understand to be embraced within that shorthand description, and perhaps

I could never succeed in intelligibly doing so. But I know it when I see it."
The "it" Justice Stewart was referring to was hard-core pornography, and
his statement underscores the importance of classification. Would he cate-
gorize various of the top money-earning movies released in the United
States in the 1990s as "hard-core pornography"? Neither he nor we can
answer this question without an explicit definition of what hard-core pornography is because the answer resides in the classification system one employs. Today, pornography is defined by "community standards," resulting
in as many definitions as there are communities. Such will simply not do
in archaeology, where we must agree on when a particular artifact is a
Clovis point or a Dalton point and when a particular ceramic sherd is a
Barton Incised or Ranch Incised.

The status quo in archaeological systematics is largely being maintained
because of a general failure of archaeologists to recognize the significance
of classification to archaeological endeavors. Many of the historical types
constructed and tested decades ago by culture historians are still referred
to by name, and they are still used for myriad analytical purposes, despite
the fact that they may be inappropriate for such purposes. Most of these
types were built specifically to measure the passage of time, a purpose that
many of them serve quite well. To expect them to be equally capable of
doing other sorts of analytical work is ill-advised, particularly in the absence of tests showing that they are in fact capable of such. There are
interesting parallels between paleobiological systematics and archaeological
systematics, but the literature on the former is less well-known to archaeologists than the literature on the latter. And yet there are important lessons
to be gleaned from paleobiology.

First, and we think most important, archaeologists must have an analytical goal. This will suggest the kinds of units to construct and the requisite
scales of resolution. Second, the analytical validity and utility of the units
must be testable—that is, it must be empirically ascertained if the units do
what they are supposed to do. This leaves open the question of analytical
goal. One traditional goal of anthropology and archaeology has been to
document and explain the diversity of cultural manifestations by phrasing
questions and hypotheses in historical terms. That goal still seems to be a
legitimate one, as does the basic approach to it, although we favor casting
the questions, hypotheses, and possible answers in Darwinian rather than
strictly sociocultural terms (Lyman and O'Brien 1997, 1998; O'Brien et al.
1998).

Archaeologists would be well-advised to heed the words of philosopher
David Hull (1970: 32):

The two processes of constructing classifications and of discovering scientific laws
and formulating scientific theories must be carried on together. Neither can outstrip
the other very far without engendering mutually injurious effects. The idea that an

extensive and elaborate classification can be considered in isolation from all scientific theories and then transformed only later into a theoretically significant classification is purely illusory.

The object lesson of the species problem in paleobiology underscores Hull's central point: systematics is more than fundamental to scientific inquiry; it is critical. To ignore it, to designate its status as second class, and to use it without thinking, all endanger the success of scientific research.

ACKNOWLEDGMENTS

John Darwent and Steve Wolverton provided useful discussion and comments on earlier versions of this chapter. E. J. O'Brien, J. Hart, J. Terrell, and an anonymous reviewer made us aware of various problems in a first draft.

REFERENCES

Allen, M. S. (1996). Style and function in east Polynesian fish-hooks. *Antiquity* 70: 97–116.

Ascher, R. (1961). Analogy in archaeological interpretation. *Southwestern Journal of Anthropology* 17: 317–325.

Binford, L. R. (1967). Smudge pits and hide smoking: The use of analogy in archaeological reasoning. *American Antiquity* 32: 1–12.

Binford, L. R., and S. R. Binford. (1966). A preliminary analysis of functional variability in the Mousterian of Levallois Facies. *American Anthropologist* 68: 238–295.

Bordes, F. (1961). Mousterian cultures in France. *Science* 134: 803–810.

Dunnell, R. C. (1971). *Systematics in Prehistory*. New York: Free Press.

Dunnell, R. C. (1986). Methodological issues in Americanist artifact classification. In M. B. Schiffer (ed.), *Advances in Archaeological Method and Theory*, vol. 9. Orlando, FL: Academic Press, pp. 149–207.

Eldredge, N. (1985). *Unfinished Synthesis: Biological Hierarchies and Modern Evolutionary Thought*. Oxford: Oxford University Press.

Eldredge, N. (1989). *Time Frames: The Evolution of Punctuated Equilibria*. Princeton, NJ: Princeton University Press.

Eldredge, N. (1999). *The Pattern of Evolution*. New York: Freeman.

Eldredge, N., and S. J. Gould. (1972). Punctuated equilibria: An alternative to phyletic gradualism. In T.J.M. Schopf (ed.), *Models in Paleobiology*. San Francisco: Freeman, Cooper, pp. 82–115.

Ford, J. A. (1954a). Comment on A. C. Spaulding's "Statistical techniques for the discovery of artifact types." *American Antiquity* 19: 390–391.

Ford, J. A. (1954b). On the concept of types: The type concept revisited. *American Anthropologist* 56: 42–53.

Gasche, H., and O. Tunca. (1983). Guide to archaeostratigraphic classification and terminology: Definitions and principles. *Journal of Field Archaeology* 10: 325–335.

Gould, S. J., and N. Eldredge. (1977). Punctuated equilibria: The tempo and mode of evolution reconsidered. *Paleobiology* 3: 115–151.

Gould, S. J., and N. Eldredge. (1986). Punctuated equilibrium at the third stage. *Systematic Zoology* 35: 143–148.

Gould, S. J., and N. Eldredge. (1993). Punctuated equilibrium comes of age. *Nature* 366: 223–227.

Hooton, E. A. (1926). Methods of racial analysis. *Science* 63: 75–81.

Hughes, S. S. (1998). Getting to the point: Evolutionary change in prehistoric weaponry. *Journal of Archaeological Method and Theory* 5: 345–408.

Hull, D. L. (1970). Contemporary systematic philosophies. *Annual Review of Ecology and Systematics* 1: 19–54.

Hull, D. L. (1997). The ideal species concept—and why we can't get it. In M. F. Claridge, H. A. Dawah, and M. R. Wilson (eds.), *Species: The Units of Biodiversity*. London: Chapman and Hall, pp. 357–380.

Huxley, J. S. (1940). Toward the new systematics. In J. S. Huxley (ed.), *The New Systematics*. Oxford: Clarendon Press, pp. 1–46.

Kornbacher, K. D., and M. E. Madsen. (1999). Explaining the evolution of cultural elaboration. *Journal of Anthropological Archaeology* 18: 241–242.

Krieger, A. D. (1944). The typological concept. *American Antiquity* 9: 271–288.

LeTourneau, P. D. (1998). The "Folsom Problem." In A. F. Ramenofsky and A. Steffen (eds.), *Unit Issues in Archaeology: Measuring Time, Space, and Material*. Salt Lake City: University of Utah Press, pp. 52–73.

Lipo, C., M. Madsen, R. C. Dunnell, and T. Hunt. (1997). Population structure, cultural transmission, and frequency seriation. *Journal of Anthropological Archaeology* 16: 301–334.

Lyman, R. L., and M. J. O'Brien. (1997). The concept of evolution in early twentieth-century Americanist archeology. In C. M. Barton and G. A. Clark (eds.), *Rediscovering Darwin: Evolutionary Theory in Archeological Explanation*. Archeological Papers No. 7. Arlington, VA: American Anthropological Association, pp. 21–48.

Lyman, R. L., and M. J. O'Brien. (1998). The goals of evolutionary archaeology: History and explanation. *Current Anthropology* 39: 615–652.

Lyman, R. L., and M. J. O'Brien. (1999). Americanist stratigraphic excavation and the measurement of culture change. *Journal of Archaeological Method and Theory* 6: 55–108.

Lyman, R. L., and M. J. O'Brien. (2000). Chronometers and units in early archaeology and paleontology. *American Antiquity* 65: 691–707.

Lyman, R. L., M. J. O'Brien, and R. C. Dunnell. (1997). *The Rise and Fall of Culture History*. New York: Plenum.

Lyman, R. L., S. Wolverton, and M. J. O'Brien. (1998). Seriation, superposition, and interdigitation: A history of Americanist graphic depictions of culture change. *American Antiquity* 63: 239–261.

Mayden, R. L. (1997). A hierarchy of species concepts: The denouement in the saga of the species problem. In M. F. Claridge, H. A. Dawah, and M. R. Wilson (eds.), *Species: The Units of Biodiversity*. London: Chapman and Hall, pp. 381–424.

Mayr, E. (1942). *Systematics and the Origin of Species*. New York: Columbia University Press.

Mayr, E. (1959). Darwin and the evolutionary theory in biology. In B. J. Meggers (ed.), *Evolution and Anthropology: A Centennial Appraisal*. Washington, DC: Anthropological Society of Washington, pp. 1–10.

Mayr, E. (1968). The role of systematics in biology. *Science* 159: 595–599.

O'Brien, M. J., T. D. Holland, R. J. Hoard, and G. L. Fox. (1994). Evolutionary implications of design and performance characteristics of prehistoric pottery. *Journal of Archaeological Method and Theory* 1: 259–304.

O'Brien, M. J., and R. L. Lyman. (1998). *James A. Ford and the Growth of Americanist Archaeology*. Columbia: University of Missouri Press.

O'Brien, M. J., and R. L. Lyman. (1999). *Seriation, Stratigraphy, and Index Fossils: The Backbone of Archaeological Dating*. New York: Kluwer Academic/Plenum.

O'Brien, M. J., and R. L. Lyman. (2000). *Applying Evolutionary Archaeology: A Systematic Approach*. New York: Kluwer Academic/Plenum.

O'Brien, M. J., R. L. Lyman, and R. D. Leonard. (1998). Basic incompatibilities between evolutionary and behavioral archaeology. *American Antiquity* 63: 485–498.

Phillips, P., and G. R. Willey. (1953). Method and theory in American archaeology: An operational basis for culture-historical integration. *American Anthropologist* 55: 615–633.

Ramenofsky, A. F., and A. Steffen (eds.). (1998). *Unit Issues in Archaeology: Measuring Time, Space, and Material*. Salt Lake City: University of Utah Press.

Simpson, G. G. (1943). Criteria for genera, species, and subspecies in zoology and paleozoology. *New York Academy of Sciences, Annals* 44: 145–178.

Simpson, G. G. (1944). *Tempo and Mode in Evolution*. New York: Columbia University Press.

Simpson, G. G. (1945). The principles of classification and a classification of mammals. *American Museum of Natural History, Bulletin* 85.

Simpson, G. G. (1961). *Principles of Animal Taxonomy*. New York: Columbia University Press.

Spaulding, A. C. (1953). Statistical techniques for the discovery of artifact types. *American Antiquity* 18: 305–313.

Spaulding, A. C. (1954). Reply to Ford. *American Antiquity* 19: 391–393.

Spencer, C. S. (1997). Evolutionary approaches in archaeology. *Journal of Archaeological Research* 5: 209–264.

Sylvester-Bradley, P. C. (ed.). (1956). *The Species Concept in Palaeontology*. London: The Systematics Association.

Valentine, J. W., and C. L. May. (1996). Hierarchies in biology and paleobiology. *Paleobiology* 22: 23–33.

Whittaker, J. C., D. Caulkins, and K. A. Kamp. (1998). Evaluating consistency in typology and classification. *Journal of Archaeological Method and Theory* 5: 129–164.

Willey, G. R. (1953). Archaeological theories and interpretation: New World. In A. L. Kroeber, *Anthropology Today*. Chicago: University of Chicago Press, pp. 361–385.

Chapter 6

Complexity

John Kantner

INTRODUCTION

Since the time of Charles Darwin, complexity has most often been regarded as a typical result of evolutionary processes, both in popular and scholarly literature. Complexity is clearly not a necessary result of **natural selection**, the primary process for evolutionary change that simply refers to the reduction of variation according to the differential replicability of an entity's characteristics. Nevertheless, the history of life on earth is still seen as the story of increasingly complex organisms, a story with close parallels in discussions of the evolution of other systems such as human sociocultural formations. Accordingly, considerable scholarly effort is expended on explaining how or even if evolutionary theory, in either its classic or contemporary forms, can explain why change seems so closely linked with increasing complexity.

These issues, of course, beg the question of what exactly we mean by the term "complexity." A 1995 article in *Scientific American* presented a list, compiled by Seth Lloyd, of over 30 different ways that the concept has been used in a variety of disciplines (Horgan 1995). With definitions ranging from "the amount of entropy in a system" to "the amount of computer memory required to describe a system," the word "complexity" has increasingly become a symbol of uncertainty and incomprehension, so much so that many people consider it to mean "something too complicated to understand" or "something we have no means of understanding" (Segraves 1982: 288).

Dictionaries are not particularly helpful, usually defining complexity as "the state of being complex" but also offering "intricacy, entanglement" as definitions (*Webster's Revised Unabridged Dictionary* 1998). The fact that the term can be used as either an adjective or a noun further confuses the issue. Perhaps a definition that captures the essence of all other dictionary entries can be paraphrased from the *American Heritage Electronic Dictionary* (1992): "The quality or condition of consisting of interconnected or interwoven parts." In anthropology, the word has been used primarily as a noun. So we often hear expressions such as "the complexity of human behavior" and "sociopolitical complexity," all of which tend to revolve around the dictionary's definition of the term as representing an entity of "many interwoven parts." In practice, however, anthropology's use of the term often approaches the more colloquial view that the item of interest is too complicated to fully understand.

HISTORY

Although anthropologists have employed the term "complexity" in a number of different contexts, it has primarily been used to describe sociocultural forms. This application of the term has a long history. For example, at the turn of the century, Herbert Spencer, inspired by Charles Darwin's work, used the concept of complexity in his theories of human sociocultural evolution. Although **evolution** can probably best be defined simply as "change over time," Spencer viewed this as a process of progressive development. He regarded sociocultural evolution as the result of necessarily increasing complexity of communal bonds, political and judicial institutions, and economic interrelationships. He explicitly regarded sociocultural complexity as increasing "through continuous differentiations and integrations" (1898).

In the first half of the twentieth century, with anthropology heavily influenced by Franz Boas' particularism, the concept of complexity was used primarily to represent the uniqueness of specific sociocultural traditions. In the 1940s, however, scholars such as Leslie White reacted to the vague application of the term by commenting that "sociologists and cultural anthropologists . . . merely assume, in the first place, that everyone knows what is meant by complexity, and, in the second place, they assume without argument that complexity means difficulty" (White 1949: 61–62). Reviving Spencer's view of complexity, White noted that "complexity is a *quality* of a phenomenon, not a measure of its size" (White 1949: 63) and elaborated on the relationship between energy, technology, and sociocultural complexity.

By the late 1950s, many anthropologists were increasingly focusing on issues surrounding sociocultural complexity. Particularly influential were attempts to distill a range of organizational variables for a given society into some "index of complexity." For example, Naroll (1956) used three **traits** (i.e., characteristics or conditions of a society) to identify and quantify differences in complexity, while Carneiro (1967) reduced over 200 organizational traits to a single index of complexity. The assumption was that greater quantities or higher values of these traits represented increasingly elaborate relationships between components of a society. The growth of sociocultural complexity was therefore seen as an increase in the quantity of components that facilitate the operation of a large society composed of many different parts.

This use of complexity as a quantitative measure of a society's parts and their connections gave way in the 1960s and 1970s to a typological approach that focused on qualitative differences between sociocultural forms. The resulting **typologies** represented systematic classifications of human societies according to shared characteristics or traits. Elman Service (1962, 1975), for example, presented his sociocultural categories of bands, tribes, chiefdoms, and states, which were often perceived and usually operationalized as normative steps within a linear evolutionary framework. Chiefdoms and states were considered to exhibit complexity; bands and tribes generally did not possess complex forms of social and political integration. Complexity was presented as an explicit but general packet of sociocultural traits that could be generalized into evolutionary categories, such as in Steponaitis' elaboration of simple versus complex chiefdoms (1978; see also Creamer and Haas 1985). While unquestionably valuable in the development of anthropological knowledge and theory, these concepts of complexity divided societies into essentialistic bundles of traits which required that change be initiated externally since internal variability was minimized.

Not all scholars in the 1960s and 1970s jumped on the typology bandwagon. Archaeologists such as Clarke (1968), for example, advocated a less categorical systems approach in which complexity of human society was viewed in the same way that biologists looked at living systems, with innumerable interacting components determining the flow of energy, matter, and information. Flannery (1972: 409) emphasized a similar view of the concept, noting that "complexity can be measured in terms of . . . segregation (the amount of internal differentiation and specialization of subsystems) and centralization (the degree of linkage between the various subsystems and the highest-order controls in society)." While this systems perspective emphasized the interrelatedness and interconnectedness of a society's components and therefore most closely parallels dictionary definitions of the term, as in unilineal evolution, change in systems models had to be initiated externally. Such stimuli from the environment were seen as promoting further elaboration of components and their relationships with one another, resulting in greater sociocultural complexity.

By the 1980s, some anthropologists reacted to the shortcomings of models of unilineal evolution by dismantling the concept of complexity. An influential article by Feinman and Neitzel (1984) demonstrated that the

discrete, discontinuous levels of complexity as defined in unilineal/typolog-
ical schemes did not exist and that no single variable could adequately
represent the concept of complexity. Other archaeologists came to similar
conclusions. McGuire (1983), for example, emphasized the fluid trajectories
of heterogeneity and inequality as the critical components of complexity,
while Steponaitis (1981: 321) called for a separation of "ordinal" views of
complexity into "several analytically separate dimensions," including food
surpluses, political centralization, and **hierarchy** (i.e., the organization of
successive grades, with each level subordinate to the one above). This return
to a focus on complexity as the interrelatedness of components paralleled
an interest in understanding how internal factors might promote increasing
sociocultural complexity.

Despite the call for a renewed focus on the specific components and
relationships that comprise sociocultural complexity, much of the research
during the late 1980s and into the 1990s continued to use the term without
explication. Complexity was still regarded as a somewhat discrete packet
of specific traits that a society either did or did not possess, perhaps still
influenced by unilineal evolutionary typologies. In Johnson and Earle's
(1987) popular summary of sociocultural evolution, for example, complexity was regarded as a set of features such as larger population scale and
greater socioeconomic integration that together defined distinct levels in
their evolutionary typology (see also Lightfoot 1987). Often lost in these
applications of complexity was an exploration of the different variables
whose interrelationships were differentially expressed in all societies, a view
of complexity that a number of scholars during this time were beginning
to explore in greater depth. For some archaeologists, complexity was essentially regarded as a quality of a society that was present or absent, while
others considered complexity to be present in all societies but with varying
numbers of parts and degrees of interconnectedness.

CONTEMPORARY USES

Use of the Concept in Archaeology

The use of the concept of complexity in archaeology and in anthropology
in general continues to be entangled in discussions of sociocultural evolution. Ambivalence in what the term "complexity" means is manifested in
the prevalent tendency to avoid defining it. Scholars continue to refer to
"the development of social complexity" (Nielsen 1995: 47) or "the upper
limits on the level of complexity" (Graves and Ladefoged 1995: 158–159)
and assume that all researchers share an understanding of the concept. This
imprecision is increasingly criticized: "What does this concept of complexity mean? There seem to be as many definitions of complexity as there are
archaeologists interested in the subject" (Price 1995: 140).

Archaeologists are still ambivalent as to whether complexity best refers to discrete states that a society may exhibit or whether the concept should be represented primarily as interrelated, continuous variables. The former perspective is still quite prominent in the literature, even while many scholars are explicitly moving away from typological approaches to the description and analysis of prehistoric polities. We therefore still see references to complexity "thresholds" between chiefdoms and states measured by the presence or absence of specific traits. Possehl (1998: 287), for example, suggests that internal differentiation and structural specialization is a level of complexity representative of a state but not a chiefdom (see also Drennan 1996: 25; Feinman 1998: 104–114). Similarly, Kosse (1994: 36) notes that "complexity is defined as the presence of vertically organized simultaneous hierarchies" and later refers to "the additional expense of complexity" as a critical factor affecting whether or not complexity would appear among a society (Kosse 1994: 46–47).

Perhaps in response to the often-criticized imprecision with which the concept of complexity is used, many scholars who still conceptualize complexity as existing in discrete states have increasingly emphasized specific sociocultural domains where they believe complexity to be most clearly manifested. For example, Hayden (1995) considers the appearance of complexity to be represented by "the emergence of socioeconomic inequalities, economically based hierarchies, and economically based complexity," while later he points to "social complexity involving socioeconomic inequalities and resource ownership" (1995: 21–22). Unfortunately, the effect of this ambiguity has been to further dilute the meager definitional precision that existed before, exacerbated by manifestations of the concept that are driven by theoretical considerations. So while Maschner and Patton (1996: 102) emphasize "social ranking and political complexity," Chapman (1996: 45) considers the appearance of complexity to indicate "the emergence of hereditary inequality and social stratification." Arnold (1996: 2) first refers to "hierarchical organization and regional integration," and later to "vertical hierarchies and sociopolitical inequalities" as the harbingers of complexity. Some scholars seem to regard complexity as separate from social ranking and inequality; others separate complexity from hierarchical organization, while still others combine all these variables with economic elaboration for their definitions of complexity. These highly diverse uses of the term "complexity" make it very difficult to develop a shared understanding of what is meant by the concept or by the phrase "sociocultural complexity."

A smaller group of scholars have focused on complexity as a quality possessed by all societies to varying degrees, referring to "an enormous range of sociopolitical complexity, from the essentially egalitarian . . . to the stratified systems" (Webster 1998: 312). This parallels a focus on the dictionary definition of the concept as scholars attempt to separate measures of complexity from theoretical considerations of what drives increasing sociocultural complexity: "I personally prefer the dictionary definition of complexity—things complex have more parts and more connections between parts" (Price 1995: 140). Accordingly, many of these scholars are focusing on two trajectories that together are considered to comprise complexity: internal differentiation of components and more intercomponent relationships (Hill et al. 1996: 107; Paynter 1989: 369). Some take an extreme position, suggesting that we discard the term "complexity" altogether to rid the discipline of imprecise unilineal and typological views of sociocultural variability (O'Shea and Barker 1996: 16). They advocate instead an exclusive focus on the specific trajectories of complexity that are really what we are interested in if we want to explain change.

In the past decade, a number of different theoretical camps have diverged from mainstream archaeology. A few groups have explicitly aligned themselves as the representatives of modern evolutionary theory and their perspectives on the concept of complexity are at least partially informed by biological theory. Two groups are especially prominent. The first, variously referred to as evolutionary archaeologists or selectionists, advocates a strict interpretation of **Darwinian evolutionary theory**, with the term "Darwinian" indicating that this approach advocates evolution by natural selection as the most efficacious approach for both describing and explaining cultural change. While much of their work up to this point has been concerned with the interface of evolutionary theory with archaeological data, the topic of complexity has been occasionally addressed. Dunnell (1995: 41), for example, has defined complexity as the "functional specialization" of individuals, resulting in "centralized decision-making, occupational differentiation, and nonkin-based organization." Dunnell further distinguishes between complex and simple societies, defining a threshold based on the point at which a society has become an aggregate of functionally differentiated individuals and is effectively an evolutionary unit that itself is subject to selective pressures. According to this perspective, a characteristic of complexity is the diversion of energy into "superfluous" and "wasteful" behaviors, which thereby increases the society's ability to reproduce itself (Dunnell 1989; Graves and Ladefoged 1995: 167). Interestingly, this selectionist perspective on complexity and on thresholds between societal complexity in some ways parallels unilineal approaches that view sociocultural evolution as proceeding through discrete stages.

The second group of archaeologists and anthropologists influenced by evolutionary theory are variously referred to as evolutionary ecologists or human behavioral ecologists. These scholars advocate a more flexible interpretation of modern evolutionary theory, especially emphasizing human decision making within the social and physical environmental context. Their research, however, has rarely touched on issues of sociocultural complexity, perhaps due to a primary focus on foraging societies. When the issue of complexity has been broached, it has generally paralleled other contemporary definitions that regard complexity as measured by the amount of internal differentiation and integration, with a special focus on hierarchy and inequality (e.g., Boone 1992).

As anthropology and archaeology move into the twenty-first century, the concept and uses of complexity continue to be refined. Despite some residual typological perspectives that still perceive complexity as a bundle of discrete traits, scholars are increasingly attempting to tease apart the components that comprise sociocultural complexity. However, one problem that we continue to face is how best to separate the definition of complexity from the **explanation** of (in other words, identifying the causes of) complexity. Some applications of the concept often verge on being teleological, including statements such as, "local political institutions continued to evolve in response to an increasingly complex society" (Ferguson 1991: 192). Another tendency seen in the literature is the avoidance of a generalized view of sociopolitical complexity in favor of the consideration of specific components. However, in many of these cases, the term "complexity" simply reemerges at new levels; instead of referring simply to "sociocultural complexity," we now see references to phrases such as "political complexity," "economic complexity," or "functional complexity." These applications of the concept of complexity still possess an undesirable degree of imprecision.

Use of the Concept in Other Disciplines

The term "complexity" is widely used across a variety of disciplines, including sociocultural anthropology, evolutionary biology, mathematics and physics, and computer science. Most of these disciplines have been more careful to explicitly define what they mean when they use the concept, revealing the diversity of ways in which the term is applied. Although most applications are loosely based on the dictionary definition of the word "complexity," different aspects of the concept are emphasized in different disciplines. The following is only a brief review of some of the uses of the concept of complexity, focusing especially on those that have in one way or another influenced archaeological method and theory.

In sociocultural anthropology, use of the concept of complexity parallels its use in archaeology. In discussions of sociocultural complexity, there is a particular emphasis on decoupling the components of complexity and focusing on these as the relevant analytical concepts. For example, in practice theory, the term "complexity" is generally discarded in favor of the use of components such as "socioeconomic differentiation," "political centralization," and "social stratification" (e.g., Giddens 1984; Ortner 1984). This avoidance of "complexity" is made easier by the fact that sociocultural anthropologists do not focus as much on diachronic change and have easier access to information on the specific components of social and cultural complexity. Use of the concept of complexity, however, does appear in the discipline. For example, Flanagan (1989: 260) refers to "the complexity of simple societies" and further elaborates on the idea of technological complexity as indicated by the presence of mechanized tools and "social-organizational" complexity as the presence of social classes.

Because archaeology has borrowed so many concepts and theoretical approaches from evolutionary biology, an examination of the use of "complexity" in this discipline is certainly relevant. In general, the term is defined with greater precision than is seen in archaeology or anthropology. Evolutionary biologists often regard the concept of complexity as representing the amount of differentiation in some biological system, especially emphasizing the number of distinct parts that are specialized in some way. The evolutionary theorist Heylighen (1995) notes:

The aspects of distinction and connection determine two dimensions characterizing complexity. Distinction corresponds to variety, to heterogeneity, to the fact that different parts of the complex behave differently. Connection corresponds to constraint, to redundancy, to the fact that different parts are not independent, but that the knowledge of one part allows the determination of features of the other parts.

Edmonds (1999) makes a point to carefully distinguish the concept of complexity from related concepts that are also used to characterize a system, such as its size, our ignorance of it (i.e., the inability to understand the system), the variety of components, its Kolmogorov complexity (the minimum length of a description of the system), or the system's level of order and disorder. Edmonds instead defines complexity as "that property [of an entity] which makes it *difficult* to formulate its overall behaviour even when given almost complete information about its *atomic* [irreducible] components and their inter-relations" (Edmonds 1999: 6) (emphasis added). He also emphasizes the need to distinguish between the complexity of description and the complexity of explanation, adding a level of separation between description and theory that is often absent in anthropological applications of the concept.

As would be expected, evolutionary theorists tend to see complexity and complex systems as arising through the process of natural selection. In their discussion of the origins of complexity in language systems (i.e., the point from which it derives), Pinker and Bloom (1990) note that

the only successful account of the origin of complex biological structure is the theory of natural selection ... we argue that language is no different from other complex abilities such as echolocation or stereopsis, and that the only way to explain the origin of such abilities is through the theory of natural selection.

However, many scholars also recognize that complex structure and functionality can also arise independently from natural selection (e.g., neural plasticity and Braille); thus, complexity does not necessarily indicate that natural selection occurred, although evolutionary biologists do tend to emphasize this in their analyses.

So-called complexity theory and chaos theory have become popular topics in many disciplines, including archaeology. Perhaps because they are so closely tied to mathematics and physics, terms used in these theoretical approaches are always carefully defined. In complexity theory, the term "complexity" is often defined as the quantity of information that is needed to fully describe a system (Cohen and Stewart 1994: 20; Gell-Mann 1994). This view parallels "algorithmic informational complexity," which is simply the shortest computer program needed to describe a system. Note that this definition does not include the idea of interrelatedness that is a seemingly essential part of most definitions of complexity. In fact, complexity theorists are not explicitly concerned with component interrelationships, instead focusing on how simple rules pursued by individual agents can result in the emergence of new, complex, non-linear properties (Holland 1995). As Cohen and Stewart (1994: 219) indicate, "complexity at any given level is a consequence of the operation of relatively simple rules one level lower down." The emphasis is therefore on identifying the simple rules of agents that promote complex effects (e.g., Axelrod 1997). Interestingly, this hearkens back to Adam Smith's (1776) discussions of how spontaneous order can emerge without **design** (i.e., the order is not an intended outcome) simply by individuals pursuing simple **goals** (i.e., objectives, or the purposes toward which endeavors are directed), an idea that influenced Charles Darwin's own thinking on evolutionary processes.

AUTHOR'S FAVORED DEFINITION

A recent issue of the *SFI Bulletin*, produced by the Santa Fe Institute, a think tank for complexity theory, includes the following discussion of "complexity" (Baake 1999):

SFI President Ellen Goldberg says that complexity involves "interacting parts with very simple rules," but she is quick to add that the term does not reduce to a constant definition across disciplines. For that reason, Goldberg likes the term; it is flexible and permits multiple definitions.

Indeed, the variability of the definitions for "complexity" has allowed it to be uniquely expressed both between and even within different disciplines, as the review of its use in archaeology clearly demonstrates. Computer science provides another example, for in this discipline, complexity is "the degree of complication of a system or system component, determined by such factors as the number and intricacy of interfaces, the number and intricacy of conditional branches, the degree of nesting, and the types of data structures" (Evans and Marciniak 1987). Here, the concept of complexity includes aspects of the dictionary definition, but the definition is further expanded to accommodate discipline-specific interests.

The problem is that with every discipline using "complexity" in a different way, crossing disciplinary boundaries and using the concept in a mutually comprehensible way becomes exceedingly difficult. This is particularly problematic for archaeology, which has a long tradition of borrowing concepts from other disciplines. With some archaeologists grounded in anthropological views of complexity at the same time that others are reaching toward evolutionary theory or complexity theory, we increasingly have a difficult time understanding how each of us is defining the concept. For this reason, I think it worthwhile to explore possible definitions that perhaps best capture the essence of complexity while allowing for some flexibility in the way it is applied.

Defining complexity as "the quantity of information needed to describe an entity" is tempting, as it provides a very simple definition with wide applicability to all circumstances in which the term has been used. However, this definition tends to minimize what seems to be a critical aspect of complexity that separates it from related concepts such as "size," "variety," or "multiplicity": the degree of systemic interrelatedness of the entity in question. Complexity refers to more than just a large, variegated entity consisting of many parts; the intensity of interrelationships among the parts is also important. This is particularly relevant for archaeology, for we are interested in complex human systems, not just large ones.

An improved definition of **complexity**, which has a precedent in Flannery's work (e.g., 1972), is provided by Paynter (1989: 369) as "the degree of internal differentiation and intricacy of relations [integration] within a system." I would further add that differentiation and integration should be measured both horizontally and vertically, with "horizontal" used in reference to components that have similar influences on the system, while "vertical" distinguishes components that have unequal influences on the system. This creates essentially four variables that together provide a scaled measure of complexity: *horizontal differentiation*, *vertical differentiation*, *horizontal integration*, and *vertical integration*. Complexity can therefore be regarded as a continuous, quantitative measure that describes a system. This definition differs from many archaeological uses of the term that tend to view integration and complexity as existing separately (e.g., Blanton et al. 1996: 13), or typological approaches that heuristically view complexity as a discrete state. The definition I advocate is also distinguishable from related concepts such as scale and boundedness, which, although important for defining the entity whose complexity is being measured, are not necessarily and invariably related to a system's complexity.

In the definition I advocate, the "system" can be perceived as any entity, ranging from stone tools to modern nations. For example, in the case of sociocultural entities, complexity is envisioned as a continuous measure of all societies and accordingly no thresholds between simple and complex polities are recognized. In accordance with the base definition, sociocultural complexity is a measure of interconnected behavioral and cultural differentiation in a **population**, or set of socially interacting individuals. As such, the definition of complexity is seen as independent of theories as to why the level of complexity changes. So, for example, a scholar may hypothesize that societies exhibit greater levels of complexity because increasing vertical differentiation (e.g., economic inequality), stimulated by internal or external factors, in turn promotes increases in vertical integration (e.g., decision-making hierarchy).

This decoupling and simplification of the concept of complexity allows the different variables that comprise complexity and the relationships between them to be examined independently. This in turn makes the concept more amenable to modeling and analysis using contemporary theoretical approaches in archaeology, such as evolutionary archaeology and behavioral archaeology, which by their very nature cannot easily accommodate qualitative representations of complexity. This view also recognizes the non-progressive nature of complexity, and it similarly avoids the "oppositional thinking" that those advocating a dialectical approach find so troublesome with mainstream uses of the term "complexity" (e.g., McGuire and Saitta 1996).

CASE STUDIES

Very few archaeologists have explicitly approached the concept of complexity in the way that I have advocated. Those who have are interested primarily in sociocultural complexity. One of the first scholars to produce a case study that teased apart the concept of complexity is Olivier de Montmollin. In his study (1989) of the Classic-period Maya of southeastern Mexico, he focused on "bundled continua of variation," a series of interrelated variables that together provided a measure of changing complexity. Informed by political science and with an interest in sociopolitical change, de Montmollin's variables included measures of centralization, differentiation, and integration in addition to hierarchy, solidarity, and stratification (1989: 16–20). His variables were therefore more specific to his research problem than those that I propose for comprising complexity, but at the root of his "bundled continua of variation" were the same trajectories that I consider to be important.

Because he avoided a typological and static view of complexity, de Montmollin was able to describe changing sociopolitical features of the polity in question and then use the different trajectories of complexity as a basis for explaining the changes. According to de Montmollin, breaking complexity into its component parts avoided a variety of problems inherent to formalist and essentialistic approaches to the concept, including "undue reification of society [and] societal types; inappropriately categorical thinking . . . ; [and] nominal definition of types, with assumed co-variation of several attribute levels and elimination of worthwhile research problems" (1989: 217). In this context, **attribute** referred to a conceptually irreducible quality or characteristic inherent in or ascribed to a society.

A more recent study that utilizes a concept of complexity very similar to the one I advocate is summarized in the recent work of James Hill, W. Nicholas Trierweiler, and Robert Preucel (1996). For their study, these scholars provide an explicit definition of complexity: "we see it primarily as the degree to which any given cultural system is internally differentiated in terms of qualitatively different organizational components or parts" (Hill et al. 1996: 107). They further acknowledge that hierarchy and the "parallel (horizontal) arrangement of organizations/institutions" are additional trajectories of complexity, as are "the interrelationships among the different organizational components of a cultural system" (1996: 108). Clearly identified are the aspects of complexity that I consider important, with differentiation and integration measured both horizontally and vertically. For their study, these trajectories are operationalized more specifically as regional social integration, political centralization, social stratification, and status differentiation.

Hill et al. (1996) use this framework for understanding complexity in their discussion of sociocultural development of Puebloan **groups** (i.e., assemblages of people considered together because of similarities among them) on the Pajarito Plateau of north-central New Mexico. Their study is not so much an examination of changing complexity as it is an analysis of changing adaptations and increasing agricultural intensification, but they do evaluate propositions for increasing horizontal and vertical integration and differentiation. Because of their perspective on complexity as a decoupled set of continuous variables, Hill et al. (1996: 121) are able to demonstrate that as social groups on the Pajarito Plateau changed over time, they experienced increasing status differentiation and perhaps social stratification but not increasing social integration and political centralization. This study demonstrates that it is possible to identify important patterning using the concept of complexity presented in this chapter.

Another study that decouples the components of complexity is Monica Minnegal and Peter Dwyer's ethnoarchaeological work in the interior lowlands of Papua New Guinea (1998). Their study is a reaction to previous views in which lowland societies of New Guinea have been contrasted with the highland societies, which are "commonly represented as an end point of socioecological evolution—as the pinnacle of 'complexity' in New Guinea" (1998: 376). Minnegal and Dwyer object to this intrinsically typological and often ecologically deterministic view of New Guinean societies, which obscures a great deal of meaningful sociocultural diversity.

Minnegal and Dwyer's approach (1998) is inspired by Hill et al. (1996), and they too focus on the productive base as the stimulus for increased complexity. However, they define the concept of complexity somewhat differently from Hill et al., focusing on three trajectories: differentiation, integration, and evaluation. The latter, which seems to be a measure of sociocultural identification and regulatory mechanisms, is somewhat unique. Minnegal and Dwyer appear to be emphasizing that their concept of complexity includes not just the "involvement of parts" (i.e., differentiation and integration), but that "individuation of form" is also a critical aspect of complexity. This refers to the boundedness and independence of the system in question that separates it from all other sociocultural systems. Although individuation of form is certainly important in discussions of sociocultural complexity, I would dispute its direct relevance to a precise concept of complexity, arguing that the boundedness of a system is not directly and invariably related to its complexity. A stone tool, for example, has very high individuation of form but may represent very little technological complexity.

Minnegal and Dwyer (1998) correlate the variables of differentiation, integration, and evaluation with differences in population density and intensification of plant food production in two adjacent societies located in the low- and middle-altitude Strickland-Bosavi region. Using this approach to complexity, they are able to demonstrate that, despite similar environmental conditions and access to **resources** (i.e., food and materials necessary for somatic and reproductive efforts), the two groups exhibit markedly different levels of complexity. Minnegal and Dwyer do not extensively consider why these differences exist, instead focusing their discussion on defining complexity for each group. However, they do suggest that variable population density and intensification have differentially affected the components of complexity in the two New Guinean societies.

All three case studies discussed above are able to separate measures of complexity from theoretical considerations of what causes sociocultural changes. Hill et al. (1996) and Minnegal and Dwyer (1998) are able to evaluate the effect of intensifying food production and variable population density on measures of complexity, while de Montmollin (1989) can look more toward the influences of specific trajectories of complexity on one another. In each study, different variables that comprise complexity are seen as differentially affected by external or internal changes according to historical or contextual contingencies. Such patterns would not have been identified using either typological definitions of complexity or definitions that are too abstract to capture the sense of interrelatedness and differentiation that dictionary definitions of the term emphasize, but which are often minimized in anthropological research.

FUTURE IMPORTANCE

In this chapter, complexity has been defined as a continuous measure of horizontal differentiation, vertical differentiation, horizontal integration, and vertical integration. This discussion has especially concentrated on the concept of complexity as it has been applied to anthropological research on sociocultural variability. Certainly, in archaeology, the term is seen most often in this context. However, other uses of "complexity" are also found in the literature, and these have not been extensively discussed in this chapter. For example, in Bettinger and Eerkens' (1997: 181) discussion of social transmission and Great Basin projectile points, they define technical complexity as the number of steps needed to produce an artifact. Whether use of the concept of complexity advocated in this chapter would have enhanced the precision of their analysis or revealed new patterns is difficult to determine. I suspect that measuring horizontal and vertical differentiation and integration even for a stone-tool technology could be a more effective application of the concept of complexity, but we need actual examples of complexity applied in this context. Other technologies such as irrigation systems may also benefit by measuring their complexity according to the variables defined in this chapter.

Ultimately, though, the value of the concept of complexity advocated here will find its greatest utility in discussions of sociocultural evolution, for this is where the most confusion regarding the term exists. As Nelson has noted (1995: 598), "the term complexity, while easy enough to grasp intuitively, refers in archaeological practice to a web of properties whose interrelationships are poorly understood." Unfortunately, with the increasing trend away from typological sequences that employ qualitative measures of complexity, archaeologists are beginning to use the term in a wide variety of ways that defy comparability. Greater conceptual precision is particularly important now, for influences from other disciplines are introducing new and unique definitions of complexity that often are not commensurate with our diverse uses of the term. A shared view of complexity that identifies a set of irreducible core components will be especially important as archaeologists attempt to apply evolutionary theory, in whatever form it takes, to describing and explaining changes in sociocultural complexity. Hopefully, the definition of complexity advocated in this chapter can direct scholars toward a more integrated understanding of a concept that has played such an important role in anthropological discussions of human behavior.

REFERENCES

Arnold, J. E. (ed.). (1996). *Emergent Complexity: The Evolution of Intermediate Societies*. Archaeological Series No. 9. Ann Arbor, MI: International Monographs in Prehistory.

Axelrod, R. (1997). *The Complexity of Cooperation: Agent-Based Models of Competition and Collaboration.* Princeton, NJ: Princeton University Press.

Baake, K. (1999). Language issues. *Santa Fe Institute Bulletin* 14(2): 28–29.

Bettinger, R., and J. Eerkens. (1997). Evolutionary implications of metrical variation in Great Basin projectile points. In C. M. Barton and G. A. Clark (eds.), *Rediscovering Darwin: Evolutionary Theory and Archeological Explanation.* Archeological Papers No. 7. Arlington, VA: American Anthropological Association, pp. 177–192.

Blanton, R. E., G. M. Feinman, S. A. Kowalewski, and P. N. Peregrine. (1996). A dual-processual theory for the evolution of Mesoamerican civilization. *Current Anthropology* 37: 1–14.

Boone, J. L. (1992). Competition, conflict, and the development of social hierarchies. In E. A. Smith and B. Winterhalder (eds.), *Evolutionary Ecology and Human Behavior.* New York: Aldine de Gruyter, pp. 301–337.

Carneiro, R. L. (1967). On the relationship between size of population and complexity of social organization. *Southwestern Journal of Anthropology* 23: 234–243.

Chapman, R. W. (1996). Problems of scale in the emergence of complexity. In J. E. Arnold (ed.), *Emergent Complexity: The Evolution of Intermediate Societies.* Archaeological Series No. 9. Ann Arbor, MI: International Monographs in Prehistory, pp. 35–49.

Clarke, D. L. (1968). *Analytical Archaeology.* London: Methuen.

Cohen, J., and I. Stewart. (1994). *The Collapse of Chaos: Discovering Simplicity in a Complex World.* New York: Penguin Books.

Creamer, W., and J. Haas. (1985). Tribe versus chiefdom in lower Central America. *American Antiquity* 50: 738–754.

Crumley, C. L. (1995). Heterarchy and the analysis of complex societies. In R. M. Ehrenreich, C. L. Crumley, and J. E. Levy (eds.), *Heterarchy and the Analysis of Complex Societies.* Archeological Papers No. 6. Washington, DC: American Anthropological Association, pp. 1–5.

de Montmollin, O. (1989). *The Archaeology of Political Structure: Settlement Analysis in a Classic Maya Polity.* Cambridge: Cambridge University Press.

Drennan, R. D. (1996). One for all and all for one: Accounting for variability without losing sight of regularities in the development of complex society. In J. E. Arnold (ed.), *Emergent Complexity: The Evolution of Intermediate Societies.* Archaeological Series No. 9. Ann Arbor, MI: International Monographs in Prehistory, pp. 24–34.

Dunnell, R. C. (1989). Aspects of the application of evolutionary theory in archaeology. In C. C. Lamberg-Karlovsky (ed.), *Archaeological Thought in America.* Cambridge: Cambridge University Press, pp. 35–49.

Dunnell, R. C. (1995). What is it that actually evolves? In P. A. Teltser (ed.), *Evolutionary Archaeology: Methodological Issues.* Tucson: University of Arizona Press, pp. 33–50.

Edmonds, B. (1999). What is complexity? The philosophy of complexity per se with application to some examples in evolution. In F. Heylighen and D. Aerts (eds.), *The Evolution of Complexity.* Dordrecht: Kluwer, pp. 1–18.

Evans, M. W., and J. Marciniak. (1987). *Software Quality Assurance and Management.* New York: John Wiley & Sons.

Feinman, G. M. (1998). Scale and social organization: Perspectives on the archaic state. In G. M. Feinman and J. Marcus (eds.), *Archaic States*. Santa Fe, NM: School of American Research Press, pp. 95–133.

Feinman, G. M., and J. Neitzel. (1984). Too many types: An overview of sedentary prestate societies in the Americas. In M. D. Schiffer (ed.), *Advances in Archaeological Method and Theory*, vol. 7. New York: Academic Press, pp. 39–102.

Ferguson, Y. (1991). Chiefdoms to city-states: The Greek experience. In T. K. Earle (ed.), *Chiefdoms: Power, Economy, and Ideology*. Cambridge: Cambridge University Press, pp. 169–192.

Flanagan, J. G. (1989). Hierarchy in simple "egalitarian" societies. *Annual Review of Anthropology* 18: 245–266.

Flannery, K. V. (1972). The cultural evolution of civilizations. *Annual Review of Ecology and Systematics* 3: 399–426.

Gell-Mann, M. (1994). *The Quark and the Jaguar: Adventures in the Simple and the Complex*. New York: W. H. Freeman.

Giddens, A. (1984). *The Constitution of Society*. Berkeley: University of California Press.

Graves, M. W., and T. N. Ladefoged. (1995). The evolutionary significance of ceremonial architecture. In P. A. Teltser (ed.), *Evolutionary Archaeology: Methodological Issues*. Tucson: University of Arizona Press, pp. 149–174.

Hayden, B. (1995). Pathways to power: Principles for creating socioeconomic inequalities. In T. D. Price and G. M. Feinman (eds.), *Foundations of Social Inequality*. New York: Plenum, pp. 15–86.

Hayden, B., and R. Gargett. (1990). Big man, big heart? A Mesoamerican view of the emergence of complex society. *Ancient Mesoamerica* 1: 3–20.

Heylighen, F. (1995). The growth of complexity. In F. Heylighen, C. Joslyn, and V. Turchin (eds.), *Principia Cybernetica, Brussels* (http://pespmc1.vub.ac.be/COMPGROW.html).

Hill, J. N., W. N. Trierweiler, and R. W. Preucel. (1996). The evolution of cultural complexity: A case from the Pajarito Plateau, New Mexico. In J. E. Arnold (ed.), *Emergent Complexity: The Evolution of Intermediate Societies*. Archaeological Series No. 9. Ann Arbor, MI: International Monographs in Prehistory, pp. 107–127.

Holland, J. H. (1995). *Hidden Order: How Adaptation Builds Complexity*. Reading, MA: Perseus Books.

Horgan, J. (1995). Trends in complexity studies: From complexity to perplexity. *Scientific American* 272(6): 104–109.

Johnson, A., and T. K. Earle. (1987). *The Evolution of Human Societies*. Stanford, CA: Stanford University Press.

Kosse, K. (1994). The evolution of large, complex groups: A hypothesis. *Journal of Anthropological Archaeology* 13: 35–50.

Lightfoot, K. G. (1987). A consideration of complex prehistoric societies in the U.S. Southwest. In R. D. Drennan and C. A. Uribe (eds.), *Chiefdoms in the Americas*. Lanham, MD: University Press of America, pp. 43–57.

Maschner, H.D.G., and J. Q. Patton. (1996). Kin selection and the origins of hereditary social inequality: A case study from the northern Northwest Coast. In H.D.G. Maschner (ed.), *Darwinian Archaeologies*. New York: Plenum, pp. 89–108.

McGuire, R. H. (1983). Breaking down cultural complexity: Inequality and heterogeneity. In M. B. Schiffer (ed.), *Advances in Archaeological Method and Theory*, vol. 6. New York: Academic Press, pp. 91–142.

McGuire, R. H., and D. J. Saitta. (1996). Although they have petty captains, they obey them badly: The dialectics of prehistoric Western Pueblo social organization. *American Antiquity* 61: 197–216.

Minnegal, M., and P. D. Dwyer. (1998). Intensification and social complexity in the interior lowlands of Papua New Guinea: A comparison of Bedamuni and Kubo. *Journal of Anthropological Archaeology* 17: 375–400.

Naroll, R. (1956). A preliminary index of social development. *American Anthropologist* 58: 687–715.

Nelson, B. A. (1995). Complexity, hierarchy, and scale: A controlled comparison between Chaco Canyon, New Mexico, and La Quemada, Zacatecas. *American Antiquity* 60: 597–618.

Nielsen, A. E. (1995). Architectural performance and the reproduction of social power. In J. M. Skibo, W. H. Walker, and A. E. Nielsen (eds.), *Expanding Archaeology*. Salt Lake City: University of Utah Press, pp. 47–66.

Ortner, S. B. (1984). Theory in anthropology in the sixties. *Comparative Studies in Society and History* 26(1): 126–166.

O'Shea, J. M., and A. W. Barker. (1996). Measuring social complexity and variation: A categorical imperative? In J. E. Arnold (ed.), *Emergent Complexity: The Evolution of Intermediate Societies*. Archaeological Series No. 9. Ann Arbor, MI: International Monographs in Prehistory, pp. 13–24.

Paynter, R. (1989). The archaeology of equality and inequality. *Annual Review of Anthropology* 18: 369–400.

Pinker, S., and P. Bloom. (1990). Natural language and natural selection. *Behavioral and Brain Sciences* 13(4): 707–784.

Possehl, G. L. (1998). Sociocultural complexity without the state. In G. Feinman and J. Marcus (eds.), *Archaic States*. Santa Fe, NM: School of American Research Press, pp. 261–292.

Price, T. D. (1995). Social inequality at the origins of agriculture. In T. D. Price and G. M. Feinman (eds.), *Foundations of Social Inequality*. New York: Plenum, pp. 129–151.

Reynolds, R. G. (1984). A computational model of hierarchical decision systems. *Journal of Anthropological Archaeology* 3: 159–189.

Segraves, B. A. (1982). Central elements in the construction of a general theory of the evolution of societal complexity. In C. Renfrew, M. J. Rolands, and B. A. Segraves (eds.), *Theory and Explanation in Archaeology*. New York: Academic Press, pp. 287–300.

Service, E. R. (1962). *Primitive Social Organization, an Evolutionary Perspective*. New York: Random House.

Service, E. R. (1975). *Origins of the State and Civilization: The Process of Cultural Evolution*. New York: Norton.

Smith, A. (1776). *An Inquiry into the Nature and Causes of the Wealth of Nations*. London: W. Strahan & T. Cadell.

Spencer, H. (1898). *The Principles of Sociology*. New York: D. Appleton.

Steponaitis, V. (1978). Location theory and complex chiefdoms: A Mississippian example. In B. D. Smith (ed.), *Mississippian Settlement Patterns*. New York: Academic Press, pp. 417–445.

Steponaitis, V. P. (1981). Settlement hierarchies and political complexity in non-market societies: The formative period of the Valley of Mexico. *American Anthropologist* 83: 320–363.

Tainter, J. A. (1988). *The Collapse of Complex Societies*. Cambridge: Cambridge University Press.

Upham, S., and F. Plog. (1986). The interpretation of prehistoric political complexity in the central and northern Southwest: Toward a mending of models. *Journal of Field Archaeology* 13: 223–238.

Webster, D. (1998). Warfare and status rivalry: Lowland Maya and Polynesian comparisons. In G. Feinman and G. Marcus (eds.), *Archaic States*. Santa Fe, NM: School of American Research Press, pp. 311–352.

White, L. A. (1949). *The Science of Culture: A Study of Man and Civilization*. New York: Farrar, Straus, and Giroux.

Chapter 7

Culture

Paul Roscoe

INTRODUCTION

Culture, the concept with which anthropology has been intimately identified for over a century, has suddenly jumped to prominence far and wide. Within academia, cultural studies are everywhere. In political science, a reductive analysis of the global political future in terms of culture blocks, or "civilizations," has become influential in international affairs (Huntington 1996). Even among the general public, "suddenly people seem to agree with us anthropologists; culture is everywhere. Immigrants have it, business corporations have it, young people have it, women have it, even ordinary middle-aged men have it, all in their own versions" (Hannerz 1996: 30).

Traditionally, anthropology has used **culture** in both a general and a specific sense. In the general sense, it refers to the belief-and-behavior complex that humans learn and practice as members of the species. This is the meaning deployed in statements such as: "culture is humanity's extrasomatic means of adapting to the external environment," and "people's perceptions and management of their environment are mediated by their culture." In the specific sense, culture refers to particular belief-and-behavior complexes exhibited by particular populations, as in references to "the peoples and cultures of the Pacific," and "the cultures included in the Human Relations Area Files."

Ironically, as anthropology's invention has achieved renown beyond the discipline, it has come under increasing attack from within. There is talk that the concept should be abandoned, or that anthropologists should "write against culture"(for a review, see Brumann 1999). In part, these critiques stem from concerns that the culture concept objectifies and essentializes an analytical abstraction; in part, they are motivated by concerns over how the concept might be deployed politically. They also trade, however, on the notion's protean nature: culture means many different things to many different people, within anthropology as much as without. This review attempts to clarify some of these variations; it then examines aspects of the concept that have special relevance for archaeological theorizing, and finally assesses some implications for evolutionary theories in archaeology.

HISTORY

According to Stocking (1963), anthropological use of the term "culture" has its roots in the nineteenth-century German romantic literary tradition. By that time, though, the term had already found fertile ground in the vocabulary. For at least the last five centuries, "culture" has referred to plant rearing—to culture a plant is to cultivate it—and by the time anthropology emerged in the latter half of the nineteenth century, this usage had been metaphorically extended to include the cultivation of human minds (OED 1981: 1247–1248). Thus, to culture the minds of children was to educate them, to rear or cultivate in them what were considered refined manners, tastes, faculties, arts, and etiquette.

It was in this sense that the moral philosopher Matthew Arnold (1883 [1869]: xi) used the term in 1869. By broad consensus, however, the first anthropological definition was proposed a couple of years later by Edward Burnett Tylor, the first anthropologist to occupy a university chair. Tylor (1958 [1871]: 1) defined culture as "that complex whole which includes knowledge, belief, art, morals, law, custom, and any other capabilities and habits acquired by man as a member of society." Many subsequent anthropologists, however, disagreed: over the next 80 years, more than 160 different definitions of culture appeared (Kroeber and Kluckhohn 1952), a number that has grown in the last half century to a point where it is difficult to claim any standard definition. Given how basic the concept is to anthropology, the existence of such differences is nothing short of astonishing, and points to the troubling likelihood that many anthropological debates about culture, not least those concerning culture and evolution, are talking past one another because they proceed from different definitional premises.

CONTEMPORARY USES

In its use of the culture concept, archaeology generally mirrors anthropology as a whole; in doing so, unfortunately, it also reproduces the same disagreement and disarray about the notion's meaning. These divergences are particularly evident in general introductory texts, the means through which new students are enculturated in the anthropological community. To the extent there is consensus, it is that culture is learned and shared. The differences are perhaps starkest over precisely what is learned and shared. In the strictest, so-called mentalist definitions, culture comprises the learned contents of mind, the "webs of significance" that humans have spun and in which they are suspended (Geertz 1973: 44). In other opinions, they variously include symbols, beliefs, knowledge, ideals, values, norms, rules, and so on—it being sometimes added that these generate and/or are reflected by behavior (e.g., Haviland 1999: 36). Some anthropologists expand this definition to include behavior, specifically behaviors that are learned rather than genetically inherited (e.g., Peoples and Bailey 2000: 366). Others broaden it further to include the material as well as the mental; thus, the material artifacts a people produces are counted as part of culture along with the ideas and/or beliefs that produced them (e.g., Scupin 1992: 418). In the most expansive definitions, culture embraces "everything that people have, think, and do as members of a society" (e.g., Ferraro 1992: 18)—in other words, what they have learned, how they behave, and the material artifacts they possess.

Ironically, the one area of consensus in these definitions—that culture is learned—is among the least defensible. A range of beliefs and behaviors that anthropologists routinely identify as "cultural" almost certainly are also partly based on a biological, somatically inherited component. A range of evidence suggests, for example, that kinship beliefs and behaviors pertaining to close consanguines (or those socialized together) are grounded in attachment behaviors that are partly genetic in origin. Likewise, even some of the most committed of symbolic anthropologists concede that incest aversion may have a genetic as well as a learned component. Natural selection also has shaped the human brain, providing us with a means for adaptive decision making. Regardless of their culture, to take a simple example, humans appear capable of assembling and deploying to their advantage observations that water aids plant growth, and they have probably inherited this faculty through evolutionary processes. Growing evidence suggests that the structure of human taxonomizing, once thought to be a learned, culturally specific property, is broadly shaped by genetically inherited faculties. This is not to argue that culture is therefore the product of biology, for human biology is probably the product of culture in much the same degree. Rather, it is to argue that biology and culture have interacted—co-evolved—in the evolution of humans and humanity. Unfortunately, this important insight tends to be drained away in standard definitions of culture.

The second manner in which culture is used follows from the first. Culture being a set of shared and learned traits comprising what humans have, think, and/or do, then cultures (plural) are the particular sets of learned traits that are shared by particular groups of humans. Thus, in addition to human culture in the generic sense, there is also American culture, Zulu culture, Arapesh culture, and so on. This second usage emerged rather later than the first. For early anthropologists such as Tylor and Frazer, there was, in essence, only one human culture. It extended along a fixed, evolutionary path, and the different peoples of the world were scattered along it according to the level of their mental and moral development—rather as, in the idiom of the day, children were thought to acquire more refined "cultural" tastes, habits, and faculties as they matured. The idea that there were cultures (plural) in the world was not prominently asserted until Franz Boas (1940 [1896]) attacked this idea of uniform cultural evolution.

The definition of how cultures, in this particularistic sense, are to be distinguished from one another is important to those cultural materialist and group-selectionist arguments that present cultures as the units on which natural selection works. Unfortunately, there is neither a standard nor defensible definition of culture in this sense. Although there are some explicit attempts to define a "cultural unit," more commonly the term simply gets mapped onto a second term, **society**: a culture is the particular set of cultural traits shared by members of a society. As a result, a culture (in the particularistic sense) commonly ends up defined as a population that shares a common territory, speaks a common language, and/or is interdependent (e.g., Haviland 1999: 36; Scupin 1992: 423). These definitions work adequately enough when applied to politically centralized nation states. The culture of the French can be distinguished from that of the Germans (separate territories, separate language) and that of the United States from that of Britain (same language, different territories). Even in these contexts, though, the definition can crumble. Do the Swiss constitute one culture or four? They have a single territory, but the inhabitants speak four, quite separate, territorially differentiated languages: Italian, French, German, and Romansch.

Beyond these Western theaters, the definition becomes increasingly problematic if not misleading. Part of the problem is the equation of language and culture. In defining different societies (= cultures) in terms of a common language, the presumption is that speakers of the same language share the same culture, but this is patently false. Language distributions do not correlate well with the distribution of cultures (e.g., Terrell et al. 1997: 166–168). The Boiken "language" of New Guinea, for example, embraces people adapted to such different environments as islands, coasts, thin-soiled mountains, fertile foothills, and infertile grassplains, and to claim that the speakers of Boiken share a common culture is absurd. Subsistence depends on fishing and sago in some areas, gardening and sago in others, and hunting and sago in yet others. Preferred marriage patterns range from sister exchange to marriage with the father's mother's brother's son's daughter. In some areas, competitive exchange focuses on domesticated pigs; in others, on long yams; in others, on giant yams, sago, turtles, and/or wild pigs;

and in yet others, there appears to be no competitive exchange. The Boiken language can be divided into seven "dialects," but even these exhibit considerable cultural heterogeneity: the western Yangoru Boiken copied the initiation houses and long-yam cults of their neighbors, the Kaboibus Arapesh and Eastern Abelam, while the central Yangoru Boiken, speakers of the same Yangoru dialect, exchanged pigs and had a quite different, palisaded initiation enclosure.

Most archaeologists who attempt to extend Darwinian theory to human social systems sidestep these difficulties because they posit units of selection other than groups and cultures, most frequently cultural elements, traits, attributes, or memes. Unfortunately, the nature of these entities and the precise manner in which they articulate to form culture is rather vague, often deliberately so, most selectionists preferring to leave these issues open to future research. In seeking to apply Darwinian processes to the analysis of cultural change, however, they do attribute certain minimal properties to culture. Culture is a system with the capacity to generate variability in behavior and that enshrines mechanisms for the faithful transmission and preservation of that variation between generations (e.g., Jones et al. 1995: 13–14; Rindos 1984: 74–76). (A third requirement—the existence of selective criteria that affect the viability of variants relative to one another—concerns extracultural processes that operate on culture rather than the nature of culture itself.) The mechanisms by which this behavioral variation is generated and transmitted, however, are left unspecified or are outlined in rather reductive and vague terms. Variation, for example, is often (though not always) attributed to "random generators"; transmission is portrayed in terms of "copying," "replication," and the like.

Selectionists justify this minimalist model of culture on two grounds. First, what is important from a Darwinian perspective are "behavioral acts and not the predelictions, reasons, or symbolic functions underlying these acts" (Rindos 1984: 75). This claim is fragile, however, insofar as it presumes, without warrant, that the relationship between mental phenomena and cultural behavior is precisely isomorphic with the relationship between genes and biological behavior.

Second, evolutionary archaeologists note, an ignorance of genes, their nature, and their interaction did not prevent Darwin from theorizing biological evolution. Consequently, a minimalist model in which the nature of culture is left vague should not hinder the development of a Darwinian model of cultural evolution. Had Darwin known of genes, of course, he would have been remiss not to have incorporated them into his theory. It is therefore important to stress that we actually know quite a lot about the cultural equivalents of genes and gene processes, and so we would be likewise remiss if we did not attempt to embed these findings in any model of cultural evolution. Of particular interest are significant advances made by a number of social theorists within and beyond anthropology in understanding the processes by which culture is generated and transmitted. In these theories, the "faithful" transmission of culture (replication, copying, etc.) is commonly termed **cultural** (or social) **reproduction,** and the generation of variability is called **cultural** (or social) **transformation.** The remainder of this review briefly outlines the nature of these processes, and in conclusion sketches some of the difficulties they present to selectionist theorizing. The aim in so doing is not to issue another cautionary tale to archaeologists, but rather to try to illuminate more clearly the proper place of Darwinian theory in relation to the evolution of culture.

Cultural Reproduction (Replication, Copying)

Although some aspects of what are commonly considered cultural beliefs and behavior have a genetic component, vast areas of human belief and behavior are nonetheless learned and therefore truly cultural. Anthropologists have customarily distinguished three forms of cultural learning: situational, social, and symbolic. **Situational learning** is learning from experience, from trial and error: the individual adopts or alters a behavioral response to a stimulus on the basis of experience. Among the Yangoru Boiken of New Guinea, by way of example, stories are told of instances in the pre-contact period in which an ancestor conducted quite elaborate toxicity tests on a new plant that had spread into the region. To begin with, the ancestor fed the new plant to a pig, an animal considered physiologically similar to humans. When the pig showed no signs of sickness, he tested it on a dog, considered even closer to humans physiologically than pigs. When the dog showed no ill effects, the ancestor ate the plant himself and, surviving unscathed, deemed it safe for human consumption. Today, as a result of this situational learning, these plants have become part of the Yangoru diet.

Whereas situational learning stems from one's own experience, **social learning** involves learning by observing someone else's experience. The individual copies a behavioral response to a stimulus that he or she sees another individual adopt or alter on the basis of experience. In the Yangoru Boiken toxicity trials, the ancestor who tested the new plant is said to have called his close kin together to observe the final trial on himself, commending them to avoid the plant if he died. Through this social learning experience, his relatives learned in fact that the plant was safe.

Symbolic learning involves learning that is remote from experience. Individuals adopt or alter a behavioral response on the basis of observing neither their own nor another's experience, but on the basis of information communicated to them through symbols. Today, the Yangoru Boiken do not themselves have to test the toxicity of the plant their ancestors tested; they learn this information by being told—through the medium of words, that is, symbols—and they then adapt their behavior accordingly.

Conventionally, anthropologists have considered the transmission of culture to occur through social and symbolic rather than situational learning. More recently, so-called practice models of culture and society (e.g., Bourdieu 1990; Giddens 1984; Sahlins 1981) present a more complex and more unified picture of enculturation in which learning is all, in a sense, situational. In this model, enculturation is not just a process of active teaching (e.g., by adults) and passive learning (e.g., by children), though clearly this is an important dimension of the process. As reflexive creatures, humans actively teach themselves culture. We continuously monitor the flow of our activities and the social and physical environments in which we move, and we routinely maintain a continuing "theoretical understanding" of the grounds of this activity. More prosaically, as we move through our lives, we keep ourselves constantly aware of what is going on around us, and we try on an ongoing basis to make sense of it. We keep track and try to make sense of what people say to us and to one another, how they say it, and how they react non-verbally to what is said and done. We continuously monitor how close people stand to us and to others, and we seek to maintain an understanding of the rules governing this positioning. We observe the myriad of customary actions going on around us—the gifts people give one another, and reactions to these gifts—and we seek to deduce and update on an ongoing basis the rules and values that explain these actions.

In the main, humans are oblivious to the fact that they conduct this continuous monitoring and rationalization. We do it effortlessly, as though we were genetically programmed to execute it, which no doubt we are. The product of this reflexive monitoring and rationalization of behavior is culture, stocks of knowledge about the physical and social world that any individual needs in order to "go along" in those worlds—to make sense out of what is going on and to respond to it appropriately. These stocks of knowledge are huge. They include such varied types of knowledge as all the linguistic rules required to speak properly; how far away to stand from people; the nature of appropriate exchange objects in different situations; how and where to find food at different times of the year; how to behave toward kin and non-kin; how to behave in the presence of important people; what to think and how to conduct one's self in religious contexts; and so on.

Several important features of enculturation follow from this model. First, culture is not so much transmitted as it is situationally reconstructed anew by every individual born. Second, culture is not so much shared as it is coincident. Individuals exposed to similar routines of daily life tend to construct stocks of knowledge that are similar in content. Third, enculturation is far more than an intergenerational process in which adults teach and children learn: enculturation occurs in every waking second of life, from birth to death. In the process of reflexively monitoring action, adults as well as children continuously reaffirm to themselves that they understand reality as their culture defines it; and in their competent performance of what their culture defines as reality, they affirm this understanding to others. (If they fail to perform competently—if they insist on belching loudly in a restaurant or on replying, when offered a drink, "Squirrels are the Devil's oven mitts, you know"—they are sanctioned. In the former instance, most probably, they become the subject of gossip and ostracism; in the latter, they are likely to attract psychiatric attention. Indeed, some psychological "disorders" may simply be disorders in the ability to reflexively monitor and/or rationalize action: the afflicted individual is simply unable to build up appropriate stocks of knowledge about how to speak and behave.) Fourth, the number of agents involved in transmitting culture is far greater than the pair involved in sexually transmitting genes. The full transmission of culture involves the behavior not only of parents but of everyone—adult and non-adult—with whom a child interacts, as well as of non-human agents such as animals, artwork, and technologies like television. Finally, because the reflexive monitoring and rationalization of action happens so effortlessly, we are largely unaware of culture's constructed nature; for most people (at least those who are not social scientists), culture seems instead to be a natural property of the universe.

So far as human survival is concerned, the most important aspect of enculturation is probably its role in cultural reproduction. Cultural reproduction is the process by which many, if not most, aspects of a culture continue unchanged through time, often for very long periods. Members of a culture come and go—they get born, they immigrate, they die, they emigrate—yet, over many generations, culture will routinely survive this turnover largely unchanged. Even many aspects of modern industrial culture, which famously changes apace, survive for centuries. Despite everything that has happened in the last couple of hundred years, the United States is still governed by a Constitution, it still has a tripartite governmental structure, and it still speaks a language that people from one of its parent cultures, Britain, can readily understand. Even so-called revolutions leave culture largely intact. The French Revolution radically changed the formal political structure of France but had very little effect on the structure and organization of the French family, French towns and villages, the French language, table manners, gustatory habits, and so on.

How is cultural reproduction achieved? To some degree, it can be an intentional act. If we can see a way to ensure social reproduction, and if it is within our power to act on this knowledge, we can choose to ensure the stability of social institutions. A lot of what goes on in Congress and the White House is intentionally aimed at reproducing aspects of culture. Inflation and interest rates go up, and politicians and technocrats intentionally take action to try and bring them back down. The Constitution and the laws built on it are deliberate attempts to ensure the reproduction through time of the "freedom of the individual," as this is defined in America. Schooling is an intentional attempt to perpetuate a particular form of democratic, technological society by ensuring an adequate flow of humans qualified and competent to perform roles such as computer technician, flight controller, economist, lawyer, and so on that industrial society requires. Civics lessons are intentional attempts to inculcate the ideology and attitudes required to reproduce American citizenship, capitalism, and government in each new generation. Like the culture heroes of many non-industrial societies, for example, the Founding Fathers are represented as god-like beings who, in their infinite wisdom, generosity, and public-spiritedness, created a set of laws that render the United States, in most of its citizens' eyes, the most perfect form of human government. (Every school child learns the story of George Washington and the cherry tree, a mythical exaltation of Washington that appears to have no basis in fact but which helps sanctify and thereby render unchallengeable the American democratic form of government that he helped found.)

As important as this sort of intentional cultural reproduction is, anthropologists have generally shown greater interest in unintentional cultural reproduction, a process that occurs in all societies and accounts for most cultural reproduction. Consider, for example, a small but vitally important and complex aspect of human culture, conversational turn-taking. When people talk, they do not all speak at once; if they did, in fact, conversation would be impossible. Instead, they take turns in a highly organized and intricate conversational choreography. Remarkably, most humans have absolutely no conscious idea either of the complex rules governing this turn-taking or of how they achieve it in everyday life. Indeed, until it is pointed out to them, most are completely unaware that the behavior exists—and yet it gets reproduced, generation after generation.

The unintentional reproduction of culture is an extraordinary feat, and it occurs through the recursive nature of human action. Although humans participate in social action in order to meet some end, their actions always have consequences that they do not intend, one of which is enculturation—of themselves and others. The prime example is speech. When we speak to one another, we do so with particular ends in mind. A husband may say to his wife, "Do I really have to feed the wretched cats while you're at your mother's?" His aim is to express his dissatisfaction at having to feed the animals in question, and he may have a half-hearted hope that his spouse will agree to lodge them with the vet while she is gone. Yet this and other speech acts have a vitally important but unintended consequence: they contribute to the reproduction of numerous cultural rules and values. Recall that we are reflexive creatures, always monitoring what goes on around us, constantly trying to make sense of it, and in the process continually adding to our stocks of knowledge about the physical and cultural world around us. This is particularly so of children. Thus, to reproduce culture into the next generation, all that adults have to do is enact the normal business of everyday life in their presence. Children will monitor what adults say, the contexts in which they say it, how they say it, and what happens after they say it; and they will attempt to rationalize these actions. They will notice that the term "cat" occurs often in the presence of a furry, four-legged, animated object, and they will learn to associate the former with the latter. They will notice that Daddy gets visibly upset at the words "feed the cats again," from which they learn particular emotional states. In addition, watching Daddy's interactions with Mommy, they will add to stocks of knowledge about how to take turns in conversation. In such ways, culture gets reproduced "behind our backs," so to speak.

The unintentional reproduction of culture is one of the most remarkable features of life on Earth, but because it happens largely beyond our attention it can have insidious consequences. In particular, it can cause people to participate in their own domination. In conversational turn-taking, for instance, ethnomethodologists and sociolinguists find that humans use an extraordinarily complex set of conventions to establish when we can interrupt and when we should give way. These include intonation, hesitation cues ("and she said . . . like . . . er . . ."), body positioning (leaning back as one comes to the end of what one is saying), and so on. We also use perceived power differentials as cues. People tend to defer to those in authority—in the extreme case, speaking only when spoken to—and this cue probably plays a significant role in the reproduction of male dominance. In everyday conversation men interrupt women with significantly greater frequency than women interrupt men. The immediate consequence is that male agendas tend to get aired and, hence, advanced over female agendas, facilitating male dominance. The more subtle and pernicious consequence is that men, women, and children observing these conversational patterns reflexively learn a set of rules that permit men to interrupt more frequently, thus unintentionally reproducing the conditions that permit men to dominate.

Nor is it linguistic behavior alone that facilitates these unintended effects. The rituals of birthdays and Christmas, for another example, appear to play a role in subtly reproducing codes of power and value associated with capitalist societies. Most Christmas and birthday gifts can be given in any direction within the family circle: books, clothing, and candy, for example, are often given reciprocally among siblings, parents, and children. The exception is money: it is acceptable for parents to give children cash, but it is generally considered inappropriate for children to give their parents money or for siblings to give it to one another (unless a wide age discrepancy is involved, in which case an elder sibling might give cash to a younger sibling).

Few in Western society are consciously aware of this asymmetry, yet it is a powerful means of enculturating a symbolic principle that equates power and prestige with the disbursement of money. Capitalist society is founded on a notion that those who pay out wages ("bosses") are entitled to exercise certain powers over those who receive these wages ("employ-ees")—a principle that ramifies throughout Western politico-economic cul-ture. The customer (who pays over money) "is always right"; politicians (whose salaries are paid by taxpayers) "serve the public" (in theory at least); and taxpayers assume an authoritarian attitude toward the lives of those on welfare, whose support they pay through taxes. Similarly, parents, who have authority over their children, may give cash to their children on birthdays and Christmas, but it is inappropriate for children, who must submit to their parents, to give money to them. To be sure, the exchange rituals of birthday and Christmas were not introduced to foster a cultural code equating power and economic resources, and there is no grand con-spiracy behind their perpetuation. At birthday and Christmas time, the Western family is simply acting according to the dictates of its culture. In so doing, however, its members and others reflexively learn and affirm this coded equation of power and money, thus unwittingly reproducing down the generations an aspect of culture that facilitates their domination in everyday life.

Cultural Transformation (The Generation of Variability)

Although standard definitions of culture usually make reference to cul-tural reproduction—a shared culture is transmitted through learning—they give few clues to its opposite, cultural transformation. Cultural transfor-mation refers to cultural change, to the appearance of behavioral variation. Its causes are complex and may be cultural or extracultural (i.e., physical). Commonly, anthropologists have tended to think of these causes under the headings of environmental change, historical accident (or contingency), and "cultural logic."

Environmental change is perhaps the most obvious cause of cultural change. If humans do not adapt to significant changes in climate or avail-able material resources, they may not survive; at the very least, they are unlikely to prosper as well as they could or did. The environmental events themselves, it should be noted, are often the result of both cultural and extracultural processes acting in concert: climate change, for example, has often been the product of the two in combination, most recently in the case of global warming.

Environmental change can be viewed as a historical accident, the result of contingent interactions of physical (and often cultural) processes. Historical contingency also encompasses accidents of cultural history, how-ever, such as the events surrounding Captain Cook's death on the island of Hawai'i. As Handy and Handy (1972: 373–384) have pointed out, when Cook arrived with his ships, the *Resolution* and the *Discovery*, the Ha-waians took him to be their god, Lono. Cook happened to arrive at the time of year when, as part of the Makahiki rites, an effigy of Lono was traditionally carried on an annual journey clockwise around the perimeter of the island. By chance, the sails on Cook's ships resembled Lono's effigy, and Cook circumnavigated Hawai'i in a clockwise direction. After Lono, the god, had finished his tour, he was supposed to leave the island, ceding it for the remainder of the year to Ku, the ruling Hawaian god-king. Unwittingly playing his part, Cook set sail from Hawai'i roughly on cue, but things then began to go wrong. The *Resolution* sprang its mast, and Cook decided to return to Hawai'i to repair it. The Hawaians were distressed to see Lono return, and a set of events ensued that culminated in Cook's murder on the beach at Kealakekua. Subsequently, these events ramified through the Hawaian cultural system, transforming it in many ways, not least, according to some authors, contributing to the later collapse of the Hawaian taboo system (Sahlins 1981).

As Sahlins (1981) has argued of the encounter between the British and Hawaians, historical accident can also set in motion a third cause of cultural transformation, what might be called the operation of cultural logic. Cultural logic is the idea that the immediate causes of cultural phenomena are other cultural phenomena; in other words, that culture is the cause of its own change. Unfortunately, this concept is rather underexamined in anthropology, but structural contradiction (or cultural antinomy) is frequently identified as an important manifestation of cultural logic at work. The idea is that two equally valid cultural rules or principles, or the inferences drawn from them, can be contradictory. If they are, then cultural change is precipitated as people resolve, or try to resolve, the dilemma.

Raymond Kelly (1977: 289) provides a linguistic example, the emergence in the English language of the word "ain't" (e.g., "You ain't nothin' but a hound dog"). We commonly contract the phrases "is not," "are not," would not," and so on, according to a grammatical rule that replaces the "o" in "not" with an apostrophe and combines the two words into one, thus producing "isn't," "aren't," "wouldn't." Now, according to this rule, "am not" should go to "amn't," but it does not because this would contradict a phonological rule that "m" cannot immediately precede "n" in the same syllable. (The apparent exceptions—e.g., "damn," "hymn"—actually prove the rule, because the final "n" in these words is unvoiced.) The resolution of this structural contradiction was a new linguistic form: "i" was substituted for the "m" in "amn't" to give "ain't." This resulted in yet further transformation because, with the elimination of "m," "ain't" became freed from the first person pronoun form. Thus, though "ain't" originally derived from "I *am* not," once it was robbed of the first-person marker "m," it also became possible to use it in "you ain't," "s/he ain't," "we ain't," and so on.

Kelly (1977) argues that social organization among the Etoro of New Guinea similarly emerges from a structural contradiction between the principles of siblingship and descent. A more familiar example might be a contradiction in Western concepts of the person that seems to have fueled the ongoing cultural changes surrounding the abortion issue. The principle of individualism in Western society has, as one of many logical consequences, the belief that a person is the ultimate arbiter of his or her own body. As a result, people have the legal right to dispose of their bodies as they see fit, to decide for themselves whether to tattoo it, pierce it, give blood, donate a kidney, have teeth or appendix out if they are diseased, or even, in the direst cases, commit suicide. This principle leads to contradictory conclusions, however, with respect to a fetus. On the one hand, the fetus can be considered part of its mother's body, in which case she has a right to dispose of it as she wishes. On the other, it can be considered a person in its own right, in which case the mother has no right to dispose of it as she wishes. Unfortunately, our core cultural principles furnished no simple, unequivocal resolution to this conundrum and, for more than 30 years, the ensuing debate has fuelled enormous change in the religious, political, legal, and ethical spheres of Western cultural life.

In and of themselves, environmental changes, historical accidents, and structural contradictions cannot bring about cultural change; human **agency**—the intended and unintended effects on material conditions and social affairs of the actions humans take in living out their lives—is the indispensable means by which cause is translated into cultural change. This may seem to belabor the obvious, but materialist, selectionist, and ideational paradigms in anthropology have consistently downplayed, sometimes even erased, human agency in the explanation of human life. In extreme forms of materialism, agency is reduced entirely to material conditions; in the selectionist model, it is frequently treated as no more than a random generator of cultural traits (random, at least, relative to selective forces acting on these traits); and in extreme forms of cultural determinism, it is reduced to the machine-like execution of "cultural principles."

None of these perspectives gives human agency its analytical due. As noted earlier, Darwinian processes have endowed humans with the cognitive and motivational capacities to model and make predictions about their physical and cultural environments, to take actions based on this predictive modelling, and to reflexively modify their actions in accordance with the results. In consequence, just as they are able to act intentionally to *reproduce* culture, humans also can act intentionally to *change* it. One important type of intentional cultural change is adaptation (where "adaptation" here means "the gamut of processes whereby human beings respond to and modify features of their physical environment" [Giddens 1984: 233–234]). In response to climatic change, for example, humans might intentionally construct dykes to control flooding and/or organize relief for people in danger of inundation. Alternatively, adaptation may involve not just reactions to environmental events but creative and transformative actions on the environment. Among the Yangoru Boiken, the author observed a man deliberately plant out what he took to be a new yam variety that had sprouted on our rubbish tip, in order to compare its performance to other varieties. It proved a success in the man's evaluation, and he named it *Barbarara mungu* (Barbara's yam), in honor of the author's wife, and adopted it into his subsistence regimen.

What cannot be stressed enough, however, is the importance of the unintended consequences of intended human actions. Among the most important of these, as noted earlier, is the reproduction of such varied cultural phenomena as language, turn-taking, and capitalist hierarchy. But the unintended consequences of human action also produce manifold cultural *changes*. The recent shift to gender-neutral language on American campuses, it can be argued, is the unintended consequence of quite unrelated economic and political developments in U.S. society that date back to the 1960s. With the success of the Civil Rights movement, according to some arguments, a number of women involved in that campaign began to reflect on the similarities between their own situation and that of African Americans. At around the same time, the financial situation of the average American family started to decline: inflation began seriously to erode family incomes at the same time that TV advertising and programming were inflating consumer expectations. Marketers aggressively encouraged people to see themselves in a home in the suburbs, with a car or two in the garage, perhaps a boat, a well-stocked cocktail cabinet, and so on (e.g., Harris 1981: 76–97).

To make family ends meet while trying to secure a higher material standard of life, women moved into the workforce in increasing numbers. In 1947, only 21% of married women worked outside the house; by 1990, this figure had reached 60%. Out in the workforce, women quickly discovered they were doing similar jobs to men for much less pay, they were barred from entering quite a few professions, and they were prevented from attaining the higher echelons in others. Despite doing a full day's work, moreover, they found they were still expected to do all of the housekeeping after hours. With their interests thwarted, they focused increasingly on trying to figure out the causes of inequities that, before, they had scarcely recognized.

One thing, among many, that they focused on as a possible cause of male dominance was gender asymmetries in language. As sociological and psychological research (e.g., Schneider and Hacker 1973) has demonstrated, use of "Man," "he," "his," in the generic sense to mean "humans," "he and she," "his and her" has a measurable effect in privileging males over females. Students instructed to write a story about "Urban Man," for example, are more likely to write a story centered on a man than students instructed to write about "Urban life." This conceptual bias has considerable effects on the situation of women. Even though the intent may be to address both men and women, a job advertisement that asks an applicant to send in "his" resumé has the actual effect of discouraging women from applying. As its proponents claimed, in other words, a shift to non-discriminatory language does help level the economic and political playing field for women. The broader point is that the economic and political actions and events that started this process in the 1960s were undertaken for reasons quite unconnected to linguistic change, but these changes were some of their many unintended consequences.

Even actions intended to *reproduce* culture can end up transforming it. Current campaign-finance laws in the United States, for example, were introduced in the late 1970s in the wake of the Nixon scandals, as an attempt to restore financial probity to U.S. political campaigns. Today, many citizens, including a number in Congress and the White House, acknowledge that matters have instead been transformed for the worse.

CASE STUDIES

This review has used case studies of U.S. culture and the Yangoru Boiken of New Guinea to illustrate the more important elements of what culture is and how it works. Culture emanates from our particular nature as reflexive beings who constantly monitor and try to make sense of what goes on around us in the daily routines of our lives. As such, culture gets created, reproduced, and transformed, both intentionally and unintentionally, its unintentional reproduction—its transmission behind our backs, so to speak—making it especially potent in structuring human lives.

Because culture is independent of any particular individual, some anthropologists have described it as an objective condition of human existence. In a sense, it is as real as the physical environment and, like that environment, it poses conditions to which any individual born into it must adapt if he or she is to survive. Culture is unlike the physical environment, however, in that it cannot exist independently of humans; indeed, it exists, it is reproduced, and it is transformed *only* through human actions, human practices. It is this property that makes culture and cultural evolution crucially different from biology and biological evolution, and it is to the consequences of this difference that this review now turns.

FUTURE IMPORTANCE

It is not overstating the case to claim that every human action produces unintended—and largely unpredictable—cultural change. The effects of our actions are usually minimal but, like the proverbial butterfly flapping its wings over China, they also can be major. Suffice it to say, the potential for social change is inherent in every social act, and it is now an axiom of social theory that the reproduction of culture is always problematic and never guaranteed. This finding poses a largely unacknowledged problem, to which theorists who would apply Darwinian selection to cultural affairs need to attend if their arguments are to survive.

The problem revolves around the evolutionary requirement that a mechanism exist for the faithful transmission and preservation of variation between generations, and it arises from a fundamental difference in the mechanics of biological and cultural transmission. Advancing the foundations of modern evolutionary archaeology, Dunnell (1980: 63) proposed that

If a given trait is heritable to a measurable degree (the mechanism need not be known) *and if it also affects the fitness of organisms possessing the trait to some measurable degree* (recognizing the possibility of neutral or stylistic traits), *then the trait must be subject to natural selection* and will be fixed in populations. (emphasis in original)

The problem is precisely the non-parenthetical component that Dunnell chose not to emphasize: "and will be fixed in populations."

As constituents of the natural world, genes are stabilized by the physical and chemical properties of the universe. Successful genes can become "fixed in populations" precisely because, once selected, their structure remains unchanged. To be sure, they occasionally mutate, but biological evolution works only because the rate at which genes mutate is far slower than the rate at which natural selection differentially selects particular genes. Were this not so, mutation would cause potentially adaptive genes to appear and then disappear before natural selection had had a chance to favor them.

Cultural traits are not stabilized by the physiochemical properties of the universe. Although it is common to suppose that they have some kind of "momentum" or "inertia" that perpetuates them through time, this view is inadequate. As explained above, the stability of a cultural trait is chronically contingent. The possibility of its change is inherent in every social act, either as an intentional or as an unintentional consequence, and in practice culture is constantly mutating. Thus, natural selection may well operate on cultural traits, but successful traits do not become "fixed in populations" in the way that genes do. In any and every human act, historical accident or the operation of cultural logic may set in motion a series of intended and/or unintended consequences that cause an adaptive trait to disappear as suddenly as it appeared.

To put this another way, archaeologists wishing to apply Darwinian models to cultural phenomena need to explain what prevents an adaptive cultural trait from disappearing once it has appeared. If they wish to argue that humans are aware of adaptive traits and act consciously to perpetuate them, then by the scientific principle of parsimony the relevance of invoking Darwinian processes in relation to cultural evolution must be questioned.

It is sufficient simply to claim that natural selection has conferred on humans the cognitive ability to recognize, and act to perpetuate, adaptive traits. If evolutionary archaeologists wish to argue instead that humans remain unaware of the adaptive consequences of their cultural behavior, then it will be necessary to explain how and why current social theory is wrong about the contingent nature of cultural traits, or to offer some description of the hitherto unrecognized process that ensures the stability of adaptive traits in the face of cultural processes that continually threaten to undermine them.

REFERENCES

Arnold, M. (1883) [1869]. *Culture & Anarchy: An Essay in Political and Social Criticism.* New York: Macmillan.

Boas, F. (1940) [1896]. The limitations of the comparative method of anthropology. In F. Boas (ed.), *Race, Language and Culture.* New York: Macmillan, pp. 271–304.

Bourdieu, P. (1990). *The Logic of Practice.* Stanford, CA: Stanford University Press.

Brumann, C. (1999). Writing for culture: Why a successful concept should not be discarded. *Current Anthropology* 40: S1–13, S21–27.

Dunnell, R. D. (1980). Evolutionary theory and archaeology. In M. B. Schiffer (ed.), *Advances in Archaeological Method and Theory,* vol. 3. New York: Academic Press, pp. 55–99.

Ferraro, G. (1992). *Cultural Anthropology: An Applied Perspective.* St Paul, MN: West.

Geertz, C. (1973). *The Interpretation of Cultures.* New York: Basic Books.

Giddens, A. (1984). *The Constitution of Society.* Berkeley: University of California Press.

Handy, E.S.C., and E. G. Handy. (1972). *Native Planters in Old Hawaii: Their Life, Lore, and Environment.* Honolulu: Bernice P. Bishop Museum Press.

Hannerz, U. (1996). *Transnational Connections: Cultures, Peoples, Places.* London: Routledge.

Harris, M. (1981). *America Now: The Anthropology of a Changing Culture.* New York: Simon and Schuster.

Haviland, W. A. (1999). *Cultural Anthropology.* Fort Worth, TX: Harcourt Brace.

Huntington, S. P. (1996). *The Clash of Civilizations and the Remaking of World Order.* New York: Simon and Schuster.

Jones, G. T., R. D. Leonard, and A. L. Abbott. (1995). The structure of selectionist explanations in archaeology. In P. A. Teltser (ed.), *Evolutionary Archaeology: Methodological Issues.* Tucson: University of Arizona Press, pp. 13–32.

Kelly, R. C. (1977). *Etoro Social Structure: A Study in Structural Contradiction.* Ann Arbor: University of Michigan Press.

Kroeber, A. L., and C. Kluckhohn. (1952). *Culture: A Critical Review of Concepts and Definitions.* Papers of the Peabody Museum of American Archaeology and Ethnology 47(1).

OED. (1981). *The Compact Edition of the Oxford English Dictionary*, vol. 1, A–O. Oxford: Oxford University Press.

Peoples, J., and G. Bailey. (2000). *Humanity: An Introduction to Cultural Anthropology*. Belmont, CA: Wadsworth.

Rindos, D. (1984). *The Origins of Agriculture: An Evolutionary Perspective*. Orlando, FL: Academic Press.

Sahlins, M. (1981). *Historical Metaphors and Mythical Realities: Structure in the Early History of the Sandwich Islands Kingdom*. Ann Arbor: University of Michigan Press.

Schneider, J., and S. Hacker. (1973). Sex role imagery and use of the generic man in introductory texts: A case in the sociology of sociology. *American Sociologist* 8: 12–18.

Scupin, R. (1992). *Cultural Anthropology: A Global Perspective*. Englewood Cliffs, NJ: Prentice Hall.

Stocking, G. W. (1963). Matthew Arnold, E. B. Tylor, and the uses of invention. *American Anthropologist* 65: 783–799.

Terrell, J. E., T. L. Hunt, and C. Gosden. (1997). The dimensions of social life in the Pacific: human diversity and the myth of the primitive isolate. *Current Anthropology* 38: 155–175.

Tylor, E. B. (1958) [1871]. *The Origins of Culture: Part 1 of "Primitive Culture."* New York: Harper.

Chapter 8

Descent

Scott MacEachern

INTRODUCTION

> **Descent: 7a.** The fact of "descending" or being descended from an
> ancestor or ancestral stock; lineage. **b.** of animals and plants; in Biology
> extended to origination of species (= EVOLUTION 6c). **c.** (figurative).
> Derivation or origination from a particular source.
>
> Oxford English Dictionary

> Thus, on the theory of descent with modification, the main facts with
> respect to the mutual affinities of the extinct forms of life to each other
> and to living forms, are explained in a satisfactory manner. And they
> are wholly inexplicable on any other view.
>
> Darwin 1859: 334

In the sense of this chapter, common usage of the term **descent** involves a
set of factors, both material and temporal. Descent entails the existence of
both an ancestral source, a process by which copies of that source are
generated through time, and the resulting offspring of that source. The
entities involved may be human beings reckoning their ancestry through
their parents and grandparents, biological organisms undergoing evolutionary change, behaviors changing through time, versions of a computer program being modified for final release, or abstract systems of thought
subjected to critique and amendment. Descent is thus a **genealogical** concept, an account of the persistence of a **lineage** of related entities through
time. Furthermore, observation of the world and the more formal strictures
of information theory imply that processes of copying are not perfect over

multiple generations, so that the characteristics of descendent and ancestral entities will be dissimilar to varying degrees.

Descent is thus a considerably more complicated concept than it might appear at first glance and, as Charles Darwin recognized, the concept is central to evolutionary theory in biology. "Descent with modification" implies the existence of lineages of units that perpetuate themselves through time, but emphasizes the vital element of variability: the particular set of attributes or properties transmitted between generations accumulate innovations, due to copying error, recombination of genetic material, and so on. These units are further subject to some processes of selection, which results through differential survivorship and increased levels of adaptation to local environments. Descent plays a vital mediating role in evolutionary definitions, because it articulates the units of evolution (the species in biology, for example) with the evolutionary processes that those units undergo through time. Further, it provides a means for examining the relatedness of evolutionary units, through conceptions of genealogy, common ancestry, and divergence. There is, however, little consideration of hybridization between evolutionary units of descent, because until relatively recently such hybridization in biology was thought to be more or less insignificant.

An evolutionarily informed concept of descent would potentially be very important within archaeology. It might in particular help in distinguishing cultural **homologies** (similarities derived through descent from a common ancestor) from cultural **analogies** (in this sense, similarities derived through adaptive convergence) and **synologies** (similarities derived from diffusion or borrowing [Durham 1992: 334]). The relevance of these concepts to, for example, hoary archaeological questions of independent invention and diffusion should be obvious. Such a concept might over time yield insights into the processes through which artifact assemblages develop through relations between cultural systems and environments, and at the same time provide models for conceiving of the human population units actually responsible for the production of the archaeological record. The human groups that produced ancient artifactual distributions are now all too often simply reduced to prehistoric exemplars of "tribes," "bands," "societies," or other categories borrowed wholesale from ethnographic research. The descent concept may thus help articulate archaeological and ethnographic approaches frequently estranged from one another. As such, we would expect that descent would also be fundamental in any evolutionarily informed theory of cultural processes in archaeology, which is, like evolutionary biology and paleontology, a discipline concerned with patterns of change through time.

There has in fact been relatively little explicit use of this evolutionary concept in archaeology, even in the self-consciously selectionist research initiatives that have labeled themselves as "evolutionary archaeology" in the United States over the last decade. This seems to be due in part to a great deal of uncertainty among archaeologists concerning the fundamental units and mechanisms of evolutionary change in cultural systems. Without agreement on matters as basic as the entities undergoing evolutionary change, consideration of relations of descent appears impossible. Archaeologists thus find themselves in a curious situation, with a theory of evolution provided by Darwin and richly elaborated by later researchers, but without a Mendel to provide an accepted theory of inheritance or even a Linnaeus to begin systematization of the variety of human occurrences they study. If a concept of descent is to be useful in archaeology, users will have to come to some agreement on the analytical units to be taken under study, and a set of important methodological issues will have to be addressed.

HISTORY OF THE CONCEPT IN BIOLOGY AND ANTHROPOLOGY

North American archaeologists can look to two different, but closely interrelated, sources for ideas about descent that are applicable to their discipline. In the first place, of course, descent has played a fundamental role in Darwinian theories of biological evolution, by establishing what Darwin saw as the essentially genealogical nature of evolutionary processes. The concept was thus directly opposed to religiously based ideas of special creation, which held that the hierarchical organization of living species studied by Linnaeus was the product of divine action and that such species were therefore perfected and immutable. Ideas of evolutionary descent were not unique to Darwin, forming as they did an important part of the intellectual equipment of theorists like Jean-Baptiste Lamarck; but Darwin furnished a mechanism—natural selection—through which evolutionary change takes place through time. Darwin also had the benefit of considerably more practical experience as a naturalist, and familiarity with the practices of plant and animal breeders both in Britain and beyond. The detailed genealogies that such breeders kept allowed them to maximize the efficiency of artificial selection on domesticated species, and the striking effects of such artificial selection provided an important conceptual model for "descent with modification" and natural selection.

We cannot overstate the importance of Darwin's synthesis within biology. Species exist as real biological entities and perpetuate themselves as lineages through time (Simpson 1961), via various systems of reproduction. Processes of natural selection generate dynamic adaptations of those species to changing environments—but also lead to the possibility of divergences, splits within lineages in response to differential selection pressures on different populations within a single species, possibly leading to the formation of new "daughter" species. "Descent with modification" thus yields a nested pattern of species clustered within ever more inclusive genealogies

(Eldredge 1999), eventually encompassing all living things within a comprehensive hierarchy of evolutionary taxa. No mechanism exists for the amalgamation of separated species, so only the relative balance of species adaptation, diversification, and extinction regulates the diversity of biological species on earth. This is not an assumption that may be made within anthropology, linguistics, or archaeology.

Paleoanthropologists and biological anthropologists frequently deal with the concept of biological descent directly, as they examine the evolution of modern human beings and of our now-extinct hominid cousins, as well as of the other primates. However, much more complex relations between Darwinian evolutionary theory and investigations of human cultural systems date from the beginning of the Darwinian synthesis in the mid-nineteenth century. The influence of Malthus' (1914 [1872]) theorization of human population growth and resource competition on Darwin's conception of natural selection is widely accepted. Stephen Alter (1999) has documented the intellectual interactions between Darwin and other evolutionists, and philologists and historical linguists, both before and after the writing of *On the Origin of Species*. He pays particular attention to the ways in which parallels were drawn between "descent with modification" in living things and the processes of differentiation then being theorized for languages and language families. Darwin (1887) himself, of course, was occupied with the origins of humans and of human culture in *The Descent of Man*. By the late nineteenth century, evolutionary theory was being misused by "social Darwinists," who among other errors drastically overemphasized the importance of biological descent and genealogy in the constitution of human populations and cultures.

Such social Darwinist approaches were widely rejected by the early decades of the twentieth century. However, descent (and closely related concepts, like that of genealogy and the lineage) also holds a central place in much more accepted realms of anthropological and archaeological practice. These are concepts frequently applied to human groups, and indeed their usage for such groups predates their application to other living things. Through the twentieth century, anthropologists have devoted a great deal of effort to the analysis of human systems for reckoning kinship and descent. They have done so because it appeared that, in the small-scale societies that anthropologists have traditionally studied, such systems were central to social organization, providing a structure for day-to-day interactions and for the mutual expectations of conduct that people hold. In these cases, descent involves the most basic elements of human reproduction, but also the persistence, divergence, and ramification of human corporate groups through time.[1]

One of the most influential expressions of such studies of descent and kinship was Evans-Pritchard's (1940) classic ethnography *The Nuer*, where the concept of segmentary lineage systems situates Nuer individuals and groups both in their cultural territories and, through descent, in history. The bifurcating hierarchies of clans, maximal, major, medial, and minor lineages in Evans-Pritchard's (1940: 192–248) monograph closely parallel the complex pedigrees used by mid-nineteenth-century Darwinists and philologists to represent the diversification of languages and species. All are genealogies, constructed to locate the relations between ancestral and descendant units through history. *The Nuer* was extremely influential in twentieth-century anglophone anthropology, and segmentary lineage systems were identified in societies around the world—although the utility of such broad application of the concept (especially outside Africa) has been widely debated. However, the concept of descent used in *The Nuer* differed fundamentally from that used in Darwinian theories of biological evolution. On the one hand, Evans-Pritchard recognized the Nuer lineage as a real thing, a group of people related through patrilineal descent from a common ancestor, but he also recognized that lineages were historical charters, with fictive relations of descent acting as justifications for narratives about social relations in the real world. As such, Nuer lineage systems could accommodate not only divergences, but also hybridizations of hitherto separate descent units, in ways impossible to conceive of according to theories of evolutionary biology. Descent in this case is conceived of as primarily a social and cultural phenomenon, not a biological process.

Concern with these systems of kinship and descent has not been restricted to cultural anthropologists: archaeologists have made use of them as well, as they seek to identify the human groups responsible for patterning in archaeological occurrences. During the early twentieth century, typological analyses of North American artifact assemblages were advanced considerably, but concepts of the human groups associated with those assemblages remained relatively underdeveloped. Consideration of lineage systems and domestic systems of production coincided with an increased interest in the social correlates of archaeological assemblages in the 1950s and 1960s. This involved, among other results, a set of well-known studies (e.g., Deetz 1965; Longacre 1970; Whallon 1968) that examined ceramic variability as the material output of relations in and between unilineal descent groups. In these cases, close parallels between the evolution of artefact assemblages and the historical trajectories of human groups were hypothesized. An important criticism of these studies has been that they tended to confuse the idealized charter of the descent group with the actual social system in action, assuming that the genealogical charts in ethnographies actually reflected how humans interacted in communities (Stanislawski 1978: 217–224).

CONTEMPORARY USAGES

Genealogical Concepts of Cultural Development

At this point, the concept of descent is not the explicit focus of theorizing in most archaeological research programs. Rather, it makes a more or less implicit appearance with a variety of circumstances and in a number of highly contrasting ways. At the most general level, archaeologists remain naturally interested in the development of human communities through time, and considerations of social fission, migration, contact, and settlement remain staples of archaeological theorizing about prehistory. Such theorizing involves consideration of relations of descent among human populations. These evolutionary issues have been addressed, for example, by Mace and Pagel (1994) and by Durham (1992), some of the few researchers to have explicitly considered descent as a historical process with implications for the archaeological studies of ancient human societies. These models conceive of "new/daughter cultures" deriving via fissioning processes from single "parental/mother cultures," and are essentially hierarchical and genealogical. A corollary of this is that similarities between elements of different cultures in the same region are seen as primarily due to homology (common descent), rather than analogy (adaptive convergence) or synology (Durham's term for diffusion or borrowing), with obvious implications for archaeological analyses. Durham (1992: 333), for example, emphasizes the importance of Transmission Isolating Mechanisms (TRIMs), which reduce the chances of interaction and hybridization between descendant units, in a direct analogy to biological descent, while Mace and Pagel (1994: 552) accord rather more importance to such processes.

This sort of evolutionary context has figured most explicitly in reconstructions of the prehistoric colonization of the islands of the Pacific, and especially Polynesia (e.g., Kirch 1984; Sahlins 1958), and Durham emphasized the importance of that work in his article. Colonization of small, relatively isolated island systems affords a natural opportunity for such analysis, since it is easy to conceive of such islands as environmentally diverse, and the adaptation of small colonizing groups to that diversity as resulting in evolutionary change. Further, colonization of empty territories and assumptions of some degree of isolation after colonization makes these evolutionary models more closely comparable to biological models of adaptation and speciation, since no provision for amalgamation of evolutionary units need be made. Kirch (1984) hypothesizes the existence of an Ancestral Polynesian Society in western Polynesia between about 500 B.C. and A.D. 300; this reconstruction is based on comparative archaeological, linguistic, and ethnographic data from across Polynesia. Representatives of these ancestral populations then colonized the rest of Polynesia over the next centuries, and Kirch illustrates a series of developmental pathways by which these groups adapted to local environments on Tonga, Hawai'i, and Easter Island. The processes by which these Polynesian societies developed are conceived of as explicitly genealogical (Kirch 1984: Figures 1, 19), and are strongly informed by "family trees" of the development of Polynesian languages (Kirch 1984: Figures 5, 7).

Similar parallels are drawn between linguistic genealogies and hypothesized lineages of descent among human communities in other areas of the world as well, although rarely with evidence of colonization processes as clear-cut as in Polynesia. Increasingly, population genealogies derived from genetic studies are also considered in the historical reconstructions undertaken by archaeologists. In Africa, for example, the social meanings of the spread of languages known as the Bantu Expansion are extensively debated: did it involve processes of migration by human populations, processes of language adoption, or both, and what are the relations between Bantu linguistic genealogies and the archaeological assemblages that cover much of Africa south of the Sahara (Chapter 9, this volume; Phillipson 1977; Vansina 1995)? In Europe, similar discussions revolve around conflicting reconstructions of the spread of Danubian/Linearbandkeramik archaeological assemblages at the beginning of the Neolithic: is this a spread of cultural systems only, or does it involve migration and colonization by farming groups from southeastern Europe (Ammerman and Cavalli-Sforza 1984; see also Zvelebil 1998)?

These reconstructions are frequently marked by a lack of attention paid to the question of comparability between the units of descent produced by studies in different disciplines: archaeological assemblages, languages and dialects, genetic populations of humans, and in other cases ethnographic or historical descriptions of societies by outsiders. The mere fact that one can produce genealogical diagrams using different kinds of data does not imply that these diagrams will reflect similar cultural processes when applied in a single area and time period. Such problems of data incompatibility either go unmarked or are dismissed, with processes of linguistic, genetic, and cultural change treated as if they were more or less identical and subject to the same sorts of evolutionary influences (Durham 1992: 333; Mace and Pagel 1994: 552).

It is by no means clear how the units of descent depicted in these genealogies are actually defined. The end points appear to be "cultures" or "ethnolinguistic groups"—the "tribes" of a previous generation of anthropologists, with their assumptions of boundedness and cultural homogeneity (Durham 1992: 332)—in the ethnographic present, but the characteristics of these units do not accord well with more recent ethnographic data on communities in different areas of the world, and the researchers ignore the reifying effects of colonization on such communities. Mace and Pagel (1994: 553–556) give an example involving presence and absence of camel herding by East African pastoral "cultures" like the Pokot, Samburu, and

Rendille—groups of humans. Higher levels in these genealogies are thus presumably equivalent ancestral "cultures," which in the past gave rise to descendants through a process of fission. The tree involved is arranged according to linguistic criteria, as a stand-in for other cultural relations of descent in the past. The large-scale parallels between linguistic and genetic data used by Mace and Pagel (1994: 551–554) to fix their genealogies are in fact rejected by most professional linguists; no common proto-language ancestral to both Nilotic or Cushitic languages is known to have existed. In practice, it would appear that these ancestral cultural units depicted in these genealogies are not "cultures," but rather constellations of traits inferred to be ancestral through comparisons between the "cultures" that exist today (Mace and Pagel 1994: 555–557)—artifacts, that is, of the system of "culture" classification, whether that system be linguistic or otherwise. It seems very difficult to conceive of how such an ancestral constellation of traits could actually generate a human "culture," a group of people like the Pokot or Samburu. Social and biological descent are being conflated in such studies, often in ways very difficult to analyze.

Reconstructions of human history that rely on genealogical models, whether they be archaeological, linguistic, or genetic, also risk not taking sufficient account of processes of contact and assimilation between descendant units—whether these be genetic exchange between biological populations, borrowings between languages, or processes of acculturation between cultural systems. Indeed, in cultural terms the validity of genealogical models of descent is predicated on a significant degree of isolation between units, as Durham (1992: 333–334) notes. However, it is by no means clear that these conditions hold, archaeologically or even linguistically (*contra* Durham 1992; see for example Dixon 1997; Lesser 1961; Terrell 2001). Cultural units of descent are, after all, not biological species, and humans are mobile creatures; the strengths of isolating mechanisms between these units would appear to be far lower than they are between biological units of descent. The degree of isolation among Polynesian populations living on their far-flung islands has been questioned (e.g., Terrell et al. 1997), and such segregation would almost certainly be less among cultures sharing a region of a continental land-mass, whether that be in Africa, Europe, or elsewhere. Reticulate models of human interaction and cultural evolution, analogous to that proposed by Templeton (1998) for the biological evolution of polytypic modern human populations, would seem to be at least as useful as genealogical models that overemphasize the importance of cultural relationships of descent and inheritance. Such reticulate models would emphasize the importance of culture contact and interchange, and seem in many areas of the world to better reflect ethnographic experience than do models that present cultures as isolated and diversifying lineages.

North American Evolutionary Archaeology

The North American studies that most directly articulate with biological concepts of "descent with modification" are radically different from these evolutionary frameworks of cultural development favored by Durham, Kirch, and their colleagues. They involve research by investigators who explicitly define their work as "evolutionary archaeology," and justify it directly as an attempt to use Darwinian theory to explain variation in the archaeological record. Their goal is thus to transform archaeology into a historical science akin to evolutionary biology. To do this, of course, the operations of prehistoric cultural systems must be reconceived using terminology and systematics commensurate with Darwinian evolutionary analysis (Dunnell 1995), which involves analysis of forces of natural selection operating on human phenotypic variability broadly conceived. Such phenotypic variability includes not only the physical and behavioral characteristics of the human organism, but also the material results of that human behavior. Artifacts are thus conceived as a part of the "extended phenotype" of human beings, and of exclusive interest to archaeologists because they persist through time and are thus amenable to observation, unlike the behaviors (and the humans) that produced them. Archaeologists study the evolution of artifacts, not of human culture.

This is archaeology with human agency and intentionality to a great degree edited out of the field of study, of interest only as one proximate source for artifactual variation, which in turn acts as grist for natural selection in the archaeological record (Lyman and O'Brien 1998: 618). Other modes for the sorting of variation also exist (Teltser 1995: 7). According to some evolutionary archaeologists, archaeology must be cut loose from its disciplinary moorings with (primarily cultural) anthropology, since the latter is chiefly engaged in telling stories about human communities in different parts of the world and will probably never be a science. Indeed, the degree to which non-evolutionary archaeological research will be compatible with the goals, terminologies, and systematics of evolutionary archaeology is not at all clear, and according to some formulations evolutionary archaeology is to be conceived more or less as a new and independent discipline (Dunnell 1989).[2]

We would expect that archaeological theorizing that focused on the effects of "descent with modification" on ancient artifact assemblages would deal quite explicitly with the concept of descent. However, this concept continues to be somewhat underdefined, even among those investigators who most explicitly utilize evolutionary paradigms.[3] Concepts of persistent lineages of design/production underlie much of evolutionary archaeological theorizing about the development of ancient artifactual systems. In some cases (e.g., Lyman and O'Brien 1998: 616, 619; Neff and Larson 1997; Neiman 1995), descent appears to be conceived of as essentially a statistical phenomenon, involving the persistence of a set of associated artifact traits under selection over time. In other cases (e.g., Barton 1997; Graves and Ladefoged 1995), it appears to involve a lineage of humans, producing artifact assemblages through cultural inheritance and subject to differential success resulting from these behavioral processes of communication, production, and use.

There may be a number of reasons for this uncertainty. In the first place, it is not obvious (to an archaeologist outside the lineage, at least) that human agency can be eliminated from the archaeological record as completely as these models might seem to require. It is difficult to see how artifacts can be actual units of reproduction and descent in the archaeological record, since it is a commonplace that neither pots nor arrowheads breed. They are thus an element of the "extended phenotype" of human beings, and it is quite true that biologists have in similar ways examined patterned artifactual production by other species of animals. However, the complexity of human artifact production and use is many, many times greater than in other species of animals, and humans function within social and ideational environments of correspondingly greater complexity. Under such circumstances, it seems difficult to remove human agency from specification of the selection pressures that work on "descent with modification." A prime example is the evolutionary archaeological conception of the style/function dichotomy, with stylistic traits defined as those that are neutral with respect to selection pressures. Such selective neutrality is to be identified through studies of the patterning of trait variability in the archaeological, involving rather long and indirect chains of inference (e.g., Neiman 1995), or through engineering studies (e.g., O'Brien et al. 1994) that are in practice quite unlikely to identify social functions of stylistic variation. The "work" of style in such cases may well have selective value, but it will be a selection located in environments that in part include human social life. To the degree to which human social and cultural systems are elements in the environments within which selection takes place, we may expect that they will play their role through recursive relations with material production systems. In such a case, humans can not be entirely eliminated from considerations of the development of artifact lineages over time.

It appears that these differences also relate at least in part to a significant limitation in evolutionary archaeology as conceived of by a number of its leading theorists: the difficulty of articulating these concepts with ethnographic data. For all of the rejection of anthropology by practitioners of evolutionary anthropology, many work in contexts where varying amounts of ethnographic data are available for the construction of ethnographic analogies useful in understanding of the archaeological record. (Indeed, it is difficult to see how evolutionary archaeologists can interpret the archaeological record in the first place without some use of such analogy.) If such data are available, their use will be almost irresistible, and human agency will then enter archaeological interpretations—but the explicit tenets of this approach make the articulation of such data with evolutionary systematics extremely difficult. It is likely that methodological uncertainty about the constitution of units of descent in evolutionary archaeology will continue for the foreseeable future.

To the present, evolutionary archaeology has generated a considerable theoretical superstructure. It has, however, generated rather fewer case studies demonstrating the specific application of the approach in interpretation of the archaeological record, and the advantages of the theoretical program over more conventional archaeological analysis. The research program of evolutionary archaeology involves drastic reductions in the ambit of archaeological research, in the things that archaeologists are supposed to be interested in, and it seems unlikely that most archaeologists will be willing to restrict their interpretative frameworks to the degree demanded by that program.

Apprenticeship and Learning Networks

Other, very different, approaches to the use of descent in archaeological research exist. On a much more localized level, a number of recent ethnoarchaeological investigations of artifact production (Gosselain 1995, 1999; Roux and Corbetta 1990; Wallaert 1998) have focused on less rigidly defined learning networks of teachers and apprentices than the ceramics-and-lineage studies of Longacre, Deetz, and Whallon noted in an earlier section of this chapter. These researchers belong primarily to a francophone school of artifact analysis (but see also Dietler and Herbich 1989), one that locates material production as the end result of different *chaînes opératoires*, sequences of social operations and choices aimed at transforming raw materials into finished product. Their studies of apprenticeship processes offer a fairly direct analogy to concepts of descent in biology, focusing as they do on group recruitment and membership, the ways in which information and practice are perpetuated through time, and the ways in which innovations are accommodated and controlled. Field research for the most part involves extremely fine-grained and detailed observation of the social contexts of artifact production and learning systems. This research is methodologically and ethnographically rich, and has yielded a great deal of information about the social correlates of specific artifact production systems.

Unfortunately, such fine-grained ethnoarchaeological studies systems are very difficult to apply to archaeological occurrences, and the time-depth of these investigations is at this point extremely short. Researchers are essentially undertaking synchronic studies of production, supplemented by producer genealogies and by oral historical accounts of how things used to be.

These studies do, however, provide a significant advance over customary archaeological models of artifact manufacture and distribution, which still all too often conceive of the units responsible for such production of material culture as monolithic, homogeneous "bands" or "tribes."

CASE STUDIES

There appear to be serious limitations in the roles played by the concept of descent within evolutionary frameworks in archaeology. This may be in part because, as noted in the introduction to this chapter, "descent" is a relatively high-order concept, one that articulates the units of evolution (artifact groups, human populations, languages) with the evolutionary processes that those units undergo through time. To usefully speak of descent in evolutionary terms thus demands that these other concepts be reasonably precisely defined, and that these definitions be widely accepted within the discipline. This may be the case in biology today—although we should note that vigorous debate about very basic questions, concerning both units and processes of evolution, continue. It is demonstrably not the case in archaeology, where far less agreement exists about fundamental units of analysis, the relations of those units of analysis to one another, and their conceptual relations to equivalent units of analysis in other relevant social sciences. It is thus reasonably easy to identify cautionary tales, cases where considerations of descent and genealogy are being misused in reconstructions of prehistory. The developing enthusiasm for genetic analyses of population histories over the last decade, and the publications of synthetic reconstructions of population history that routinely and explicitly conflate genetic, archaeological, and linguistic typologies (e.g., Cavalli-Sforza et al. 1994), furnish a nearly inexhaustible fund of such cautionary tales. (As noted above, similar conflation is characteristic of a number of cultural historical studies within anthropology.) It is much harder, however, to identify cases where concepts like descent and genealogy are being explicitly and usefully incorporated into archaeological analyses.

It may be time for some theoretical and disciplinary modesty in our expectations of the utility of the descent concept. The most direct relationship between biological concepts of descent and archaeological assemblages may lie at the point where human beings actually produce material culture. In this case, we can use ethnoarchaeological research to study the ways in which social descent generates learning environments through which the characteristic material culture of a particular community will be reproduced. The research initiatives undertaken by Belgian scholars working in Central Africa and noted above (of which Gosselain [1995, 1999] and Wallaert [1998, 1999a, 1999b] are probably most relevant to the present discussion) have involved careful and extensive ethnographic analysis of apprenticeship procedures and the relations of those procedures to the different *chaînes opératoires* through which artifact production takes place. This has involved, for example, comparative ethnoarchaeological research among a variety of ethnic groups in northern Cameroon, through which striking contrasts in apprentice recruitment and training were observed by Wallaert. Very different schema for apprentice learning and thus for the social reproduction of material culture seem to exist, even between groups within the same general region of the country. Thus, for example, Dii apprentices learn to produce pottery in a context of observation, imitation, and strict control, with teachers occupying a persistently higher level in social hierarchies. Apprenticeship innovation is actively discouraged. Fali-Tinguelin apprentices, on the other hand, learn in a context where questioning of teachers, active participation in the learning process, and the development of personal maturation are central (Wallaert 1999a). Apprenticeship innovation is actively encouraged. Wallaert then goes on to discuss the effects of these different learning schema on the production of modern ceramics in these communities, with implications that range from frequencies of left- and right-handedness among potters from these different groups to predictions of the relative stability of conceptual models for ceramic production.

FUTURE IMPORTANCE

> One of the central insights to emerge in and through critiques of "processual" archaeology is that it is a serious mistake to let methodological commitments and disciplinary ambitions determine how you conceptualise your subject.
>
> Wylie 1992: 51

In the context of study of *chaînes opératoires*, the research noted above yields data on the material correlates of social descent systems that are potentially directly applicable to detailed studies of archaeological ceramic samples. Close conceptual control over these systems of social descent exists, and inferential changes relevant to the study of archaeological assemblages are relatively short—at least in the context of Central African archaeology. Such research will necessarily be regional and most useful for relatively recent archaeological occurrences, at least until more such studies are undertaken and a database of information on variability in different societies is accumulated. However, research of this sort can work from the ground up—as Wallaert (1999a: 78) says, "one step at a time"—with comparative work undertaken over progressively larger areas while some control over the relations between conceptual units is maintained. This seems like a more useful approach than those that begin with Grand Theory and then seek to modify our understandings of human cultural activity in the past to fit that theory.

More generally, use of the concept of descent in archaeology would seem to require a balance between two opposing tendencies. On the one hand, attention has to be paid to the actual units of descent that archaeologists are interested in when they examine prehistoric artifact assemblages. Inadequate attention to the definition of such units leads to a metaphorical transition to better-understood usages in other disciplines, especially biology, so that "cultures" are conceived of as much like species and genealogical hierarchies of descent from biological systematics are imposed on prehistory. The problem is that the biological evolution of species and the cultural evolution of human societies are not the same process, and did not work in identical ways. On the other hand, a restriction of archaeological theorizing to evolutionary concepts more or less exactly as they are conceived of within evolutionary biology risks eliminating vast fields of past human activity from archaeological consideration—a price that seems too great to pay for the advances in methodological rigor that have resulted from analyses in evolutionary archaeology to this point. Concepts of descent and genealogy in archaeology have to be fitted to archaeological cases, not borrowed either implicitly or explicitly from biology. Considerations of artifact production systems as cultural systems may be a reasonable place to start.

It would seem most useful for archaeologists to make sure that our fundamental concepts are understood in as much detail as is possible on a local level, before expanding them into large-scale theoretical systems. This is particularly the case for concepts that admit of a variety of meanings in different disciplines, given the confusion that the metaphorical connotations of such concepts may engender. The constellation of meanings associated with descent, genealogy and lineages in archaeology appear to be prime examples of such a case.

ACKNOWLEDGMENTS

I would like to thank John Terrell and John Hart for their very helpful conversations about this chapter, for their suggestions of readings and possible areas of research, and for their patience and good humor in awaiting a chapter that was far too long delayed.

NOTES

1. Kuper (1988: 6–7) notes that, according to late-nineteenth-century theorists, the existence of these systems of kinship and descent was held to be fundamental to the definition of "primitive societies," and that their replacement by territorial, state-level forms of social organization marked the transition from "ancient" to

"modern" social forms. The disappearance of descent as an important element of social organization thus becomes, ironically enough, an expression of social evolution over time. Although these evolutionary concepts fell out of favor, Kuper convincingly argues that the concept of "primitive society" remained important within anthropology until very recently.

2. The development of evolutionary archaeology would itself perhaps make a suitable case for the study of descent in human cultural systems, with an apical ancestor (Robert Dunnell), a large number of theoretical and methodological offspring over several generations, and what appear to be relatively efficient mechanisms for replicating structures of theory and method from one generation to the next. Its association to related historical lineages of archaeological theory, including processual and behavioral archaeologies, could then be examined as well.

3. It is interesting to note that Dunnell (1995: 41–42) posits a change in the unit of evolution between "simple" and "complex" societies, from the individual in the former case to the functionally differentiated group of individuals in the latter. This exactly parallels the early anthropological differentiation of "primitive" and "modern" societies noted by Kuper (1988) (see note 1 above).

REFERENCES

Alter, S. (1999). *Darwin and the Linguistic Image*. Baltimore, MD: Johns Hopkins University Press.

Ammerman, A., and L. Cavalli-Sforza. (1984). *The Neolithic Transition and the Genetics of Populations in Europe*. Princeton, NJ: Princeton University Press.

Barton, M. (1997). Stone tools, style and social identity: An evolutionary perspective on the archaeological record. In M. Barton and G. Clark (eds.), *Rediscovering Darwin: Evolutionary Theory and Archaeological Explanation*. Archeological Papers No. 7. Arlington, VA: American Anthropological Association, pp. 141–156.

Cavalli-Sforza, L., P. Menozzi, and A. Piazza. (1994). *The History and Geography of Human Genes*. Princeton, NJ: Princeton University Press.

Darwin, C. (1964) [1859]. *On the Origin of Species*. Cambridge, MA: Harvard University Press.

Darwin, C. (1887). *The Descent of Man, and Selection in Relation to Sex*. New York: Appleton and Co.

Deetz, J. (1965). *The Dynamics of Stylistic Change in Arikara Ceramics*. Illinois Studies in Anthropology No. 4. Urbana: University of Illinois Press.

Dietler, M., and I. Herbich. (1989). Tich Matek: The technology of Luo pottery production and the definition of ceramic style. *World Archaeology* 21: 148–164.

Dixon, R. (1977). *The Rise and Fall of Languages*. Cambridge: Cambridge University Press.

Dunnell, R. D. (1989). Aspects of the application of evolutionary theory in archaeology. In C. C Lamberg-Karlovsky (ed.), *Archaeological Thought in America*. Cambridge: Cambridge University Press, pp. 35–49

Dunnell, R. D. (1995). What is it that actually evolves? In P. Teltser (ed.), *Evolu-*

tionary Archaeology: Methodological Issues. Tucson: University of Arizona Press, pp. 33–50.

Durham, W. (1992). Applications of evolutionary culture theory. *Annual Review of Anthropology* 21: 331–355.

Eldredge, N. (1999). *The Pattern of Evolution*. New: York W. H. Freeman.

Evans-Pritchard, E. E. (1940). *The Nuer, A Description of the Modes of Livelihood and Political Institutions of a Nilotic People*. Oxford: Clarendon Press.

Gosselain, O. (1995). *Identités techniques: Le Travail de la Poterie au Cameroun Méridionale*. Ph.D. diss., Université Libre du Bruxelles.

Gosselain, O. (1999). Poterie, société et histoire chez les Koma Ndera du Cameroun. *Cahiers des Etudes Africaines* 153(39–1): 73–105.

Graves, M., and T. Ladefoged. (1995). The evolutionary significance of ceremonial architecture in Polynesia. In P. Teltser (ed.), *Evolutionary Archaeology: Methodological Issues*. Tucson: University of Arizona Press, pp. 149–174.

Kirch, P. (1984). *The Evolution of the Polynesian Chiefdoms*. Cambridge: Cambridge University Press.

Kuper, A. (1988). *The Invention of Primitive Society*. London: Routledge.

Lesser, A. (1961). Social fields and the evolution of society. *Southwestern Journal of Anthropology* 17: 40–48.

Longacre, W. (1970). *Archaeology as Anthropology: A Case Study*. Anthropological Papers No. 17. Tucson: University of Arizona Press.

Lyman, R. L., and M. J. O'Brien. (1998). The goals of evolutionary archaeology: History and explanation. *Current Anthropology* 39: 615–652.

Mace, R., and M. Pagel. (1994). The comparative method in anthropology. *Current Anthropology* 35: 549–564.

MacEachern, S. (1998). Scale, style and cultural variation: Technological traditions in the northern Mandara Mountains. In M. Stark (ed.), *The Archaeology of Social Boundaries*. Washington, DC: Smithsonian Institution Press, pp. 107–131.

Malthus, T. (1914) [1872]. *An Essay on Population*. London: J. M. Dent.

Neff, H., and D. Larson. (1997). Methodology of comparison in evolutionary archaeology. In M. Barton and G. Clark (eds.), *Rediscovering Darwin: Evolutionary Theory and Archaeological Explanation*. Archaeological Papers No. 7. Arlington, VA: American Anthropological Association, pp. 75–94.

Neiman, F. (1995). Stylistic variation in evolutionary perspective: Inferences from decorative diversity and interassemblage distance in Illinois Woodland ceramic assemblages. *American Antiquity* 60: 7–36.

O'Brien, M., T. Holland, R. Hoard, and G. Fox. (1994). Evolutionary implications of design and performance characteristics of prehistoric pottery. *Journal of Archaeological Method and Theory* 1: 259–304.

Phillipson, D. W. (1977). *The Later Prehistory of Eastern and Southern Africa*. New York: Africana Publishing Company.

Roux, V., and D. Corbetta. (1990). *Le tour du Potier: Spécialisation Artisanales et Compétences Techniques*. Monographie du CRA 4, Centre des Recherches Archéologiques. Paris: CNRS.

Sahlins, M. (1958). *Social Stratification in Polynesia*. Seattle: American Ethnological Society.

Simpson, G. G. (1961). *Principles of Animal Taxonomy*. New York: Columbia University Press.

Stanislawski, M. (1978). If pots were mortal. In R. Gould (ed.), *Explorations in Ethnoarchaeology*. Albuquerque: University of New Mexico Press, pp. 201–227.

Teltser, P. (1995). Methodological challenge. In P. Teltser (ed.), *Evolutionary Archaeology: Methodological Issues*. Tucson: University of Arizona Press, pp. 1–11.

Templeton, A. (1998). Human races: a genetic and evolutionary perspective. *American Anthropologist* 100: 632–650.

Terrell, J. (ed.). (2001). *Archaeology, Language, and History: Essays on Culture and Ethnicity*. Westport, CT: Bergin and Garvey.

Terrell, J., T. Hunt, and C. Gosden. (1997). The dimensions of social life in the Pacific. *Current Anthropology* 38: 155–195.

Vansina, J. (1995). New linguistic evidence and "The Bantu Expansion." *Journal of African History* 36: 173–195.

Wallaert, H. (1998). Learning how to make the right pots: Apprenticeship strategies serving style duplication. Paper presented at the biennial SAfA Conference, Syracuse, NY, May.

Wallaert, H. (1999a). Manual laterality apprenticeship as the first learning rule prescribed to potters: A case study in handmade pottery from Northern Cameroon. *Urgeschichte Materialhefte* 14: 63–84.

Wallaert, H. (1999b). L'impact de l'apprentissage sur la perpetuation des styles céramiques. In J.-M. Leotard, *Méthodes d'Analyses de la Terre Tuite. Journée de réflexion Ocquier, 28 Novembre 1998*. DGATLP: Direction de Liège, Service de l'Archéologie, Liège, pp. 77–85.

Whallon, R. (1968). Investigations of late prehistoric social organization in New York state. In S. Binford and L. Binford (eds.), *New Perspectives in Archaeology*. Chicago: Aldine, pp. 223–244.

Wylie, A. (1992) Feminist theories of social power: Some implications for a processual archaeology. *Norwegian Archaeological Review* 25(1): 51–68.

Zvelebil, M. (1998). Genetic and cultural diversity in Europe: A comment on Cavalli-Sforza. *Journal of Anthropological Research* 54: 411–416.

Chapter 9

History

Sibel Barut Kusimba and Chapurukha M. Kusimba

INTRODUCTION

Although recent American archaeology has sought to distance itself from the concept of history, this concept is crucial to the way archaeologists think about what they are doing as researchers and why they are doing it. Therefore, it is not surprising that archaeologists have worked with many definitions of history and have suggested numerous ways of studying it. For example, archaeological culture historians as a rule see history as a richly detailed story about our past, a story that can be characterized by a uniquely varying succession of changing artifact types, settlement patterns, subsistence practices, and the like. In contrast, processual archaeologists are likely to see the historian's job as the rigorous accounting of certain identifiable processes of change leading human history to unfold in similar ways in different places on earth. In a volume such as this, however, the key issue is not the historian's famous question *What is history?* (Carr 1961), but instead the archaeologist's inquiry *What does evolution have to do with history?*

HISTORY OF THE CONCEPT IN ARCHAEOLOGY

History can be defined as "action in time," be it the action of humans, other species, or matter and energy in space. Thus one can talk about human history and about the history of the universe. In many ways, history is the broadest concept in this book. Concepts like descent, chance, selection, environment, adaptation, learning, and evolution are concerned with *influences* on action in time, or *how* action in time happens.

The definition of history as action in time can be expressed as a simple word equation:

$$time + action = history$$

Teasing action and time apart this way gives us a starting point for understanding how evolution and history fit together. Time is linear: it does not repeat itself. Actions, however, can be repeated. Consequently, history has two sides: repetition (or continuity) and change. Looked at from one side, history is about *how actions change over time*. From the opposite side, history is also about *why actions do not change*, and why the archaeological record, for example, shows us long periods of time when little, in fact, seems to have changed at all. Therefore, we need to ask not only how the key concept of history can help archaeologists study change, but also how the same concept can help explain why things can repeat themselves with a fair amount of sameness over time.

The key to solving the paradox that history is about *both* change *and* continuity is the idea that history is action in time. If you start with this definition, two deceptively simple questions come to mind. What leads to change over time? What leads instead to historical continuities? And do the key concepts of evolution really help us understand both of these sides of history?

Unlike **biological reproduction**, which is a kind of copying process, **cultural learning** is a creative process in which learners individually and socially create meaning and understanding, bringing to the learning process their own prior knowledge and experience. "Learning is an active, personally-conducted affair" (Dewey 1916: 335). Does this fundamental difference between biological reproduction and cultural learning mean that the key concepts of Darwinian evolution have no relevance to the study of human history? Teasing apart the changing from the unchanging is how most historians and archaeologists find process, pattern, or meaningful empirical generalization in past events. Terrell (1986) has defined a **pattern** as "a snapshot of variation in space at a single instant of time," **pathway** as a chronological series of patterns that show change through time, and **processes** as predictable, repetitive kinds or types of pathways in history. From this perspective, the recognition of processes is one way that archaeologists separate the two parts of the history equation. What might lead a society down the same pathway more than once, or down the same pathway as a group in a different time and place? What forces make people do the same thing over again? And on the other side of the coin, why would people want to do something differently? Why would a pattern cease to be repeated?

Other historical scientists also attempt to find patterns in past events. In evolutionary biology, history is often contrasted with chance and natural

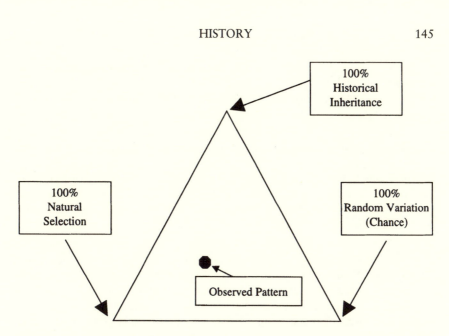

Figure 9.1. Any observed historical pattern in evolutionary biology can be thought of as a consequence of different proportions of history, natural selection, or chance (after Terrell 1986: 190).

selection. Travisano et al. (1995: 87) write that change through time "is the product of (these) three fundamental evolutionary influences. . . . Their relative contributions to evolutionary change have been the subject of intense debate." **Natural selection** describes the process through which phenotypes and their proportions, or gene frequencies, within a population change through time, through the differential reproductive success of individuals in competition. **Chance** includes mutation and genetic drift, the chance factors of reproduction that influence the appearance, passing on, or loss of traits that influence reproduction. History, in this formulation, refers to the "inherited constitution" (Travisano et al. 1995: 87) of an individual,

[history] may constrain or promote particular evolutionary outcomes according to the genetic and developmental integration of the ancestral phenotype. In this view, the set of potential adaptations is severely limited by inherent constitution, so that at every moment the course of evolution is contingent on prior historical events. (Travisano et al. 1995: 87)

The interaction of these three factors can be displayed on a triangle graph (Figure 9.1), where the relative proximity of a point representing the observed pattern represents the relative importance of history, chance, or selection on the pattern (see Terrell 1986).

Gould and Lewontin (1979) and Gould (1989) are strong supporters of

the importance of historical contingency, as opposed to selection, in influencing biological evolution. In arguing that evolutionary trajectories are
historical because the events that make them up are unique and contingent,
Gould (1989) wrote that replaying "life's tape"

would lead evolution down a pathway radically different from the road actually
taken. . . . Each step proceeds for cause, but no finale can be specified at the start,
and none would ever occur a second time in the same way, because any pathway
proceeds through thousands of improbable stages. Alter any early event, ever so
slightly and without apparent importance at the time, and evolution cascades into
a radically different channel. (Gould 1989)

Gould and Lewontin (1979) argue for the importance of biological history in establishing the raw materials for and conditions under which evolutionary forces such as natural selection, mutation, drift, and gene flow
can act. For them, organisms are "so constrained by phyletic heritage, pathways of development and general architecture that the constraints themselves become more interesting and more important in delimiting pathways
of change than the selective force that may mediate change when it occurs."
Travisano et al. (1995) tested the relative roles of natural selection,
chance, and history by examining the evolution of population size and cell
size of bacteria in controlled laboratory environments. They found that
historical constraints on change were most important in traits not strongly
subject to selection, like bacterial cell size. They conclude that "the footprint of history may be obliterated for traits subject to strong selection,
whereas the effect of history is preserved in traits that are less important."
They maintain, however, the possibility of a guiding role for history over
the long term: "Over much longer periods, the footprint of history might
eventually become too deep to be obscured even by intense selection." For
students of the fossil record, the lesson is proved that history is crucially
important, especially given the problem of determining, in the fossil record,
which traits are "subject to strong selection."
Why do things change? Why do they stay the same? Teasing out the
roles of chance, history, and selection, as do Travisano et al. (1995), may
be the key for archaeologists. There are three reasons why people might
repeat ways of doing things and why they might do things in new ways
(Figure 9.2):
    1. *Chance.* Much of what people do is still "by accident."
    2. *Agency.* Knowledge of the consequences of past events will lead in-
dividuals to copy or reject what others have done in the past. One might
also call this individual will.
    3. *Selection.* Selection is the evolutionary part of history. One might
define a type of selection among humans that is analogous to biological
natural selection. Skinner (1981) defined **selection by consequences** as the

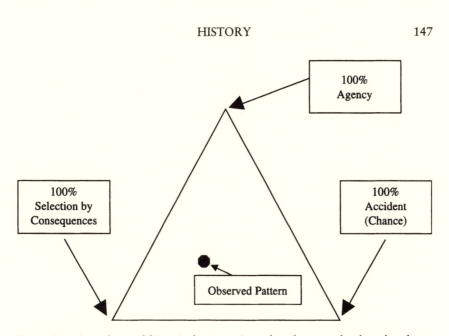

Figure 9.2. Any observed historical pattern in archaeology can be thought of as a consequence of different proportions of foresight, selection by consequences, or chance (after Terrell 1986: 190).

reinforcement of successful cultural practices that promote the success of individuals or groups. This type of reinforcement is accomplished by social institutions (like schools or churches) and ideology (for example, concepts like the sacred, the taboo, the prestigious). Selection by consequences might be positive or negative; in other words, like foresight and chance, it can select for or against particular behaviors. In other words, it can be a reason things change, and a reason things stay the same. "A better way of making a tool, growing food, or teaching a child is reinforced by its consequence—the tool, the food, or a useful helper, respectively. A culture evolves when practices originating in this way contribute to the success of the practicing group in solving its problems. It is the effect on the group, not the reinforcing consequences for individual members, which is responsible for the evolution of the culture" (Skinner 1981: 502).

Relating this three-part model of history back to the word equation of action in time, we can summarize the relationship of history and evolution. Historical change includes all change over time—the whole triangle. Some changes are accidental, although in the archaeologist's perspective, individual chance events might mark crucial historical turning points, but collectively they might not add up to processes. Others might be the result of individual motivations—those at the top of the triangle graph in Figure 9.2. Evolutionary changes, on the other hand, are a result of selection by consequences either for the individual or for the group, if the selective agent is an ideology or institution. Because of the self-reinforcing nature of selection by consequences, evolutionary changes are also often directional and repetitive, and to some extent predictable—forming *processes*. These sorts of evolutionary changes would plot on or near the lower left-hand corner of the triangle of history in Figure 9.2.

CONTEMPORARY USES OF THE TERM "HISTORY" IN ARCHAEOLOGY

Rather than seeing evolution as one corner of a triangle of history, as we do in Figure 9.2, archaeologists have tended, as in the major traditions in historiography summarized by Fogel and Elton (1983), to create a long-standing dichotomy between history and evolution. For many archaeologists, the word "evolution" refers to general laws, trajectories, patterns, or processes, while "history" is about empirical details or unique sequences of events. **Cultural history**, for example, involves the creation of unique local chronologies based on stylistic change.

In contrast to history, evolution in the eyes of many archaeologists is about general laws that apply across history, often established by identifying patterns across particular events (White 1959: 30). In archaeology and anthropology, the association of history with particular happenings and empirical details—rather than with global, repetitive events, is strong. As Richards (1992: 19–20) has phrased it, "history has seemed to be the pursuit of pedestrian minds, grubbers of disparate detail who rarely raise their heads to gaze upon Empyrian heights where facts reach to general law."

Evolutionary biologists and historians have employed similar definitions of history. They contrast history defined as the study of unique, ever-changing, time- and space-dependent events with the physical sciences, which are said to study the unchanging properties of matter and energy:

The unchanging properties of matter and energy [chemistry, mechanics, physics] and the likewise unchanging processes and principles arising there from are immanent in the material universe. They are nonhistorical, even though they occur and act in the course of history. The actual state of the universe or of any part of it at a given time, its configuration, is not immanent and is constantly changing. It is contingent . . . or configurational. . . . History may be defined as configurational change through time. (Simpson 1963: 24–25)

One might argue that the contrast between the **historical sciences** (those that deal with action in time) and the **natural sciences** (those that deal primarily with immanent processes) is not that great. Natural scientists, historians, and evolutionary biologists are all involved in interpreting change through time—even an experiment can only be performed exactly the same way once.

The natural sciences can, through experimentation, contrive natural phenomena to control context. Nevertheless, as the study of physical science goes deeper and deeper into the atom, and toward the description of more and more complex and context-dependent systems, the differences between historical and natural sciences may indeed wane. Physics, for example, has been penetrating into fundamental particles, grappling with uncertainty, probability, and chaos theory, the "falling leaf on a blustery Chicago day," for much of this century. Hawking (in Gleik 1987: 6) has noted: "We have advanced to a stage where we spend millions of dollars on experiments whose results we cannot reduplicate."

Travisano et al. (1995) used experimentation with bacteria to apportion their evolution to the relative influences of chance, history, and selection. In this biological context, history becomes a constraint on evolution. How do historians and archaeologists define continuity and change? How can they find patterns and determine the relative roles of history, chance, and selection by consequence in the creation of those patterns? The historian's methods are fundamentally different from those of the natural scientist, who searches for laws and often uses experiments to test laws. To some historians, history is "a concern with the description of particular events of the past rather than with the search for general laws which might govern these events" (Hempel 1965 [1942]: 231). It is through description—specifically narrative description—that the historian explains. The word "history" has a common lay meaning as a *story*, or narrative, of what happens. By this definition, history is what historians write: stories or accounts describing "a chronologically-ordered and somehow unified or related sequence of events with a beginning, middle, and end" (Pluciennik 1999).

Accompanying this common lay meaning of history is the belief that historical narratives must be based on written records. Societies without written records of one kind or another, therefore, are societies without history—they are "prehistoric" societies. Since the 1960s, however, most historians would accept that all human societies have histories, and that historical evidence can be pieced together from many different sources, both written and non-written (Vansina 1990). Writing about precolonial African societies, for example, Newbury (1997: 300) remarks that "some societies recognized several distinct genres of historical recitation: fixed dynastic poetry, free verse, open narrative, or ritual prescription with historical exegesis, often associated with a given category of narrators."

A **narrative**, be it written or not, is a story in which events are defined, situated in space and time, and linked to other events. In a recent edited volume (Nitecki and Nitecki 1992), several evolutionary biologists and philosophers of science argued that the narrative was the scientific form of explanation employed by all sciences of action in time, whether of humans or other life forms: "All explanations of events in time are ultimately narrative in structure" (Richards 1992: 46).

Features of Narrative

Creating a narrative or story is a complex process of defining events and characters and relating them through a plot structure (Pluciennik 1999). Characters may be individuals or collectives. Events are usually unified sets of occurrences with antecedents, beginnings, and ends, which are to a large extent defined by the analyst, not objective reality. The plot gives a wider meaning to a series of events and characters and shows their interrelationships. Narratives typically explain the unique context of historical events and have a "particularizing quality" (Spaulding 1968: 35). Much of a narrative is presented within a worldview, philosophy, or **meta-narrative**, such as Marxism or neo-Darwinism, that is a part of the narrator's present intellectual and cultural milieu (Pluciennik 1999: 15).

As Spaulding (1968: 35) put it, explanatory generalizations implicit in the narrative, and shared by reader and narrator, make a historical narrative "skillful (and) satisfying." The success of a narrative can be judged on the "tightness" with which it can demonstrate the interrelationships of causation among events. Good narratives "enmesh central events in causal networks that fix them with inevitability" (Richards 1992: 23). From our own perspective, a good narrative should also isolate the interaction of agency, chance, and selection by consequences through which historical patterns are created.

A Brief and Selective Historiography of Historical Narratives

Guilderhus (1996) has recently argued that concerns with historical accuracy and the authority of the historian have become more and more important throughout Western historiography. The challenge that history must explain the past has always existed in tension with the reality that different historians throughout time have operated under different meta-narratives and held different ideas of what truth and explanation are and ought to be. Fogel and Elton (1983) summarize this tension between the "traditional" and "scientific" views of history.

The Traditional View. The traditional view of history, as championed by Elton (Fogel and Elton 1983), argues that historians must examine the existing evidence in as open-minded a way as possible, and then interpret it with the understanding that historical actors respond to their situations in historically determined ways resulting from their worldview and perspective. Collingwood (1956: 223) argued that one must understand both the outside of an event (the actions of bodies and objects) and the inside of an event (the agency, or thoughts and motivations, of historical actors).

The Scientific View. In a view oppositional to the traditional view of history, other historians and philosophers such as Voltaire, Comte, Popper, Hempel, and Fogel have sought to infer general rules or processes of history that are external to human actors. In nineteenth-century France and England, positivists led by Comte and Mill focused on repeatable and generalizable events and hoped to find universal laws of history. Carl Hempel (1965 [1942]) argued that general laws could be found in history through the application of "covering laws" that both explained and could predict similar future happenings under similar conditions. The positivist insistence that rational investigation can either create or apply universal rules or covering laws to the explanation of history has been a persistent but minor and somewhat unconvincing voice in historiography (Guilderhus 1996). "Most 'laws' of social science are in fact empirical generalizations about the history of human development" (Kelley and Hanen 1988).

The polarization of science from history has existed at least since the early nineteenth century, when Hegel and Dilthey separated *naturwissenschaft* (natural science) from *geisteswissenschaft* (humanities or arts). In one of the more recent works on archaeology by a philosopher, Bell (1994) argues that scientific narratives are very different from historical narratives. According to Bell, scientific narratives aim at isolating causal process and creating explicit empirical generalizations. Historical narratives, on the other hand, are more likely to describe the interrelationships of complex and numerous events, causes, and conditions, and they are informed by assumed, implicit explanatory generalizations or meta-narratives (Bell 1994: 124; Pluciennik 1994).

New approaches to epistemology argue that the challenges of explanation in history and natural science are more similar than Dilthey's division or even Bell's would suppose. Realist conceptions of science show that implicit assumptions, worldviews, bias, and imperfect knowledge are a part of all disciplines (Gibbon 1989). Furthermore, the methodologies of science and history are not that far apart either. Pluciennik (1999: 18) has pointed out that, in their structure as forms of knowledge, scientific explanations can be considered to be types of narratives. Even a chemical equation, although simple, retains the essential features of narrative, describing an interrelationship between chemical compounds. Both science and history involve isolating and describing events and their relationships in time and space,

> the coherence of a narrative describing a sequence of events could be given equally by, for example, physical causality in the context of a particular chemical equation, or by the demonstration of a particularly complex intersection of physical and cultural conditions and social processes. (Pluciennik 1999: 15)

One could easily criticize Pluciennik's overemphasis on similarities between science and history. Nevertheless, Pluciennik argues successfully that the differences between science and history have been overemphasized, particularly among archaeologists.

Nonetheless, the association between history and "disparate detail" has been long-standing in archaeology. One reason lies in the perceived inferior status of archaeology as a science. Archaeology developed as an "auxiliary science" (Carr 1961: 8) of history in Europe and of anthropology in the Americas. Carr believed archaeology's function was merely to provide basic facts of chronology and evidence, such as "the origin and period of a fragment of pottery or marble . . . the raw materials of the historian rather than of history itself" (Carr 1961: 8). Broadening of the definition of historical sources to include not just written records but cultural forms, behaviors, social institutions, and their material correlates (Newbury 1997) has been important in changing the perceived role of archaeology as a discipline and its relationship to history and anthropology. Like all historical scientists, archaeologists try to explain, not just generate facts.

Franz Boas, a key figure in the establishment of American anthropology as a science, argued for the solid documentation of historical sequences and affirmed that the same phenomena do not always have the same causes. However, Boasian empiricism has been blamed for the eventual descriptive excesses of culture history approaches to prehistory. Harris (1968: 676) wrote of archaeology during the Boasian era,

if the hand of historical particularism rested heavily upon the study of cultural regularities among ethnologists, its weight was even more deadening among the archaeologists . . . the archaeologist concentrated upon the pattern of rim sherd incisions found at his site and possibly at one or two adjacent localities . . . culture . . . was a thing of sherds and scrapers and little else.

The "New Archaeology" of the 1960s and 1970s argued that culture historians did little more than establish chronologies based on artifact style change. It strove to "disassociate archaeological explanation from historical narrative" (Bell 1994: 125). Binford (1968) argued forcefully that archaeologists were not historians' handmaidens, not simply "strange historians working at a disadvantage, that is, without written records" (Binford 1983: 20).

Binford rejected the Collingwoodian prescription that one must empathize with prehistoric actors' motivations, arguing that historians have no way of understanding these motivations or of knowing whether they are right or wrong about them. In other words, archaeologists should avoid writing historical narratives because of their inherent untestability, a view also held by the philosopher Bell (1994: 125).

The fact that people are not always honest inevitably presents the historian with the problem of understanding the motives that individuals might have had. . . . But, while material things most certainly do communicate coded information, they are very rarely coded for the purposes of deceit. (Binford 1983: 20)

Certain historians have proposed that the best method for finding out about the past is empathy—that is, merely to imagine what actions or circumstances would bring about the conditions observed. . . . But (this) is just the first step—far more important is how we evaluate these ideas. Without some methodology for evaluating ideas, we are in the position of having a free hand to generate lots of stories about the past, but not having any means of knowing whether these stories are accurate. (Binford 1983: 21)

Gibbon summarizes that in much of the rhetoric of New Archaeology:

Key terms like culture, archaeological data, science and analogical interpretation were given new definitions; others like process, system, model and explanation were promoted to a new importance and also redefined; still others, especially diffusion, taxonomy, and history, were demoted in importance. (1989: 63)

A major criticism of traditional archaeology was that it treated the recovery and description of data as an end in itself, and that understanding of the past could emerge by itself with the amassing of facts. New Archaeology specifically allied history with particularism and reconstruction rather than with the generalizing and explanatory goals of anthropology. (1989: 67)

Overall, the history/evolution dichotomy has not led to new understanding in archaeology. Archaeologists since the 1960s have used a ladder of stages of sociocultural integration, such as the band, tribe, chiefdom, and state categories, to try to describe general or global processes of culture change. In this way, both New Archaeology and culture history conceived of history as a progression of stages or "a sequence of homogeneous periods or systems rather than as continuous change" (Dunnell 1996: 116). Unfortunately, the consequences of both the "culture history" and neo-evolutionary views are that the "synchronic view of time" (Plog 1974) makes it impossible to construct historical narrative that can skillfully describe the interaction of foresight, chance, and selection. As an example, we examine changing interpretations of the "Bantu Expansion."

CASE STUDY

One of the fundamental questions that Africanist historians and anthropologists have been concerned with is determining the evolution of ethnicity in Africa. Across much of central, eastern, and southern Africa, Bantu languages are spoken. These languages share many similarities of vocabulary and grammar, even though the languages themselves appear over a vast area of over 500,000 square kilometers. As Phillipson (1977: 106) wrote:

"It has been a prime goal for students of African history to elucidate the processes responsible for this remarkably widespread linguistic distribution." The relative similarity and broad geographical expanse of Bantu suggest that their speakers had a common geographical point of origin and a recent migration out from that point of origin, say, within the last 2,000 years (Phillipson 1977). Oliver and Fagan (1975: 30, 77–80) were some of the first to develop the currently influential expansion scenario. They argued that the initial home of speakers of proto-Bantu was in the Cameroonian grasslands, where present-day linguistic variation is highest; these ancestors of the Bantu cultivated root crops and made pottery and stone tools. From here, the proto-Bantu group moved into the Congo Basin, acquired iron, and "expanded east and west, south and north" (Oliver and Fagan 1975: 30).

Early Iron Age sites in eastern and southern Africa have been interpreted as evidence of precisely such an expansion by Bantu-speaking peoples (Huffman 1982: 136; Phillipson 1977), based on what is seen as a sudden appearance of iron-working technology, agriculture, and permanent settlements, and in some areas, the first appearance of pottery (Sutton 1990). Linguistic studies argue that central Cameroonian proto-Bantu-speakers spread southward and eastward into the Great Lakes Region. Many believe that archaeological evidence supports this hypothesis, in particular the early appearance of Urewe pottery in the Great Lakes Region around 500 B.C. Numerous pottery styles have been mapped on to early linguistic communities, and are believed to represent the spread of sub-branches or separate streams of Bantu-speakers (Phillipson 1977).

Since Oliver and Fagan, the Bantu expansion has often been portrayed as a massive population spread and migration from the postulated Bantu heartland across much of sub-Saharan Africa. This migration, it is said, was fueled by the population explosion that followed the introduction of farming and, later, metallurgy. "The migration rolled like a giant 'wave,' divided in several 'streams,' over the subcontinent and soon overwhelmed the autochthonous foragers." (Vansina 1995).

According to some views, the conjectured massive population increase was the medium through which hunting and gathering populations were replaced or absorbed by food producers possessing iron tools, cattle, and later, cereals. In other words, the presumed Bantu expansion was also a culture-historical transition from the Stone Age to the Neolithic/Iron Age stage in East Africa.

According to some authorities the main expansion of the Bantu-speakers was vast and fast, not a series of gradual stages as some have argued, but neither was it a matter of purposeless wandering, nor of organized military conquest. It was a remarkable process of colonization in the true sense of the word—the opening up of essentially empty lands (Sutton 1981: 580).

This interpretation of a Bantu expansion as a purposeful "colonization" into "empty" lands has been widely accepted. It has been assumed that because the Bantu language distribution was so large, only a single large process could have caused it. Vansina (1995: 189) notes that

scholars have been mesmerized by the huge extent of the present distribution of Bantu languages and could only think of a single process, an equally huge human migration, "the Bantu expansion," to explain it. . . . The unvarying success of these Bantu migrants came to be attributed to a vast technological differential; they were sedentary, they were potters, they were farmers, and later metallurgists, awhile the autochthons were just nomadic foragers.

This model of a Bantu expansion as a progressive migration event maps it in the top corner of our triangle of history (Figure 9.2). A much more historical view of the process through which these related languages spread throughout Africa sees a much more complex view of the situation. Rather than assuming that a single and repeating cause or process led to a unified Bantu expansion, a historical view incorporates all three causes of change as interacting throughout the historical pathway of the African Iron Age. At any particular point in time, one of the three causes of change might be primary; but placing successive historical snapshots end to end shows how all three forces are combining. In other words, the vast geographical range of Bantu languages is a product of many causes and processes.

Vansina (1995) has made three cogent criticisms of the prevailing migration theory. First, the theory assumes that only a human migration could cause the wide geographical distribution of Bantu languages. Yet languages may, in fact, spread without involving human migrations, as waves of water can spread out in a pond (Vansina 1995: 189). Second, the scenario collapses one to several millennia's worth of history into a single migration event which seems doubtful if the present pattern is, in fact, the result of numerous processes and events that unfolded over sub-Saharan Africa during this time period. Finally, the tree generated by a clustering analysis of modern language similarity has been interpreted as a phylogenetic tree, rather than just the most parsimonious branching diagram that can explain present-day language differences. This type of misinterpretation is common among scholars attempting to use present similarities and differences to infer past population histories, such as among students of the origins of modern humans (Relethford 1995).

Vansina proposes a wave model to replace the tree model, in which languages may have one or more parents and more than two descendant languages. The wave model attempts to account for the continuous nature of language change both within and among languages, focusing on individual innovations or traits of idiolects and dialects, and how they spread within and among languages. Archaeological and linguistic research has shown that the alleged Bantu expansion was actually a series of different kinds of population movements, interactions, and technological and linguistic transfers. The archaeological record has also shown that the origin of metallurgy, food production, or pottery is not coterminous with the appearance of "Bantu" pottery (Mapunda 2000; Schoenbrun 1993). In many cases, pottery, food production, and metallurgy could have spread without population movements and predate the appearance of pottery attributed to "Bantu" speakers in any given area. Indigenous groups were not technologically simple and highly mobile; many were sedentary fishers or they already possessed domesticates (Ehret 1995; Vansina 1990, 1994–1995, 1995). The first iron technologies in the Great Lakes Region around 800 B.C. probably post-date the split between eastern and western Bantu streams. Although many proponents of the expansion scenario (Phillipson 1979) were aware of some of the archaeological evidence of pre-Bantu iron working or food production, they still accepted the hypothesis of a single historical process to explain the distribution of Bantu pottery.

An increasing number of archaeologists are finding empirical reason to reject the Bantu expansion model. But to turn to one of the questions we posed at the beginning of this paper: *What does evolution have to do with history?* If the Bantu expansion is the end result of numerous different, unique processes or events, is its history in any way "evolutionary"? Returning to the triangle graph in Figure 9.2, is the concept of selection by consequences, the kind of gradual, reinforcing, selective change that is evolution, relevant to the spread of Bantu languages at all? We would argue that it is. Selective forces were some of the prime determinants of the shifting patterns of language, food production, and technology that existed in the Iron Age. Environmental selective forces, for example, constrained much of the movements of peoples and technologies and defined the conditions of interaction that made linguistic borrowing advantageous or not. Much of the success of a Bantu-speaking group over the peoples they encountered, for example, may have depended on successful relationships with autochthonous people, either Bantu or not, for the exchange of technology, knowledge, ritual authority, or foodstuffs. But in each case, a different strategy may have been required, given the differing environmental and cultural context of each case. Many Bantu languages died out or were replaced by non-Bantu languages (Vansina 1995: 192). In other words, it was not that "the Bantu" possessed some superior cultural arsenal. Rather, selection by consequences operated in different contexts. Advantageous forms of interaction and knowledge were self-reinforcing. Over evolutionary time, these forms of interaction and knowledge will include major transitions like the gradual spread of food production and metallurgy.

THE IMPORTANCE OF HISTORY IN ARCHAEOLOGY

The evolution/history debate was also waged throughout the twentieth century in the social sciences and history (Guilderhus 1996). However, rather than opposing evolution and history, archaeologists should accept the role of selection in the creation of historical pathways, along with chance and foresight. In other words, evolution is a corner on the triangle of history.

As this review has discussed, history is both the past itself, the configurational change through time, and our narrative explanations of the past and the present, whether written, spoken, performed, ritualized, or experienced. Ultimately, these two definitions of history are one and the same. "The so-called past life is nothing else but our understanding of that life" (Nitecki 1992: 15). When the actual writing of prehistory is concerned, all archaeologists have used the narrative form of explanation. The definition of characters, events, and plot is a question of chosing one's scale, and is in large part up to the narrator. That scales of analysis are chosen by the narrator means that the difference between historical and evolutionary narrative is a matter of degree rather than of kind. Are the topics that archaeologists write about, such as "The Origins of Agriculture" or "The Origins of Modern Humans" historical questions or evolutionary ones? As Pluciennik points out, they are both, depending on the narrator's choice of scale for the building blocks of the narrative such as events, processes, and characters.

Thankfully, the debate over historical particularism and neo-evolutionism has waned in recent years. Among archaeologists today, perhaps the greater conflict is not between particularism and evolutionism, but between those who use the present to infer the past (the adaptationist or evolutionary ecology school; Boone and Smith 1998) and those who use the record of the past to reconstruct it (Lyman and O'Brien 1998).

These debates aside, many recent developments in archaeology reflect an increasing concern with the interconnectivity of events and the importance of human agency. In the study of social complexity, for example, the evolutionary model has largely been replaced with concepts like heterarchy, which seek to describe how individual actions and concerns can influence shifting political, economic, and social relationships among interacting societies (Crumley 1995). In any case, archaeology would benefit if it came to see history not as the description of the particular and unique, the background noise behind the pattern in human actions, but as the interaction of selection, chance, and human foresight.

ACKNOWLEDGMENTS

We would like to thank Rahul Oka and John Terrell for their very helpful comments and for providing us with numerous helpful writings and references.

REFERENCES

Bell, J. A. (1994). *Reconstructing Prehistory: Scientific Method in Archaeology.* Philadelphia: Temple University Press.

Binford, L. (1968). Some comments on historical versus processual archaeology. *Southwestern Journal of Anthropology* 24: 267–275.

Binford, L. R. (1983). *In Pursuit of the Past: Decoding the Archaeological Record.* New York and London: Thames and Hudson.

Boone, J. L., and E. A. Smith. (1998). Is it evolution yet? A critique of evolutionary archaeology. *Current Anthropology* 39: S141–S173.

Carr, E. H. (1961). *What Is History?* New York: Vintage Books.

Collingwood, R. G. (1956). *The Idea of History.* New York: Oxford University Press.

Crumley, C. (1995). Heterarchy and the analysis of complex societies. In R. Ehrenreich, Carole Crumley, and J. E. Levy (eds.), *Heterarchy and the Analysis of Complex Societies.* Archeological Papers of the American Anthropological Association No. 6. Washington, DC. American Anthropological Association, pp. 1–5.

Dewey, J. (1916). *Democracy and Education: An Introduction to the Philosophy of Education.* New York: Macmillan.

Dunnell, R. C. (1996). Evolutionary theory and archaeology. In M. J. O'Brien (ed.), *Evolutionary Archaeology: Theory and Application.* Salt Lake City: University of Utah Press, pp. 30–67.

Fogel, W., and G. R. Elton. (1983). *Which Road to the Past? Two Views of History.* New Haven, CT: Yale University Press.

Gibbon, G. (1989). *Explanation in Archaeology.* Oxford: Basil Blackwell.

Gleick, J. (1987). *Chaos: Making a New Science.* New York: Viking.

Gould, S. J. (1989). *Wonderful Life: The Burgess Shale and the Nature of History.* New York: Norton.

Gould, S. J., and R. Lewontin. (1979). The spandrels of San Marco and the Panglossian paradigm: A critique of the adaptationist programme. *Proceedings of the Royal Society of London B* 205: 581–598.

Guilderhus, M. T. (1996). *History and Historians: A Historiographical Introduction.* Englewood Cliffs, NJ: Prentice Hall.

Harris, M. (1968). *The Rise of Anthropological Theory.* New York: Harper.

Hempel, C. (1965) [1942]. The function of general laws in history. In C. Hempel (ed.), *Aspects of Scientific Explanation.* New York: The Free Press, pp. 231–244.

Hill, M. F. (1949). *Permanent Way: The Story of the Kenya and Uganda Railway.* Nairobi: East African Literature Bureau.

Huffman, T. (1982). Archaeology and ethnohistory of the African Iron Age. *Annual Reviews in Anthropology* 11: 133–150.

Kelley, J., and M. P. Hanen. (1988). *Archaeology and the Methodology of Science.* Albuquerque: University of New Mexico Press.

Lyman, R. L., and M. J. O'Brien. (1998). The goals of evolutionary archaeology: History and explanation. *Current Anthropology* 39: 615–652.

Mapunda, B. (2002). Fipa iron technologies and their implied social history. In C. M. Kusimba and S. B. Kusimba (eds.), *New Approaches in East African Archaeology.* Philadelphia: University of Pennsylvania Museum Press, in press.

Newbury, M. (1997). Historiography. In J. Middleton (ed.), *Encyclopedia of Africa South of the Sahara.* New York: Charles Scribner's Sons, pp. 299–305.

Nitecki, M. (1992). History: La grande illusion. In M. Nitecki and D. Nitecki (eds.), *History and Evolution.* Albany: State University of New York Press, pp. 19–53.

Nitecki, M., and D. Nitecki. (1992). *History and Evolution.* Albany: State University of New York Press.

Oliver, R., and B. Fagan. (1975). *Africa in the Iron Age, c. 500 BC to AD 1400.* Cambridge: Cambridge University Press.

Phillipson, D. W. (1977). The spread of the Bantu language. *Scientific American* 236: 106–114.

Phillipson, D. W. (1993). *African Archaeology.* Cambridge: Cambridge University Press.

Plog, F. (1974). *The Study of Prehistoric Change.* New York: Academic Press.

Pluciennik, M. (1999). Archaeological narratives and other ways of telling. *Current Anthropology* 40: 653–678.

Polkinghorne, D. (1983). *Methodology for the Human Sciences.* Albany: State University of New York Press.

Popper, K. (1966). *The Poverty of Historicism.* New York: Harper Torchbooks.

Relethford, J. (1995). Genetics and modern human origins. *Evolutionary Anthropology.* 4: 53–63

Richards, R. (1992). The structure of narrative explanation in history and biology. In M. Nitecki and D. Nitecki (eds.), *History and Evolution.* Albany: State University of New York Press, pp. 8–15.

Schoenbrun, D. (1993). We are what we eat: Ancient agriculture between the Great Lakes. *Journal of African History* 24: 1–31.

Simpson, G. C. (1963). Historical science. In C. C. Albritton, Jr. (ed.), *The Fabric of Geology.* Stanford, CA: Freeman Cooper, pp. 24–48.

Skinner, B. F. (1981). Selection by consequences. *Science* 213: 501–504.

Spaulding, A. C. (1968). Explanation in archaeology. In S. L. Binford and L. R. Binford (eds.), *New Perspectives in Archaeology.* Chicago: Aldine, pp. 33–39.

Sutton, J. (1990). *A Thousand Years of East Africa.* Nairobi: British Institute in East Africa.

Terrell, J. (1986). Causal pathways and causal processes: Studying the evolutionary prehistory of human diversity in language, customs, and biology. *Journal of Anthropological Archaeology* 5: 187–198.

Travisano, M., J. Mongold, A. Bennett, and R. Lenski. (1995). Experimental tests of the roles of adaptation, chance, and history in evolution. *Science* 267: 87–90.

Vansina, J. (1990). *Paths in the Rainforest.* Madison: University of Wisconsin Press.

Vansina, J. (1994–1995). A slow revolution: Farming in sub-equatorial Africa. *Azania* 29–30: 15–26.

Vansina, J. (1995). New Linguistic Evidence and "The Bantu Expansion." *Journal of African History* 36: 173–195.

White, L. (1959). *The Evolution of Culture: The Development of Civilization to the Fall of Rome.* New York: McGraw-Hill.

Chapter 10

Individuals

Dean R. Snow

INTRODUCTION

Scientific archaeology depends on a suite of well-defined, fundamental concepts, as does anthropological science, the larger discipline in which it is embedded. Among the most fundamental of those concepts is that of the basic unit of selection in evolution. I argue here that the individual human being is that basic unit in cultural evolution, just as the individual organism is the basic unit in biological evolution. This is consistent with usage by scholars such as Boyd and Richerson (1985: 7). However, long-standing practice, recent debates, and inconsistent usages by other scholars all indicate that this is by no means an obvious choice.

An **individual** is defined here as a single human being, as contrasted with a social group, institution, or culture. The individual is thus also an indivisible entity that cannot be separated into parts without altering the character and significance of the parts. Larger entities such as social groups or cultures are aggregates of individuals. These are **populations**, as defined and used in this and other chapters in this volume. By implication, perceived changes in the populations can be described in terms of the addition, subtraction, or metamorphosis of the constituent individuals.

I argue that for individuals to form a population they must either derive from some reproductive process carried out by older individuals of like type, whether or not the older individuals are still alive and part of the population, or they must be capable of transforming themselves such that they can join a population of which they were not previously a part. Although there are exceptions in human cultural populations, it is usually the case that at least some individuals in the population are capable of reproducing others of their kind independent of outside mediation.

These may be regarded by some as narrow definitions of individuals and populations. Indeed a much more inclusive definition of population is possible, for one could define it as Lyman and O'Brien (1998: 643) do in one place, as any group of like individuals, such as Clovis points or shell-tempered pottery vessels. These are artifacts, which I define as any object whose design is culturally coded. Adopting this definition allows one to talk of sets of artifacts as populations even though the individual artifacts are not capable of reproduction or transformation without outside, specifically human, mediation. However, O'Brien, as well as several other theorists, does not consistently hold this position when pressed (Leonard and Jones 1987: 215; O'Brien et al. 1994), and I judge that they are correct when they imply that unmediated reproduction is required of any group defined as a population. Hector Neff (1992), following Hull (1980), takes a very different view, for he allows for sets of artifacts to be defined as populations of **interactors**, which in turn are usually defined as are individuals in a breeding population. This view is discussed in more detail below.

The fundamental process in biological evolution is that of natural selection. In biological evolution transformation is impossible except through mutation, and individuals must derive mainly from some reproductive process carried out by older individuals of like type. Individual organisms vary in form, and those that are more adaptive tend to reproduce more successfully, thus passing adaptive traits along genetically. Existing organisms die and thus leave the group we commonly call the "species." While alive they typically reproduce, and those that have adaptive traits tend to do so more successfully. As a consequence, the individuals that are added to the species through reproduction carry the genetic material of adaptive predecessors more often than that of less adaptive ones. The metamorphosis of a maladaptive individual into a more adaptive one is possible to a small degree, but it is limited by genetic constraints. In any case an individual cannot pass along acquired traits because biological reproduction is constrained by genetics.

An analogous but different process is constantly at work in cultural evolution. Maladaptive individuals are less successful in reproducing themselves in a cultural system, but this process is largely overridden by the capacity of individuals to undergo transformational cultural change. Thus in cultural evolution the more important fundamental process is that of **transformation**. Because of this distinction it is not possible to transfer many concepts from biological evolution into cultural evolution in unmodified form. Indeed, the effort to adapt the principles of biological evolution to archaeological theory has not previously produced many useful results. I judge that the main problem has been that some archaeologists have attempted to adopt principles of biological evolution without properly amending them to fit cultural phenomena. Specifically, many archaeologists have adopted the mechanisms of biological evolution but have shifted the locus of selection. A much more successful approach is to keep the locus of selection on the individual human organism but to revise the mechanisms to suit cultural evolution.

A problem with the word "selection" in either biological or cultural evolution is that an English verb like this one typically implies the existence of an agent. If selection is going on, then by implication some agent must be doing the selecting. Much has been written on this subject (see Graves-Brown 1996, and references therein). Rather than abandon the term "selection" because of this problem, I use it here with the stipulation that it is a mindless process, both in biological and cultural evolution. This stipulation is similar to that implied by any geomorphologist discussing the sorting of gravel according to grain size by river currents. Concern with implied agency is a logical detour that, while perhaps interesting, is not an impediment to productive research. Thus we can get on with it by stipulating that there is no agent of selection, either supernatural or natural. This is true even in the case of human cultural evolution, where it can be argued that foresight and intentionality play important roles. My position in this case is that human foresight and intentionality are limited in scale, both temporally and spatially, and at the scales that archaeological analysis typically investigates aggregate human behavior, they are largely irrelevant.

HISTORY OF THE CONCEPT

The concept of culture has been at the core of anthropology for decades, but it has not served the discipline well. We still have no definition of the term that is at once generally accepted and heuristic. Despite this fundamental problem and a poor track record, many anthropologists continue to assert that culture is our most basic unit of analysis. This is true whether they are speaking of specific cultures defined in one way or another as aggregates of individual humans, or of culture in a more general sense.

Nineteenth-century notions of culture led to the concept of **acculturation**. This was typically presented as a process through which specific native cultures lost traditional traits as they absorbed new ones from dominant and expanding European culture(s). This essentialist definition of culture promoted the view of all cultural change as loss. Ironically, native cultures themselves also promoted the same view through strategies designed to maintain solidarity and continuity through time. Small, politically subordinate ethnic minorities are often insistent about supposedly unchanging traditions even as native languages fall into disuse, economic systems evolve rapidly, and modern technology overtakes them. The image of an American Indian of obviously mixed genetic background wearing feathers while talking on a cell phone clearly requires a more sophisticated model of cultural evolution.

I have adopted Durham's ideational definition of culture in general and specific cultures in particular in order to facilitate the development of such a model. **Cultures** are "systems of symbolically encoded conceptual phenomena that are socially and historically transmitted within and between populations" (Durham 1991: 8–9). In other words, a culture is a program, software rather than hardware. Many earlier theorists have failed to distinguish clearly between culture and the social system, that is, between the program and its consequences. Durham's definition allows us to escape that problem as well as the fatal problems that are inherent in using "culture" as a unit of analysis. The units of interest are thus populations and the individual human beings that constitute them. Yet neither this nor any other definition of culture has gained wide acceptance.

If the most fundamental concept of a discipline lacks a generally accepted definition it should not be surprising that other related concepts are also defined and used in varieties of ways. Thus a general discussion of cultural ecology by Kottak (1999) does not cover cases of it being done well with a few contrasting cases of it being done poorly. Instead, Kottak discusses a range of alternative ecologies, each of them schools of thought. This is typical of most recent discussions of fields within cultural anthropology. One reason that there are so many alternative schools of thought in anthropology is that anthropologists tend to allow any intellectual construct to qualify as theory. In contrast, but like the other authors in this volume, I use **theory** to mean a body of principles that is designed to explain a related set of phenomena and that is capable of generating testable hypotheses. In practice a theory is a well-substantiated explanation of some aspect of the natural world. A **hypothesis**, in turn, is a statement that can be tested by experiment or observation as a means to improve theory. These deliberately narrow definitions exclude most literary theory, social theory, and folk definitions of theory in order to focus on what scientists regard as interesting and productive problems. I see nothing to be gained from squabbles between schools of thought so long as the propositions they promote defy empirical testing.

The arguments and case studies that follow below suggest that it is appropriate to assume that in cultural evolution it is the individual human being that is the unit of selection. Furthermore, we can stipulate that the process of selection in cultural evolution is often transformational at, but not above, the level of the individual. That means that the composition of the aggregate of humans that make up a population does not change only through the processes of differential reproductive success, as is the case in biological evolution. Instead, the cultural evolution of a group allows for individuals to change their behaviors by means of innovations and learning from other individuals. In this sense cultural evolution allows for the transformation of individuals so that they may often become more adaptive than they previously were.

Although transformation occurs at the level of the individual, selection appears to operate simultaneously at multiple levels (or scales). This is because corporate groups may grow as individuals are born or recruited into them, or be driven to extinction as individuals die or leave them. Nevertheless, it is always the individual that is the basic unit. Selection also operates at the level of the individual in biological evolution, but in that case the traits of the individual are locked in its genetic code, and the individual does not have the option of changing its genetic code or moving to the breeding population of another species. Analogues to these biological constraints do not exist in cultural evolution, where selection at the individual level can be and usually is transformational. People can and do change group memberships all the time.

Intentionality and agency come up once again in the context of transformation and selection in cultural evolution. It is useful to assume that no matter what an individual does, it seems to that individual to be a good idea at the time. It is also useful to remember that all individuals are agents, although the effects of their actions vary considerably in degree and duration. But the reach of these phenomena is not long.

It is generally true that the more experienced (i.e., older) or more intelligent an individual is the more able (s)he is to predict the longer-term consequences of any action. So people vary, sometimes predictably, in their abilities to anticipate consequences. An infant has very little predictive power but an adult has much more. Nevertheless, even the most sage individual will experience the effects of unintended consequences over the long term. When we consider the aggregate actions of many individuals over time spans that exceed the lifetimes of any of them, we come to understand why non-transformational selection tends to operate at a larger scale than does transformation in cultural evolution. Faced with selective pressures, an individual human being possessed of reasonable foresight can transform himself (or herself) by changing his behavior as a means to avoid death or (less dramatically) increase his or her adaptive advantage. But really bad ideas are still sometimes misperceived as good ones, and some people still get selected out of the population for committing what everyone else may well regard as blunders. Moreover, because we live as groups of interdependent individuals, the blunder of one might have grave consequences for one or many others. In some cases the agent of the blunder might not be among those who suffer for it or even among those who know about it. In the end, intentionality is not really an important consideration for most purposes, and to focus on it can cause investigators to miss the point.

Examples also suggest that, as in the evolutionary process of natural selection, notions of progress are inappropriate in **specific cultural evolu-**

tion. Societies evolve over time as a number of processes operate on individuals and groups at several scales. Whether that evolution is progressive or not is irrelevant to any discussion of those processes. Failure to recognize this fundamental principle doomed nineteenth-century theories of cultural evolution. White's (1949) revival of cultural evolution entailed a useful distinction between general and specific evolution so that some notion of progress could be implied by the tendency for increasing complexity in **general cultural evolution.** Even biological evolution has come to accommodate the general observation that modern life forms are more complex than their early single-cell ancestors (Mayr 1999).

THE MEANINGS OF THE CONCEPTS

The Elements of Darwinian Evolution

Both cultural evolution and biological evolution require the following elements:

1. units of transmission
2. sources of variation
3. mechanisms of transmission
4. processes of transformation
5. sources of isolation

Given that biological traits are variable, heritable, and unequally adaptive, and given sufficient time, biological evolution is inevitable. Darwin's discovery was simple and elegant even before the genetic code (the mechanism of trait transmission) and mutation (the process of biological trait transformation) were understood.

It is rational to presume that at least some of the elements of biological evolution might be used to understand cultural evolution. However, because the mechanisms of transmission differ, a major question has to focus on the basic unit of cultural transmission. Dawkins (1976, 1999) has proposed the **meme,** a cultural analogue to the gene. Harold Blum (1968) longer ago proposed "mnemotype" for the same purpose. One can use a thesaurus to find alternative terms like "idea," "premise," "concept," and so forth. The advantage of the term "meme" is that it does not give a special anthropological definition to a common English word like "idea." Its disadvantage is that it reifies what is at best a metaphor. No one currently proposes that "meme" can be defined in molecular terms in the way that "gene" can be.

Ideas or memes are subject to copy error and conscious modification. Barnett (1953), who was interested mainly in how the basic unit of transmission mutated, preferred "innovation." However, a problem with that term is that because of a trick of the English language it can be either a process or its product, an ambiguity that bothers some theorists. Lyman and O'Brien (1998: 617) argue that "novelty" is a better choice because the term avoids this problem and because it does not imply intent.

Much ink has been spilled over the issue of human intentionality. Variation is produced by both copy error and intentional innovation, but we are all also familiar with the phenomenon of unintended consequences. At the end of the day it may matter little whether we regard cultural evolution as proceeding because of human intelligence or in spite of it. Adaptive memes, which are popularly and perhaps more lucidly called "good ideas," arise through a variety of processes. The success of their future replication is not necessarily predicted by the number of people seeking to claim credit for them. Thus the role of intent is difficult to assess, often impossible to specify (especially by archaeologists), and ultimately irrelevant to most or all of the processes we are trying to understand. Human intentionality is not causative; rather, it is part of the phenomena that we seek to explain (Dunnell 1980: 61).

Whatever term is used, the meme or its synonym has to be the unit of information that is conveyed from one human brain to another. Various people have objected to the use of any such unit on grounds that it is either little more than a metaphor or that it imputes a false concreteness. I use "meme" because it is short and does not require me to impose a special usage on any more common English word. But I do so with the stipulation that unlike genes, memes mutate in the course of most, perhaps all, transmissions, and that we cannot often be sure how intentional the modification is. One need only observe a group of children playing "telephone" to confirm these features. Cultural evolution thus "focuses on differential social transmission rather than on differential reproduction" (Durham 1991: 192).

One can argue, as many have, that a unit as mutable as "meme" cannot be very useful in understanding the specific mechanisms of cultural evolution. However, recent research has shown that "gene" is similarly neither as easy to define nor as immutable as we once thought. Nevertheless, molecular biology shows no signs of giving up in despair (Pennisi 1999). The frequent mutation of meme due to innovation or copy error is what gives humanity the qualities that most cultural anthropologists celebrate. If that makes it impossible for us to develop a deterministic model of cultural evolution, I should expect them to be delighted.

Thus "meme" is a useful concept not despite its mutability but rather because of it. It follows that memes are not necessarily adaptive, or that a particular meme might be adaptive in one situation, maladaptive in another, and neutral in still another. Thus changing environmental contexts might cause formerly adaptive memes to become maladaptive, and vice versa. When one adds human misperception to the mix, the results might seem to be fatally chaotic. Occasionally, in human history they have been, of course, but the very rapid selection that occurs in cultural evolution can usually winnow just as rapidly. By definition, while every human action seems like a good idea to the actor at the time; replication and propagation of that action is another matter altogether.

The Larmarkian Character of Cultural Evolution

Jean-Baptiste de Monet, Chevalier de Lamarck should have been an anthropologist. In cultural evolution innovations are heritable as learned behaviors. Lamarck's attempts to argue that acquired biological traits could be passed on to offspring in a similar way subsequently earned him derision from biologists and historians of science. He was wrong about the mechanisms of transmission and the processes of transformation with regard to biological populations, but he would have been right about cultural ones.

Whether we view people as adaptive agents or unconscious subjects of transformation or selection depends on the nature and scale of what we are trying to explain. Intentional transformation according to anticipated consequences covers much of anthropological interest, and it is appropriately invoked in situations where unconscious transformation is insufficient to explain the phenomenon. Intention is thus not merely a commonsense folk category. Both conscious and unconscious transformation may be necessary to explain phenomena that cannot be explained by natural selection acting alone. But in no case should we lose sight of the individual humans, because they are the loci of the various processes, whether the specific process is selective or transformational.

Thus memes are "heritable," but not in a genetic sense, and they mutate persistently. An important point is that definition of the precise unit of transmission ("meme" or whatever) is not necessary to the development of an effective model. Just as Darwin succeeded even though he was unable to specify a precise mechanism prior to the discovery of genes, we can understand cultural evolution even in the absence of a well-understood transmission mechanism.

Transformation versus Selection

Biological evolution depends on variation within breeding population, heritability of traits, and differential survival of those traits. Natural selection focuses on the individual organism, for that is the unit of selection for adaptive traits and against maladaptive ones. Because mutation is rare, heritability is usually unambiguous.

Attempts to adopt this set of principles directly into cultural evolution have not been successful and have even led to humorously preposterous propositions. For example, there has been much recent discussion of the adoption of snowmobiles by Cree hunters. Snowmobiles are artifacts, admittedly very complex ones. If some Cree hunters are advantaged by having snowmobiles they will out-compete those Cree hunters lacking them. But we need not wait for generations of natural selection to select for hunters with snowmobiles who pass the trait on to their offspring. Individuals without snowmobiles can and will acquire them by various other means, thus transforming themselves. The population becomes transformed as a consequence of this process of individual transformation, which is much faster than the process of natural selection.

Furthermore, it is useful to think of Cree hunters as forming two social groups, those with snowmobiles and those without them. A hunter lacking a snowmobile transforms himself by acquiring one, thus moving from one group to the other. The process is a simple one in which individuals transform themselves by joining or leaving groups of various types, which are defined at various scales. Groups may be nearly permanent or very ephemeral; membership may be mandatory or optional for individuals. Individuals may be forcibly recruited or just as forcibly expelled, but whether the case involves buying a snowmobile, joining the army, or boarding an airplane the process is the same, and it is not at all like the process of natural selection.

IMPORTANCE

The Archaeological Agenda

Archaeology is the study of past human societies through their physical remains. Much that is invisible in the archaeological record we must infer from the scanty remains we have available for study. For archaeologists to succeed in this task they must also have a coherent body of theory that is as robust as biological evolutionary theory is for human paleontologists. The key concepts outlined in this volume enable us to explain change over time. Consequently, one of those concepts must identify the locus of change. In other words, patterns of cultural change we are able to discern and changes in those patterns that take place over time must be the cumulative consequences of fundamental transformations at the level of individuals.

It is possible to focus on various alternative loci of transformation. It is even possible to argue that there is more than one locus operating simultaneously in cultural evolution. However, I argue here that it is logical, convenient, and scientifically sufficient to focus on the individual human being as the locus of transformation.

In cultural evolution it is the individual human that is the unit of selection, but the process of selection is transformational at, but not above, that level. Culture would not exist if transmitted solutions were not the norm. Artifacts are a step removed from the processes of cultural evolution, proxies really. That is why archaeological systematics are so important. That is why archaeology requires units that can both monitor cultural continuity over time and monitor functional variations in artifacts.

In cultural evolution selection appears to operate simultaneously at multiple levels (or scales), in the sense that corporate groups may grow as individuals are born or recruited into them, or be driven to extinction as individuals die or leave them. That is why patterns can change so rapidly. Nomadic buffalo-hunter societies no longer exist on the Great Plains. The pressures that led to their extinction involved both selection and transformation of individuals, with transformation dominating. These societies are extinct even though the genes of the individuals that comprised them survive in transformed descendant societies of living people.

Closely tied to this is the observation that individual human beings typically belong to multiple social populations, some of them subsets of others. Individuals are situationally active or inactive in these alternative social populations. Because adaptive pressures operate simultaneously at multiple levels, it is possible for one social population to disappear while another grows, even though the two were earlier overlapping sets. Thus, style can be selectively neutral at one level or at one time, but not so at another level or time. This makes sense when it is remembered that the artifact styles observed by archaeologists reflect social groups in flux. By **groups** I mean social groupings of vastly different sizes and durations, everything from global organized religions to the express checkout line at the supermarket.

While it is important to bear in mind that the individual is the locus of transformation in cultural evolution, it is not necessary for the archaeologist to be able to study individuals empirically. By analogy, biologists often study species as sets of anonymous individuals rather than the individuals themselves. In these cases it is sufficient to know that the observed patterns have been produced by selective forces acting on individuals in the case of biological evolution, or by transformational forces acting on individuals in the case of cultural evolution. Most archaeologists must deal with the latter processes. Only a relative few work at scales or time depths that require them to deal with both kinds of evolution simultaneously.

Historical contingencies are important because there are often two or more neutral or equally adaptive solutions to selective pressures. This is true in biology as well. It seems likely to me that bluebirds are blue and cardinals are red as a result of some unique set of historic contingencies rather than because those specific colors were more adaptive than some others. But the role of historical contingencies and drift has to be much greater in cultural evolution. Indeed, much of the variation that has been traditionally interesting to archaeologists lies in the realm of neutral traits. Drift occurs rapidly in things such as ceramic decoration, allowing archaeologists to use patterns of non-adaptive change over time to discover sequences and carry out relative dating. While Boyd and Richerson (1985) might argue that these kinds of historically contingent features are less interesting than those that are selected for, it remains true that much of the variation archaeologists study is historically contingent.

Historical contingencies also deserve attention because they can condition optimization. In other words, archaeologists need history and an understanding of cultural trajectories if we are to fully understand a phenomenon like the extinction of the Norse in Greenland, which occurred even as their Inuit neighbors were thriving in the same environment. Traits that were initially neutral (or nearly so) became fatally maladaptive to the Norse when the environment changed. Their stubborn adherence to maladaptive norms doomed them, tragic proof that intentionality is sometimes relevant to our study.

The Nature of Ethnogenesis

If processes of cultural evolution operate at many levels simultaneously, then many cases support the view that cladistic models are largely inappropriate for the description of specific cultural evolution. Cladistic models are appropriate for a large array of biological and linguistic processes, and this circumstance has contributed to their popularity in anthropology generally. Once a breeding population has split into two breeding populations and enough time has passed for them to be biologically unable to interbreed, their merger becomes impossible. This circumstance enables biologists to represent the proliferation of species over time as a branching (dendritic or cladistic) process, one often illustrated by graphic trees. The model also works for the evolution of languages, which usually diverge and only rarely merge over time.

But a cladistic model rarely works for the illustration of evolving cultures, or even for evolving classes of artifacts. Moore (1994) concludes that rhizotic models of ethnogenesis are, generally speaking, more appropriate in the domain of cultural anthropology. Such models derive cultural forms from multiple root sources. Moore's conclusion extends to the domain of archaeology as well. His rhizotic models allow for human social groups to both merge and diverge rapidly and at a wide range of scales, as individuals form and dissolve social bonds.

Co-Evolution

There are valid theories for the genetic evolution of social behavior, but it is useful to separate culture, as I have defined it, from human biology. Durham has attempted to clarify cultural evolution and biological evolution as two sets of theory, and to bridge the gap between them with his principles of co-evolution. Both have the system requirements for evolution. Durham defines "reference group" as something as big as a society or as small as a nuclear family (Durham 1991: 427). It can cross-cut other group definitions as in the case of organized religion, or be as confining as caste. It is nowhere near as limited (or as limiting) as breeding population. Consequently, cultural transmission cannot obey the equivalent of the Hardy-Weinberg law governing genetic transmission. "It is people, not 'nature,' who do most of the selecting in cultural evolution, and it is communication, not reproduction, that is the principle mechanism of transmission" (Durham 1991: 458).

CONTEMPORARY USES

For an evolutionary view of human culture to be productive the archaeologist must focus on human populations and their subsets. Thus, an assemblage is the collection of artifacts once used by a group that we might wish to define as a community. The artifacts are proxies for the group that is of interest. Similarly, we are interested in the population of individuals who once used a particular artifact type, not that type as a population in and of itself.

It is useful to distinguish here between "replicators" and "interactors." In biological evolution the **replicators** are genes and the **interactors** are individuals in a breeding population. In cultural evolution the replicators are memes (or any of that term's synonyms) and the interactors are individuals in a social population. The last might be the same as a breeding population or it might be some subset of it. In any case, the individual interactor is always the individual organism; in the case of Homo sapiens it is the individual human being. Because humans evolve both biologically and culturally, we must consider both genes and memes as replicators. Cultural evolution tends to dominate most archaeological analyses because they tend to focus on relatively short time scales in which biological evolution can have little expression.

Many archaeological problems that are defined at large scale are basically demographic ones. The ebb and flow of archaeological cultures, the evolution of regional settlement systems, and the success or failure of adaptations are all subjects that if not entirely demographic in character, at least have important demographic dimensions.

If one considers together the concept of the individual as the unit of transformation and the concept of intentionality, it is easy to understand why there has been much recent interest in the significance of agency. However, in my judgment the issue of agency has been overblown, especially in the largely anonymous domain of archaeology. If intentionality has only limited effects, as I judge it does, then the ascription of agency, whether it is conceived as individual or collective, is also of only very limited utility.

ALTERNATIVE CONCEPTS

Culture as the Unit of Selection or Transformation

I have adopted an ideational definition of culture, as discussed above. In other words, a culture is a program; software rather than hardware. This definition allows us to escape the fatal problems that are inherent in using "culture" as a unit of analysis. The units of interest are populations and the individual human beings that constitute them. Yet the older culture concept is so strong that even those who argue that it is not a useful unit of analysis can lapse into using it as if it were. Durham adopts a view of culture as program, along with the view that the individual is the proper unit of analysis. But even he contradicts himself at least twice by presenting arguments that implicitly assume that the cultural system is the unit of transformation (Durham 1991: 184, 461). This appears in a work that otherwise assigns that function to the individual human being. The example is important because it illustrates the degree to which the old essentialist definition of culture can persist in careful works that otherwise eschew it. It should be clear from the repeated failures of attempts to use culture as a unit of selection that faced with a choice, Goldilocks would find it too big to serve.

The Artifact Assemblage as the Unit of Selection or Transformation

Lyman and O'Brien (1998: 616) have asserted that "in evolutionary archaeology, the population is artifacts, which are viewed as phenotypic features." They follow Teltser (1995: 53) in arguing further that "change [over time] is conceived in terms of frequency changes in analytically discrete variants rather than the transformation of a variant." This position recognizes that artifacts do not reproduce. Individual artifacts are also not conceived as the units of transformation. By their reasoning, populations of artifacts must be the units of transformation, also referred to as the "interactors." They also assert that paleobiologists assume that fossils are interactors, and that this usage lends support to their position (Lyman and O'Brien 1998: 644).

The problem with this approach is that, according to it, the population is by definition what the archaeologist or paleobiologist happen to have at hand, which are inevitably incomplete and probably biased samples of material remains. In fact, paleobiologists assume that living populations of animals were the interactors and that fossils are merely their surviving remains. That the approach of assuming fossils to be interactors has not been adopted by paleontologists is sufficient evidence that it is not a productive one for them. It is similarly difficult to see how such an approach can be used productively in archaeology. Artifacts are in one sense an extension of the human phenotype and their frequencies are mediated by the human cultural program. This means that the basic unit of transformation must be the individual human, not sets of artifacts used and deposited by sets of humans.

The Artifact as the Unit of Selection or Transformation

Hector Neff (1992) has raised the possibility that individual organisms are not the only interactors (basic units of selection or transformation). He argues that artifacts can be interactors and aggregates of artifacts can be populations. Some critics have simply dismissed the idea out of hand, arguing that it is merely an idea that occurs to archaeologists because artifacts are what they happen to have in abundance. However, given that memes are both ethereal and ephemeral, the proposal is not necessarily so absurd as to justify facile dismissal.

An attraction of allowing for the possibility that artifacts can be treated as interactors is that it permits one to account for change in artifacts over brief periods of time when there is little change in the population of individual (human) organisms making and using the artifacts. However, while it may be correct to say that in a case of this kind there is no change in the biological composition of the human population, to say that there is no change in its cultural composition would be false. The individuals have changed through transformation, by acquiring some new artifacts, dropping some others, or both. The artifacts are defined here as attributes of the individuals. Thus the population has changed, but through cultural evolution only. The change might be selected for, or it might be a simple matter of drift.

We do not have complete human organisms in the archaeological record; we have only artifacts and (sometimes) bones. Neff argues we can and do mostly sample artifacts, but his argument is analogous to that of a paleoanthropologist who proposes that we assume that fossil bones are the populations of interest and that individual bones are the basic units of selection. Such an approach might have some value if we are interested only in bones, just as Neff's proposal might have some value if we are interested only in artifacts. This, in turn, explains why many archaeologists prefer "trait" to "meme." Traits are the physical manifestations they can observe on artifacts, while memes are merely invisible ideas that are no more clearly understood today than genes were to Charles Darwin. However, for most archaeologists an understanding of artifacts remains a means to other ends. The populations of interest for most of us are the past populations of individual humans that made the artifacts, not the populations of artifacts themselves. For this reason alone Goldilocks would find artifacts too small to serve.

Neff's example of the Cree adoption of snowmobiles explicitly refers to snowmobiles as traits, and it is hard to think of them in any other way. But I judge that we gain nothing from thinking about a population of reproducing snowmobiles, complete with differential heritability of specific traits. The problem is that the characteristics of, reproduction of, and the very existence of artifacts are all mediated by human beings, so they must be traits of human beings, not populations in their own right. That is why artifacts should not be considered as evolutionary interactors and why collections of artifacts should not be considered as populations.

Neff also cites the paradoxical example of ceramic change that occurs over time, even if the population of humans making and using the ceramics stays constant. This, he proposes, is evidence that the ceramics must be considered a population in and of itself. But the population is not truly constant. Individuals age and change through the processes of individual transformation described above. When it is remembered that individual humans are basic units of transformation, then the paradox disappears. Pots are just traits after all.

The Nature of Phenotype

Neither is it particularly useful to think too seriously of snowmobiles or other artifacts as components of the human phenotype. I judge that while the notion that artifacts and behavior are part of human phenotypes is a striking image, it has little or no heuristic value. Slavish adherence to the mechanisms of biological evolution is, in my judgment, a principal reason for the failings of evolutionary archaeology up to now. So I cannot agree with Leonard and Jones (1987) that artifacts are components of the human phenotype. They could be so only if the behaviors that produce them were genetically coded as specifically as other phenotypic traits are. So the proposition is not only debatable, it is indefensible.

CASE STUDIES

Cheyenne Ethnohistory

Moore's argument for a rhizotic model of ethnogenesis is based on his research into Cheyenne ethnohistory. The modern Cheyenne are among those descendant groups of Plains Indian nomads that no longer exist. The members of Cheyenne bands of two centuries ago were recruited or coerced into sedentary reservation societies and nomadism disappeared.

Earlier evolutionary changes were at least as dramatic. In the seventeenth century most of the biological ancestors of the Cheyenne were wild-rice gatherers living in northern Minnesota. In the eighteenth century they were maize farmers living in villages in southern Minnesota and eastern North

Dakota. In the nineteenth century they were nomadic bison hunters. Through three centuries of rapid change some bands even joined various Lakota and Dakota bands. There was considerable intermarriage with these and other nations, and a considerable amount of language switching by individuals. The sequence would be impossible to track by archaeological means alone. Indeed, some archaeologists would minimize the importance or representativeness of the case because of its difficulty. But cases like this one are much more common than we might prefer to believe.

The Cheyenne have been very different societies in each of four consecutive centuries. Despite the traditional continuities that both the Cheyenne and anthropologists might like to insist prevailed throughout that time, it is clear that this was a case of very rapid cultural evolution that was facilitated by a multitude of transformations at the individual level (Moore 1987, 1996).

Iroquoian Ethnohistory and Archaeology

Although they did not begin in Iroquoia until 1634, smallpox and other epidemics resulted in the same sudden and dramatic population declines observed in other cases of virgin soil epidemics. Over 60% of the Mohawk population died in a few months in A.D. 1634, and population was only 23% of its 1634 size by 1646.

The Mohawks and other Iroquois nations survived in the long term by successfully recruiting refugees and war captives through the period of population decline. There is little or no evidence that Mohawk fertility increased significantly during the general decline. For a variety of reasons, the Mohawks did not opt to increase fertility, which was the remedy for increased mortality adopted earlier by most European populations.

Other kinds of recruitment also went on simultaneously at several scales. Before European contact, the Mohawks had successfully recruited the other four Iroquois nations into a confederacy. Later, French Jesuit missionaries recruited individuals, families, and whole nations to Catholicism. Still later, English politicians recruited individuals and groups as allies. Although intentionality was important and outcomes were predictable at and just above the level of the individual, such choices often had unpredicted and unintended consequences for the Iroquois at larger geographic and temporal scales (Snow 1996).

Hurons were successfully recruited by Jesuits, but were soon either exterminated, dispersed, or forcibly recruited by the Iroquois nations. Some refugee Hurons and Petuns fled westward, where they reformed as the Wyandots. Similar processes prevailed elsewhere in the Eastern Woodlands from the seventeenth to the nineteenth centuries. Refugee bands merged in multiethnic villages in many places. Smaller refugee or disaffected groups joined larger ones and lost their separate identities. The Delawares actually dissolved into a number of scattered bands then reformed in Ohio, along with a large minority of recruits from other nations. Most, if not all, modern reservation communities now have nominal identities that mask the multiple ethnic identities of their ancestors. Although the speed and pervasiveness of these processes may have been much greater from the seventeenth century on, it would be ingenuous to presume that they were rare prior to European contact.

Scottish Origins

There were no significant numbers of Scots in Scotland until around A.D. 400. One of the petty kingdoms of Early Christian Ireland (A.D. 400–1177) was Dál Riata, which occupied a corner of County Antrim at the northeasternmost part of the island. Sometime around A.D. 400, people from Dál Riata began to settle across the Irish Sea along the Scottish coast in County Argyll. The migrants from Irish Dál Riata were known to the Romans as "Scotti" and they would eventually give their Gaelic language and their name to all of what is now known as Scotland (Mallory 1992; McCormick 1995).

So far as we know, the only people already living in Scotland in A.D. 400 were the Picts, first mentioned by Roman writers in A.D. 297. This was in connection with an attack along Hadrian's Wall, which was breached at least three times in less than two centuries. On this occasion the Picts had the help of Irish (Scotti) allies, so connections across the Irish Sea must have already been good. But the Picts spoke a Celtic language related much more closely to British than to the Celtic language(s) of Ireland.

Settlers from Irish Dál Riata apparently established themselves along the west coast without much opposition. The Roman legions pulled out of Britain in A.D. 407, and by A.D. 490 the population of Scotti was large enough that the head of the little kingdom moved the family seat across from Ireland. The Scotti alternately cooperated with and fought with the native Picts for the next few centuries until the two were unified into a single kingdom of Picts and Scots in A.D. 844. After that the Pictish language disappeared, along with the symbol stones and other archaeological traits that had distinguished the Picts from the Scotti.

In this case small numbers of pioneering men and their families probably moved first, followed by others in chain migration. The very first moves might have been nothing more than raids. There was probably some return migration, but a net positive flow from Ireland to Scotland over a period of decades or a couple of centuries. Initial settlements were probably unopposed in this thinly populated part of northern Britain. Intermarriage with Picts followed and although we cannot yet specify the process precisely, the Gaelic language of the immigrants proved to be dominant in the long run.

The Scots and the Picts are generally thought to have practiced very similar economies, but the Scots may have had an adaptive advantage in their dairying economy. There were also differences in social organization that provided political advantage to men who could claim Scottish descent through their fathers and Pictish descent through their mothers. This advantaged Scottish ethnicity in the aggregate.

The Scots also did what most migrants have usually done throughout human history. They were reinventing themselves as part of the process of expansion. The difficulty, of course, is tracking the movements of people who are changing, sometimes dramatically, at the same time as they are moving. Fortunately, in this case the Christianity of the expanding Scots left a clear archaeological signature.

Around the end of the eighth century still another new threat arrived that changed everything. The Vikings began raiding Ireland in A.D. 795. For the next 50 years the Vikings raided, established trading colonies, and began settling portions of both Ireland and Scotland. The Norse threat may have actually accelerated the merger of Scots and Picts.

FUTURE IMPORTANCE

All of the case studies show that the individual person is the basic unit of transformation in any human society. Societies and their subsets recruit new members by reproducing biologically, but they also do so by other means, such as intermarriage, adoption, enslavement, and so on. Dominant societies may expand their numbers and their territories rapidly, particularly if their economic and political dominance over their neighbors is relatively great. Expanding societies, unlike expanding species, succeed by *both* displacing (sometimes annihilating) and absorbing individuals belonging to the subordinate societies they contact.

When individuals make major realignments in their multiple group memberships they alter the character of not only themselves but also of the collective characters of the groups they are leaving, joining, creating, or dissolving. Physical movement typically accompanies these changes, whether it is only the movement of a single woman from one household to another when she marries, or the collective movement of a horde of Mongols from Asia to central Europe. The sum of changes and movements made by a large group of people can often appear to the observer as a major migration accompanied by radical cultural reinvention. Strong founder effects require very small populations in biological evolution, but much larger populations can exhibit founder effects in cultural evolution. For example, the Puritans of Massachusetts were mutually recruited from a much larger English population in the seventeenth century. While archaeologists can attest that they were clearly derived from a parent population in northern and eastern England, they were clearly a self-selected subset of it, and once in New England they expressed a culture that was new and different.

Migrating groups are often minorities compared to the populations against which or into which they are expanding. The key to their expansion is their dominance, which might be economic, political, organizational, or even religious. There are cases in which such groups expand at the expense of others but do so through mechanisms of recruitment that make their languages subordinate. In these cases dominant societies come to speak the languages of the societies they dominate (Barth 1969). Much depends on the size of the migration, the distance involved, the nature of intermarriage, literacy, and so on. I leave all the contrary cases aside and simply point out that the Scottish case is a fairly standard one in which an economically dominant group proved to also be socially, politically, and linguistically dominant.

Migrations into previously unoccupied territory can also be studied archaeologically. While these might appear to be simpler cases, the recent literature identifies more than a few false preconceptions about the nature of cultural evolution. People adapt to new environments and transform themselves as they move. That is why it is inappropriate to discuss Polynesian origins as if the Polynesians existed as a culture prior to their settlement of the Polynesian islands. The colonization of islands in the central Pacific probably originated by way of Vanuatu, but it involved so much transformation on the part of the self-selected founders that it is inappropriate to speak of them as Polynesians before that time.

This, of course, contradicts both popular native rhetoric and some traditional anthropological views, both of which prefer to think of cultures as well-bounded and durable packages. This traditional essentialist view of culture is politically astute because it facilitates things such as land and repatriation claims. But it does so at the cost of denying a host of fairly obvious empirical observations. No ethnic group in existence today is identical with one having the same name two centuries ago, if only because birth and death have completely changed the cast of characters. In most cases transformations over that much time have also made pervasive changes in the expression of the traditional culture.

What the Scottish, Cheyenne, and Polynesian cases and others like them tell archaeologists is that change has been more constant and that migrations both large and small have been much more common in human history than many modern archaeologists have been willing to admit (much less assume). Adoption of cultural evolutionary theory that embraces rather than denies these features can only advance archaeological research.

REFERENCES

Barnett, H. G. (1953). *Innovation: The Basis of Cultural Change*. New York: McGraw-Hill.

Barth, F. (1969). Pathan identity and its maintenance. In F. Barth (ed.), *Ethnic Groups and Boundaries*. Prospect Heights, IL: Waveland Press, pp. 117–134.

Blum, H. F. (1968). *Time's Arrow and Evolution*. Princeton, NJ: Princeton University Press.

Boyd, R., and P. J. Richerson. (1985). *Culture and the Evolutionary Process*. Chicago: University of Chicago Press.

Dawkins, R. (1976). *The Selfish Gene*. New York: Oxford University Press.

Dawkins, R. (1999). *The Extended Phenotype: The Gene as the Unit of Selection*. New York: Oxford University Press.

Dunnell, R. C. (1980). Evolutionary theory and archaeology. In M. B. Schiffer (ed.), *Advances in Archaeological Method and Theory*, vol. 3. New York: Academic Press, pp. 38–100.

Durham, W. H. (1991). *Coevolution: Genes, Culture, and Human Diversity*. Stanford, CA: Stanford University Press.

Graves-Brown, P. (1996). In search of the watchmaker: Attribution of agency in natural and cultural selection. In H.D.G. Maschner (ed.), *Darwinian Archaeologies*. New York: Plenum, pp. 165–181.

Hull, D. L. (1980). Individuality and selection. *Annual Review of Ecology and Systematics* 11: 311–332.

Kottak, C. P. (1999). The new ecological anthropology. *American Anthropologist* 101: 23–25.

Leonard, R. D., and G. T. Jones. (1987). Elements of an inclusive evolutionary model for archaeology. *Journal of Anthropological Archaeology* 6: 199–219.

Lyman, R. L., and M. J. O'Brien. (1998). The goals of evolutionary archaeology. *Current Anthropology* 39: 615–652.

Mallory, J. P. (1992). Migration and language change. In E. Straume and E. Skar (eds.), *Peregrinatio Gothica III, Fredrikstad, Norway, 1991*, Universitetets Oldsaksamlings Skrifter, Ny rekke, Nr. 14. Oslo, pp. 145–153.

Mayr, E. (1999). Understanding evolution. *Trends in Ecological Evolution* 14: 372–373.

McCormick, F. (1995). Cows, ringforts and the origins of early Christian Ireland. *Emania* 13: 33–36.

Moore, J. H. (1987). *The Cheyenne Nation: A Social and Demographic History*. Lincoln: University of Nebraska Press.

Moore, J. H. (1994). Putting anthropology back together again: The ethnogenetic critique of cladistic theory. *American Anthropologist* 96: 925–948.

Moore, J. H. (1996). *The Cheyenne*. The Peoples of America. Cambridge: Blackwell Publishers.

Neff, H. (1992). Ceramics and evolution. In M. B Shiffer (ed.), *Archaeological Method and Theory*, vol. 4. Tucson: University of Arizona Press, pp. 141–193.

O'Brien, M. J., T. D. Holland, R. J. Hoard, and G. L. Fox. (1994). Evolutionary implications of design and performance characteristics of prehistoric pottery. *Journal of Archaeological Theory and Method* 1: 259–304.

Pennisi, E. (1999). Gaining new insight into the molecular basis of evolution. *Science* 285(5427): 654–655.

Snow, D. R. (1996). Mohawk demography and the effects of exogenous epidemics on American Indian populations. *Journal of Anthropological Archaeology* 15: 160–182.

Teltser, P. A. (1995). Culture history, evolutionary theory, and frequency seriation. In P. A. Teltser (ed.), *Evolutionary Archaeology: Methodological Issues*. Tucson: University of Arizona Press, pp. 51–68.

White, L. (1949). *The Science of Culture: A Study of Man and Civilization*. New York: Farrar, Straus.

Chapter 11

Learning

Stephen J. Shennan

INTRODUCTION

Learning is a concept with which everyone is familiar. A standard psychological definition describes it as referring to "relatively permanent but modifiable changes in an individual that can be detected in its behaviour and that are caused by specific experiences" (Russon 1997: 176). In contrast to what is often the case, the technical definition corresponds quite closely to the everyday idea. For example, we readily recognize that not every sensory stimulus from the outside world produces an effect that could be described as learning; much is more or less immediately forgotten.

Within an evolutionary context, learning may be seen as a form of adaptation which enables individuals to respond flexibly and appropriately to the contingencies they encounter; it is a form of phenotypic modification characteristic of most animals. Within archaeology learning has received very little explicit attention until recently, even though assumptions about the subject have been implicit in most theoretical positions within the discipline, right from its very beginning. The culture-historical archaeologists who first attempted to create a space-time framework for their subject by identifying and describing cultural traditions and their distribution in time and space took learning largely for granted. They assumed that cultural traditions were passed on by learning from the older generation and it was this that provided the basis for regarding cultures as representing peoples. Interestingly, some authors at the time drew an analogy between the passing on of culture through the generations in this way and the passing on of genes in biological reproduction (Lyman et al. 1997).

The New Archaeology of the 1960s explicitly rejected the relevance of learned norms for the understanding of variation and change in the archaeological record. All that mattered was the role of cultural phenomena in the process of adaptation, so the important thing was to reconstruct the social and economic context in which a particular phenomenon made adaptive sense. People would learn what was necessary to respond appropriately.

However, since the 1970s learning as an issue has gradually made its way up on the archaeological agenda, as a result of the growing influence of evolutionary ideas within the subject. This influence has had an impact in several ways. First, it has been pointed out that adaptations cannot be understood simply by looking at the present. The cultural resources which people use in adaptation represent what has been handed down to them from previous generations, not some ideal toolkit for the present job. Therefore, to understand adaptation we also need to understand history, just as in biological evolution. Second, it has been shown that learning processes vary and those variations have a significant impact on their outcome, in terms of what people actually do and how cultures change. Learning processes cannot be ignored as a constant which can be left out of account. Third, evolutionary approaches see all phenomena from the point of view of costs and benefits, so variations in learning processes should be potentially explicable in terms of their costs and benefits in particular situations.

All these factors point toward a consideration of the role of learning in affecting the key evolutionary processes relevant to individuals during their lifetime: survival, reproductive success, and successful parenting. More important than any of these points, however, has been the proposal that cultural traditions can be seen as analogous to genetic lineages because the process of acquiring information handed down from previous generations is closely similar in the way it operates to the process of information transfer by genetic transmission, albeit in individuals' minds, rather than in the DNA of their reproductive cells. In particular, the learning process of imitation provides a basis for seeing cultural, like genetic, transmission as a kind of copying process. Within anthropology the most influential proponents of these ideas have been Cavalli-Sforza and Feldman (1981) and Boyd and Richerson (1985), all of whom have taken the analogy as a starting point for the modification and development of mathematical models derived from population genetics as a means of understanding cultural change. However, in the wider world, by far the best-known suggestion regarding the analogy between cultural and genetic transmission is Richard Dawkins' concept of the **meme** (1976, 1982: 109–112), "A unit of particulate inheritance, hypothesized as analogous to the particulate gene, and as naturally selected by virtue of its 'phenotypic' consequences on its own survival and replication in the cultural environment."

Obviously, the concept of social learning as the passing on of memes from one person to another by a process of imitation provides a very clear basis for seeing stability and change in cultural traditions as the outcome of a Darwinian process, but it raises two important questions. Is it satisfactory to see social learning as a process of memetic copying? If not, is a Darwinian approach to culture in terms of heredity, variation, and selection still a viable one that illuminates our understanding of cultural change in the archaeological record?

This chapter reviews current knowledge of learning processes in general and social learning in particular among humans and other animals. It goes on to argue that, despite the problematic nature of the "meme" idea, social learning provides the basis for maintaining that cultural traditions are passed on from one person to another through time, and are maintained and modified by Darwinian processes. This conclusion has significant implications for specific attempts to understand culture change, as the archaeological case studies described below demonstrate.

HISTORY

The Processes of Learning

If learning is to provide a means of responding appropriately to contingencies in ways conducive to fitness maximization, as the standard evolutionary view proposes, it requires the recognition of cause-and-effect relations, or the association between situations or events (Plotkin 1997: 195). Such **associative learning** occurs in many animal species. Two general forms are distinguished by psychologists. The first of these involves the recognition of links between events in the world over which the individual has no control but which nevertheless may have a significance for that individual. The best-known example of this is Pavlov's experiments with dogs, in which the sound of a metronome preceded feeding. From the regular repetition of the event the dog came to recognize the association and would salivate on hearing the metronome, which it had not done prior to the experiment. In effect, it came to "predict" the second event, feeding, on the basis of the first (Plotkin 1997: 195). This sort of associative learning is known as **classical conditioning**.

The other general form is known as **operant conditioning** or **trial-and-error learning**. What distinguishes this type of learning is that the association is between the behavior of the learner and some consequence of that behavior. The individual learns that an action on its part has a particular effect. The classic experiments here were by Skinner in the 1930s. Rats learned that pressing a lever resulted in the delivery of a food pellet. Learning could be demonstrated by the fact that a hungry rat, once it had learned the association, would go immediately to the lever, press it, and collect the food when it was placed in the experiment box (Plotkin 1997: 198).

Classical and operant conditioning involve animals learning from experiences with the world around them. Such **individual learning** has come to be distinguished from **social learning**, "learning that takes some input from other individuals [of the same species]" (Russon 1997: 176). In other words, social learning identifies, in broad terms, a way in which information is acquired, rather than a particular kind of information. Some psychologists argue that the only thing which differentiates social from individual learning is the source of the information: in social learning the sources are conspecifics but the mechanisms involved are the same processes of classical and operant conditioning by which other information about the world is acquired. Others argue that, for some species at least, additional mechanisms are involved. The one which has been most discussed, and which is most controversial, is **observational learning**, or **imitation**, "learning to do an act by seeing it done" (Russon 1997: 178). On this view, the difference between observational learning and operant conditioning or trial-and-error learning is that observational learning does not require reinforcement. Furthermore, social learning experiments have shown that humans abstract rules from episodes of observational learning, which they are capable of using appropriately, and that once the observational learning capacity has been developed it is impossible to prevent people from learning what they have seen (Boyd and Richerson 1985: 43).

However, it seems likely that the presence or absence of reinforcement varies from context to context. Experiments by Whiten (1998) in which chimpanzees were shown how to perform a complex motor task indicated that they imitated the procedures increasingly successfully after repeated cycles of demonstration and their own attempts. In other words, trial-and-error individual learning led to better imitation rather than to increasing deviations from what was being shown. Anyone who has tried to learn to ski by imitating the demonstrated movements of a ski instructor will empathize with the situation.

Furthermore, we cannot assume that individuals will always be willing to learn by imitation. Where this is not the case, sanctions may be employed to make sure that they do.

Regardless of the role of reinforcement, all are agreed that imitation is a very complex cognitive process because it involves the copying of an observed behavior, a process which requires the translation of information received by one means, visual or aural, into an output produced by another, a pattern of action, which matches the original. It has proved extremely difficult to demonstrate the existence of "real imitation" in non-human animals, because there is a great variety of mechanisms by which the behavior of one individual animal can come to resemble that of another without involving the complexity of imitation. On the contrary, most of these mechanisms are relatively simple in cognitive terms (Whiten and Ham 1992). The current view (e.g., Russon 1997) is that the great apes can imitate in the sense defined above but that monkeys cannot, and that imitative abilities expanded considerably in the course of human evolution (Boyd and Richerson 1996).

CONTEMPORARY USES

Costs and Benefits of Social Learning

In general, social learning is beneficial where individual learning is costly in terms of risk or time/energy expended and when those costs can be cut by social learning. This would appear to suggest that social learning will always be superior to individual learning as a source of adaptive information which can be acquired at little cost (Boyd and Richerson 1988: 30). The problem is that as social learners become more common, they are increasingly likely to have learned their behavior from another social learner who has also learned from a conspecific rather than by individual learning. If the environment changes over time or the population moves to a different area, then the behavior available to be learned socially may no longer be adaptive. Boyd and Richerson (1988) developed a model to explore the conditions under which social learning provides a better basis for learning about the environment than individual learning, and concluded that its effectiveness depended on two factors:

1. the accuracy of individual learning (or the closely related cost of improving this accuracy);
2. the chance that an individual's social models experienced the same environment that the individual experiences. (Boyd and Richerson 1988: 43)

In general, when individual learning is not all that accurate in leading to the adaptively correct decision, or obtaining the information to make an accurate decision is costly, and when the environment is not changing too quickly, then relying mainly on information from other conspecifics (whatever the mechanism involved) will be adaptively more successful than relying mainly on individual learning. Occasionally making use of individual learning when the evidence for making a particular decision is very clear is all that is required to keep the social learning system on track.

There is increasing evidence of the importance of social learning in a great variety of species and situations (see, for example, Box and Gibson 1999; Heyes and Galef 1996; and Zentall and Galef, 1988). Moreover, such work provides evidence not just of social learning but of the existence of learned traditions, based in most cases on mechanisms which are much simpler than true imitation.

Laland and Williams (1998) have carried out "transmission chain" experiments showing that learned traditions can persist over time in groups of guppies even when members of the shoal are replaced by others, and none of those who originally learned the behavior remain present. Galef (1988) has shown that naïve rats use olfactory signals to learn from others what they have recently eaten, and that they then bias their subsequent food selection in favor of the foods identified from their recently fed informants. Work on Indigo Buntings (Payne 1996) has shown that yearling males copy the song themes of older males in the vicinity, forming song traditions that are known to have lasted up to 30 years in a single area, even when there is a turnover of population; and that such traditions gradually change through the accumulation of new improvisations. Even bears, whose social organization does not lead to extensive interaction with other conspecifics, show evidence of learning and social transmission of behavior from mothers to cubs (Gilbert 1999). Finally, of course, we have the extensive evidence for social learning in the great apes, both in terms of observation of processes of social learning and the existence of local, learned traditions (e.g., Boesch and Tomasello 1998; Whiten et al. 1999); for example, the well-known Tai forest chimpanzee nut-cracking. At least some of these probably involve true imitation (Russon 1997).

The examples of socially learned traditions of behavior in different animal species also show that a variety of transmission routes exist for such traditions. In the case of the guppies and the rats we have examples of what has come to be known as **horizontal transmission**, in which information is passed between animals of the same age/generation. The bears and at least some of the primate socially learned traditions, such as nut-cracking, provide evidence of **vertical transmission**, the transfer of information from parents, usually the mother in the case of mammals, to offspring. Finally, in the case of the Indigo Buntings, we have a case of **oblique transmission**, in which information is passed to a younger individual from an older one, but the older one is not a parent. Young male Indigo Buntings move away from their natal area and learn their song from older males already occupying the area to which they move.

In conclusion, learning in general, and social learning in particular, is widespread in the animal world, presumably because the conditions in which the benefits outweigh the costs are also relatively widespread; that is to say, individual learning is not especially accurate, or it is costly to make it so, and evolutionary environments have had a degree of spatial and temporal variability. The mechanisms by which such traditions are maintained are very variable and cover a broad range of cognitive complexity. Horizontal, vertical, and oblique transmission of information by social learning are all found within the animal world.

The Role of Social Learning in Humans

Like other animals, humans make extensive use of trial-and-error learning, but by common consent cultural traditions passed on by social learning play a far greater role in human adaptations than they do in those of other species. That is to say, the adaptive change which learning involves is achieved by doing what others do, often without too much reflection or experimentation; in other words, by copying, or at least attempting to copy. Obviously, if everyone copied slavishly all the time then the process would simply lead to adaptive disaster; but, of course, the same would be true if the copying of genes were perfect. The lack of complete perfection is precisely why the system works.

In terms of the factors which emerged from Boyd and Richerson's model as giving an adaptive advantage to learning from others as opposed to learning for oneself, one of the most important in the human case concerns the accuracy of individual learning.

Humans are unique in the demands they make on parental investment in offspring, since even in traditional, small-scale societies children are not energetically independent of parents until at least adolescence and in some cases later (Kaplan 1996: 100). Kaplan (1996: 103) proposes that the reason for this difference between the life history pattern of humans and other primates lies in dietary differences, because primate diets are largely composed of foods that are relatively easily collected, while the most important food resources for foragers are nutrient-dense plant foods and hunted game, whose exploitation demands considerable knowledge. Acquiring such knowledge takes a long time: among the Hadza the tubers that provide the bulk of the calories are rarely acquired even by adolescents (Kaplan 1996: 103); among the Ache even 18- to 20-year-olds only acquire on average 1,530 calories of meat per day whereas 25- to 50-year-olds acquire about 7,000 calories per day (Kaplan 1996: 105). It is apparent then that the production of successful human offspring in a foraging context requires major parental investment, both in provisioning and in teaching of relevant practical knowledge. Significantly, one of the few instances where primates do make use of resources which are difficult to extract, the nut exploitation of the Tai forest chimpanzees, provides one of the relatively few known examples of teaching in primates, and the techniques of extracting the contents of the nuts take years to learn (Boesch 1993).

Such techniques, as well as the complex motor skills involved in craft activities, could not be passed on horizontally to any great extent, because they must be transferred from experienced to inexperienced individuals, and take a long time to learn. Furthermore, insofar as they involve a teaching effort, it seems probable that in general they will be taught by biological parent to offspring, since outside the parent–offspring relationship there would be little benefit to outweigh the costs. In the case of the parent, if it invests in teaching practical knowledge, it not only gains the indirect benefit of increasing the survival and reproductive chances of its offspring, but also the direct benefit of enhancing the offspring's ability to gain access to key feeding resources and thus reducing its dependence on provisioning (Shennan and Steele 1999: 372).

Shennan and Steele (1999) compiled a table of information from eth-nographic sources relating to the transmission of traditional craft skills and found that in all cases transmission was mainly if not entirely vertical/ oblique, rather than horizontal. In the vast majority of cases where the information was available, transmission was mainly from parent to off-spring, and specifically to offspring of the same gender. In virtually all cases where information was available the skill concerned took quite a long time to learn and was acquired during childhood/adolescence.

In some cases, non-parental teaching is institutionalized in the form of apprenticeships. Where the teacher is not a parent, or at least a closely related member of the parental generation, the issue of the cost of the training process to the teacher has to be explicitly addressed by the parties involved, as the apprenticeship literature shows (Coy 1989). Apprentice-ships arise when the costs and benefits of the social economy shift, so that it is perceived to be worthwhile to learn a new skill rather than imitate one's parents, for example, with an expanding division of labor. A study of craft traditions in Yoruba towns in the early 1950s (Lloyd 1953) showed that traditional crafts were taught by fathers to sons, whereas the new technical skills of modernization, such as cycle repair, had to be learned in the context of "master–apprentice" relations.

Interestingly, the data collected by Shennan and Steele (1999) showed that this pattern of vertical/oblique transmission of complex skills, espe-cially parent to same-gender offspring, was prevalent in agrarian societies, where there is at least some evidence that parental influence and vertical transmission may have been of less importance in other areas of life than it was in foraging communities, as a result of increasing peer group inter-action among children. A study by Draper and Cashdan (1988) looked at the impact of the adoption of a sedentary way of life on the interactions between parents and children among !Kung foragers in the Kalahari desert. They found that children were increasingly involved in interaction with peers rather than adults, because the new structure of work in sedentary communities was more demanding and time-consuming for adults, and kept parents out of the village for longer periods. Peer interaction provides increasing opportunities for horizontal transmission of information and practices among children but, as one might expect from the nature of the activity, is not relevant to the teaching of craft skills.

It obviously follows from this, and indeed from the results of Boyd and Richerson's (1988) model described earlier, that we are likely to find stronger evidence of continuities over time in some kinds of behavior—for example, those that require complex learned techniques, knowledge of which has built up cumulatively over generations—than in other areas of social life where appropriate responses to contingencies can be identified and produced on the basis of individual experience, or are learned from peer groups (Cavalli-Sforza and Feldman 1981). This observation implies that we must proceed with great caution when trying to draw conclusions about continuities in social patterns; for example, from continuities in artifact production over time.

Social Learning in Humans: Memes and the Nature of Cultural Inheritance

So far we have seen that many social practices are learned from others, rather than by individuals attempting to work things out for themselves from first principles, not least the complex techniques required to produce and use the artifacts which we find in the archaeological record. It is this process which leads to the creation of cultural traditions. We have also seen that there are good evolutionary reasons for this, which affect humans even more than they do other animals. In learning such skills the role of direct observation of other individuals is of central importance and true imitation is the most sophisticated mechanism of observational learning, restricted to humans and great apes, and to birds in the aural domain.

We saw in the introduction to this chapter that imitation provides a basis for seeing learning as a process in which copies of something are passed on from one person to another. This in turn provides a basis for seeing cultural transmission as analogous to genetic transmission. As we saw in the introduction, the best-known version of this view is Dawkins' meme concept.

Dawkins saw **memes** as **replicators**, analogous to genes in the sense that they are things in the physical world which produce copies of themselves. They are subject to the same sorts of evolutionary forces as genes, especially selection, because they are passed on/inherited; they are simply in a different medium (Dennett 1995). In order to be successful a meme must be characterized by fidelity of copying, so that it changes only slowly; by **fecundity**, in that it must be capable of generating multiple copies of itself; and by sufficient **longevity** to be able to affect its own rate of replication. One consequence of this framework is that, just as genes can be considered "selfish" in that the "interests" of the gene may clash with and even override the interests of the individual in whose body they are instantiated at a particular time, so memes too can be considered as acting as **cultural viruses** (Cullen 1996), parasitizing the minds of individuals so that they act in the interests of the success of the propagation of the memes rather than in their own interests (although what "their own" means here raises a lot of questions) or that of their genes. Cullen has suggested that items as diverse as pottery types and megalithic tombs can be seen in this way.

Many authors have doubts about the meme framework. Some emphasize social learning as a process of construction by the learner, involving interaction with a more experienced individual who provides **scaffolding** for the learning of the task (Whiten 1999); that is to say, certain parts of the task are controlled or assisted by the more experienced individual in a way which points the efforts of the inexperienced individual in a particular direction, rather than actions being copied (see, e.g., Whiten 1999). Sperber (1996: 100–118) criticizes the idea of learning as copying as a kind of essentialism: "It is tempting to see all the concrete representations that can be identified by means of a prototypical version as being the same content, with only negligible variations, thus as imperfect replicas of one another but replicas nevertheless" (1996: 100). In other words, similarities between things tend to be exaggerated by us (for good evolutionary psychological reasons). Sperber's view is that what he calls "representations," including everyday knowledge, do not replicate but transform in the process of transmission, and do so as a result of constructive cognitive processes, which go on both at the stage of representing inputs in the mind and at the subsequent stage of producing public outputs (1996: 101, 118).

Lake (1998: 86) has differing reservations, pointing out that "Imitation is not a mechanism of cultural replication because it cannot effect the direct transmission of symbolic structure: the idea for an action is not directly transmitted, but retrieved from the action itself." Clearly, this is very different from the way that genes operate.

Boyd and Richerson (1999) make a similar point, emphasizing that we cannot assume that the information in the second brain is the same as in the first. In fact, they cite a linguistic example to demonstrate that, in some cases at least, "even though there is no difference in the phenotypic performance between parents and children, children do not acquire the same memes as their parents" (Boyd and Richerson n.d.: 9). More problematical still for the meme as replicator concept is the fact that situations can exist in which there is little heritable variation at the individual level but heritable differences between groups (Boyd and Richerson 1999: 10).

The meme as replicator model would therefore appear to have considerable difficulties. The question is whether rejection of the meme concept also involves rejecting the idea of social learning as providing an inheritance mechanism which makes it possible to analyze learned traditions in Darwinian terms. Boyd and Richerson (1985: 46–55) reviewed an extensive range of psychometric and sociological evidence supporting the view that social learning acts as an inheritance mechanism by producing significant similarities between learners and those they learn from which cannot be accounted for by genetic transmission or correlated environments. They concluded that

The calculated heritabilities for human behavioural traits are as high as or higher than measurements for behavioural and other phenotypic characters in natural populations of non-cultural organisms. . . . Thus it may be that [social learning] is as accurate and stable a mechanism of inheritance as genes. (Boyd and Richerson 1985: 55)

Archaeological evidence also points in the same direction. Some specific practices acquired by social learning can show considerable similarity over time, even in the absence of strong functional constraints; ceramic decoration practices defining regional traditions provide one obvious example. Accordingly, it seems reasonable to regard social learning based on imitation/observation as resulting in a cultural inheritance system leading to successful adaptation. Of course, the effects of observation/imitation may be further enhanced by the exercise of social sanctions to ensure correct imitation in certain circumstances.

How does the process work? Individuals are born into communities with already existing cultural practices. They learn an initial version of those practices during childhood and adolescence from those closest to them, by observational learning, strengthened in some cases by reinforcement and sanctions, for the good adaptive reasons described above. As we have just noted, many of those practices continue largely unchanged for long periods of time. Others change more readily. There is a variety of mechanisms of change, all involving learning and all producing modifications in the form and/or frequency of preexisting practices.

One source of change is simply copying error during learning. If those errors are incorporated in an individual's repertoire, for example, of pottery-making, then they are likely to become part of the repertoire of that individual's children. If that kin group founds a new settlement at a time of colonization or migration then the errors may form a starting point for a whole new cultural tradition.

Other changes may be more deliberate. The fact that people learn the initial version of a practice from someone else does not mean that they make no attempt whatsoever to evaluate outcomes of particular practices on the basis of their own experience. For example, a copper smelter might discover by accident or by occasionally trying variations on the usual practice that the yield of copper can be improved by pumping the furnace for longer or adding new ingredients to the furnace charge. If this was the case, the smelter might switch to the new method and if others learned of the increased success they might imitate the new procedure, leading to a population-level change in smelting technique which would become the version passed on to future apprentice copper smelters. Over time there might be a cumulative improvement in the effectiveness of copper smelting.

On the other hand, this might not happen. If the original smelter was a despised member of the community the innovation might simply be ignored. Equally, it might not be at all obvious what had produced the greater success in that particular case: it might be ascribed to a slightly different version of the ritual for success in copper smelting used that day, so the next time it was tried, with the normal furnace charge, the success would not be repeated.

But evaluation of practical outcomes is not the only basis for adopting a practice different from that initially learned. Someone who moves to a new village on becoming married, for example, may find it essential from the point of view of social relations to try to learn the local style of pottery making to conform to local practices.

In short, what we see is a phenomenon closely analogous to the genetic Darwinian framework, in which the form and frequency of entities (cultural practices), which can be regarded as in some sense having a continuous existence through time as a result of initial social learning, are potentially altered in the context of subsequent learning and decision processes. The latter are analogous to mutation and selection. Furthermore, like gene frequencies, cultural practices may also be affected by drift when population numbers are small. Again as with genes, changes to cultural practices acquired by subsequent learning and drift are cumulative. It is the altered versions which provide the basis for initial social learning by later generations.

CASE STUDIES

The Archaeological Context

Two recent case studies illustrate the potential offered by an archaeological analysis of the implications of social learning and its consequences, in which transmission is once more accepted as an essential factor in explaining change.

Neolithic Technical Traditions in the Western Alps. Pétrequin (1993) studied the history of neolithic technical traditions in the area of eastern France/western Switzerland. The region is interesting because it was the zone where two broad traditions with different histories came together. One was the Central European Neolithic tradition, which had spread from Greece through Central Europe via the Balkans; the other was the Mediterranean tradition, which had spread from the same source but along the north coast of the Mediterranean and then up the Rhone valley. In the zone where the two traditions met, a shifting cultural frontier was formed.

Pétrequin begins by showing that there was a great deal of interaction across the boundary, in terms of the exchange of raw materials (1993: 45). Moreover, dendrochronological dates suggest that the first appearance of many artifact types occurred more or less simultaneously on both sides of the frontier (1993: 45). Nevertheless, this did not necessarily lead to adoption, and a border was maintained despite the interaction, confirming the point that traditions of cultural practices must be regarded as distinct from the populations that make use of them, and that their integrity through time can be maintained despite significant amounts of contact (Collard and Shennan 2000). Thus, in the third millennium B.C., the Corded Ware beaker, which originated on the eastern side of the frontier, became known on the western side and "clumsy attempts [were made] at imitating them" (1993: 46) before they were rejected. However, certain aspects of the Corded Ware ceramic assemblage were adopted and Pétrequin shows how this involved the acceptance and learning of a new technical process.

In particular, the communities on the western side of the frontier were used to making round-bottomed ceramic vessels, because that was part of the southern tradition, but changed to making flat-bottomed ones. However, this was not straightforward. It required the learning of a new technique of building up the vessel and a sequence of stages in moving from a round-bottomed to a flat-bottomed technique which seems to have taken two to three generations (known because of the dendrochronological dating of the sites producing the vessels):

> To make a flat bottom, the . . . potters first built up a round bottom with a horizontal stabilising cordon; sometimes the round bottom was even hidden by adding clay along the inside of the annular cordon; from the outside it looked exactly like a flat-bottomed vessel, built up directly from a lump of clay. In this case, the technique of the true flat bottom became known and adopted only after a long period of trial-and-error; the idea had been transmitted without a proven technique to go with it. (Pétrequin 1993: 48)

In other words, it is not sufficient to introduce a new form into local cultural environments and assume that people can easily reverse engineer it and produce it themselves. The relevant skills need to be taught and learned.

A similar distinction between the two zones existed with regard to the use of the axe and the adze—the two having very different cultural lineages—one derived from Central Europe, the other from the Mediterranean. In each area the hafting system changed in response to the same selective pressures derived from the changing nature of the forest to be cleared—from primary forest with large trees to secondary forest with saplings and bushes—but the changes maintained the distinct axe and adze traditions. As with the distinction between round- and flat-bottomed vessels, there is more to the difference between axes and adzes than first meets the eye. As Pétrequin (1993: 55) points out, "the working positions, the gestures and the norms for sharpening the stone blades of the two tools are radically different." Even where innovations from outside were adopted, those selected tended to be from communities with similar traditions, thus reinforcing the differences between the two sides of the frontier.

These sequences only make sense in the context of the perspective proposed in this chapter. Cultural traditions based on observational learning, especially if this occurs in childhood/adolescence (as seems likely for the traditions discussed by Pétrequin given the findings of Shennan and Steele [1999]), have the properties of inheritance systems outlined above. They do not readily lose their identity when exposed to new influences but undergo changes which are plausibly seen as the result of the operation of selection processes; for example, the changes in axe form in response to deforestation.

Stylistic Change in the Woodland Period of Illinois

A rather different example of the insights to be gained from considering archaeological artifact traditions as the outcomes of inheritance systems maintained by social learning is given by Neiman's (1995) analysis of Illinois Woodland ceramic assemblage variation. The analysis focused on variation in exterior rim decoration and explored the implications of assuming that the decoration system represents a tradition maintained by social learning in which the only relevant evolutionary forces accounting for change through time in the form and frequency of decorative attributes in a given ceramic assemblage are mutation and drift, because stylistic variation is regarded as adaptively neutral and therefore not subject to selection. Drift represents the chance element in social learning traditions: even if we assume that all potters and/or all decorative motifs are equally likely to be taken as models in an episode of social learning and subsequent ceramic production, in any finite population not all potters or motifs will be copied the same number of times. For smaller populations the chances of such random variation are particularly great. By the time a few "generations" of ceramic decoration copying/production have gone by, some of the motifs will have disappeared altogether while others will be present at high frequency. Eventually, only one will prevail and the time taken for this to happen will depend on the population size.

Mutation refers to the introduction of novelty into the decorative repertoire of a particular group. This can come from local innovation or from the adoption of new motifs from other groups. To the extent that groups are in contact with one another, the drift-driven changes in the different groups should go in step with one another. Neiman (1995) carried out a simulation to demonstrate that, for a given population size, higher levels of intergroup transmission produce lower equilibrium values of intergroup divergence. It follows from the theory and its mathematical specification that when drift and neutral innovation are the only forces operating, then, if we examine the relationship between the variation within an assemblage and the differences between different assemblages, as one decreases the other will increase (Neiman 1995: 27).

An analysis of the differences between a number of Woodland ceramic assemblages from different sites, for a series of seven successive phases, showed a trend of decreasing then increasing difference between them. It also showed the pattern of inverse correlation between intra- and intergroup variation just mentioned: as interassemblage differences went down, the variation within assemblages increased. Neiman (1995: 27) therefore concluded that the trends through time in interassemblage distance were indeed a function of changing levels of intergroup transmission, which started low, reached their highest level in Middle Woodland times, and sank to new low levels in the Late Woodland period. The Middle Woodland was also the time of the "Hopewell Interaction Sphere," evidenced by the widespread appearance of exotic trade goods.

He went on to suggest that since the attribute being studied was decoration on cooking pots, and since ethnoarchaeological work suggests that successful transmission of ceramic traditions requires a long-lasting relationship between teacher and learner (Shennan and Steele 1999), then the changes in level of intergroup transmission must relate to changes in the level of long-term residential movement of potters between groups. He also pointed out that his conclusions about the patterns of interaction through time in this period and area correspond to those of the culture historians who had studied the phenomenon, rather than with those of subsequent analyses undertaken within a New Archaeology framework. These had suggested that the end of the Middle Woodland and the cessation of exotic goods exchange represented the replacement of gift exchange relations by more frequent, routine, everyday forms of contact. This does not appear to be the case.

FUTURE IMPORTANCE

Complex social learning of the kind that characterizes the human species produces cultural traditions in many aspects of life which can be regarded as having the characteristics of Darwinian inheritance systems; seen as generic phenomena, affected by such forces as selection, mutation, and drift. This is so even though we do not understand the psychology of the process; in this respect we are simply in the same situation as Darwin was in not knowing the mechanism of genetic transmission.

If our understanding of learning and of the way cultural practices are maintained and changed through time is to be improved, future work is needed in several areas. First, we need more detailed ethnoarchaeological field studies of the processes by which specific cultural practices are learned, and their costs and benefits with regard to different spheres of activity, and also to the importance of sanctions. The reason for this is that currently most accounts are anecdotal, on the one hand, and normative, on the other, disregarding variation. Second, we need ethnographic studies of patterns of kinship, social learning, and linguistic and genetic descent in recent/present-day contexts where we know the historical patterns of interaction among the people concerned, so that we can see how they relate together. Third, more computer simulations of the implications of specific learning processes and their diachronic and population-level outcomes are required.

However, a prerequisite of this improved understanding is the recognition that continuity of material culture environments—for example, the presence of ceramic vessels of particular kind—is insufficient in itself to account for the continuity of cultural traditions in many spheres of social life. It is not possible to make a cake simply on the basis of looking at one and tasting it. It is necessary to see how it is done and thus acquire a "procedural template." Whatever the specific psychological mechanism of the "handing-on" process, traditions must be taught and learned if the behavior patterns and beliefs of later generations are to resemble those of earlier ones, as they so often do.

REFERENCES

Boesch, C. (1993). Aspects of transmission of tool-use in wild chimpanzees. In K. R. Gibson and T. Ingold (eds.), *Tools, Language and Cognition in Human Evolution*. Cambridge: Cambridge University Press, pp. 171–183.

Boesch, C., and M. Tomasello. (1998). Chimpanzee and human cultures. *Current Anthropology* 39: 591–604.

Box, H. O., and K. R. Gibson (eds.). (1999). *Mammalian Social Learning: Comparative and Ecological Perspectives*. Cambridge: Cambridge University Press.

Boyd, R., and P. Richerson. (1985). *Culture and the Evolutionary Process*. Chicago: University of Chicago Press.

Boyd, R., and P. Richerson. (1988). An evolutionary model of social learning: The effects of spatial and temporal variation. In T. R. Zentall and B. G. Galef (eds.), *Social Learning: Psychological and Biological Perspectives*. Hillsdale, NJ: Lawrence Erlbaum, pp. 29–48.

Boyd, R., and P. Richerson. (1996). Why culture is common but cultural evolution is rare. In W. G. Runciman, J. Maynard-Smith, and R.I.M. Dunbar (eds.), *Evolution of Social Behaviour Patterns in Primates and Man*. Oxford: Oxford University Press, pp. 77–93.

Boyd, R., and P. Richerson. (1999). Memes: Universal acid or a better mousetrap? Paper presented at King's College, Cambridge, Conference on Memes, June 1999.

Cavalli-Sforza, L. L., and M. W. Feldman. (1981). *Cultural Transmission and Evolution: A Quantitative Approach*. Princeton, NJ: Princeton University Press.

Collard, M., and S. J. Shennan. (2000). Processes of culture change in prehistory: A case study from the European Neolithic. In C. Renfrew and K. Boyle (eds.), *Archaeogenetics: DNA and the Population Prehistory of Europe*. Cambridge: MacDonald Institute for Archaeological Research, pp. 89–97.

Coy, M. W. (ed.). (1989). *Apprenticeship: From Theory to Method and Back Again*. Albany: State University of New York Press.

Cullen, B. (1996). Social interaction and viral phenomena. In J. Steele and S. J. Shennan (eds.), *The Archaeology of Human Ancestry: Power, Sex and Tradition*. London: Routledge, pp. 420–433.

Dawkins, R. (1976). *The Selfish Gene*. Oxford: Oxford University Press.

Dawkins, R. (1982). *The Extended Phenotype*. Oxford: Oxford University Press.

Dennett, D. (1995). *Darwin's Dangerous Idea*. London: Allen Lane, The Penguin Press.

Draper, P., and E. Cashdan. (1988). Technological change and child behavior among the !Kung. *Ethnology* 27: 339–365.

Galef, B. G. (1988). Communication of information concerning distant diets in a social, central-place foraging species: *Rattus norvegicus*. In T. R. Zentall and B. G. Galef (eds.), *Social Learning: Psychological and Biological Perspectives*. Hillsdale, NJ: Lawrence Erlbaum, pp. 119–140.

Gilbert, B. K. (1999). Opportunities for social learning in bears. In H. O. Box and K. R. Gibson (eds.), *Mammalian Social Learning: Comparative and Ecological Perspectives*. Cambridge: Cambridge University Press, pp. 225–235.

Heyes, C., and B. G. Galef (eds.). (1996). *Social Learning in Animals: The Roots of Culture*. New York: Academic Press.

Kaplan, H. (1996). A theory of fertility and parental investment in traditional and modern human societies. *Yearbook of Physical Anthropology* 39: 91–135.

Lake, M. W. (1998). Digging for memes: The role of material objects in cultural evolution. In C. Renfrew and C. Scarre (eds.), *Cognition and Material Culture: The Archaeology of Symbolic Storage*. Cambridge: McDonald Institute of Archaeology, pp. 77–88.

Laland, K. N., and K. Williams. (1998). Social transmission of maladaptive information in the guppy. *Behavioral Ecology* 9: 493–499.

Lyman, R. L., M. J. O'Brien, and R. C. Dunnell. (1997). *The Rise and Fall of Culture History*. New York: Plenum.

Neiman, F. D. (1995). Stylistic variation in evolutionary perspective: Inferences from decorative diversity and interassemblage distance in Illinois Woodland ceramic assemblages. *American Antiquity* 60: 7–36.

Payne, R. (1996). Song traditions in Indigo Buntings: Origin, improvisation, dispersal and extinction in cultural evolution. In D. E. Kroodsma and E. H. Miller (eds.), *Ecology and Evolution of Acoustic Communication in Birds*. Ithaca, NY: Cornell University Press, pp. 198–220.

Pétrequin, P. (1993). North wind, south wind. In P. Lemonnier (ed.), *Technological Choices: Transformations in Material Cultures Since the Neolithic*. London: Routledge, pp. 36–76.

Plotkin, H. (1997). *Evolution in Mind: An Introduction to Evolutionary Psychology*. London: Penguin.

Russon, A. E. (1997). Exploiting the expertise of others. In A. Whiten and R. W. Byrne (eds.), *Machiavellian Intelligence II: Extensions and Evaluations*. Cambridge: Cambridge University Press, pp. 174–206.

Shennan, S. J., and J. Steele. (1999). Cultural learning in hominids: A behavioural ecological approach. In H. O. Box and K. R. Gibson (eds.), *Mammalian Social Learning: Comparative and Ecological Perspectives*. Cambridge: Cambridge University Press, pp. 367–388.

Sperber, D. (1996). *Explaining Culture: A Naturalistic Approach*. Oxford: Blackwell.

Whiten, A. (1998). Imitation of the sequential structure of actions by chimpanzees (*Pan troglodytes*). *Journal of Comparative Psychology* 112: 270–281.

Whiten, A. (1999). Parental encouragement in *Gorilla*: Implications for social communication. In S. T. Parker, R. W. Mitchell, and H. L. Miles (eds.), *The Mentalities of Gorillas and Orangutans in Comparative Perspective*. Cambridge: Cambridge University Press, pp. 342–366.

Whiten, A., and R. Ham. (1992). On the nature and evolution of imitation in the animal kingdom: Reappraisal of a century of research. In P.J.B. Slater, J. S. Rosenblatt, C. Beer, and M. Milinski (eds.), *Advances in the Study of Behaviour*. San Diego, CA: Academic Press, pp. 239–283.

Whiten, A., J. Goodall, W. C. McGrew, T. Nishida, V. Reynolds, Y. Sugiyama, C.E.G. Tutin, R. W. Wrangham, and C. Boesch. (1999). Cultures in chimpanzees. *Nature* 399: 682–685.

Zentall, T. R., and B. G. Galef (eds.). (1988). *Social Learning: Psychological and Biological Perspectives*. Hillsdale, NJ: Lawrence Erlbaum.

Chapter 12

Models

Bruce Winterhalder

INTRODUCTION

Models represent observed or hypothesized relationships of structure and function in simplified or abstract form. They transform a reference situation, usually a complex system or process, in order to make it more accessible or tractable. Maps scale down a landscape in order to guide the newly arrived over unfamiliar terrain. The logistic equation isolates key demographic variables in order to guide the analysis of exponential population growth in a finite environment. Everything important about a model is shaped by its being an instrument of prediction or investigation. Because of this, the properties of models and the capacities expected of them are nearly as varied as are the goals in using them.

Models are ubiquitous in archaeology, biology, and related historical-evolutionary sciences. They are particularly useful in these fields because the subject matter is complex (which puts a premium on orderly techniques for simplification), multidisciplinary (which puts a premium on devices facilitating clear communication), and in the very early stages of scientific development (which puts a premium on instruments that balance the development of abstract ideas and empirical investigations of their explanatory potency). Models in these fields are non-denominational, in that their use is not restricted to particular theoretical approaches. To the degree we are clear in thinking and communicating about the practice of modeling itself, models bring order and rigor to analytic efforts. This claim recognizes that modeling is an activity (the common use of the gerund gives it away), not a concept, a problem, or a field of knowledge. Skill in modeling develops with experience, but it can be helped along by understanding the place of modeling in scientific investigation.

What follows is a schematic framework for thinking about the place and use of models in anthropology, archaeology, and cognate fields, particularly ecology. Consistent with the pedagogical objectives of an encyclopedia, it is a thin essay draped over a more substantial skeleton of definitions, concepts, taxonomy, and sources. I begin with a brief historical overview. The following sections discuss kinds of models, their uses, usefulness and drawbacks, testing, analytical compromises, and the relationship of models to narrative, metaphors, and reductionism. Three case studies are followed by some modest divination about the future uses of models in the fields mentioned above.

HISTORY

The beginnings of widespread use of explicit, quantitative models in ecology can be dated to the last 50 years. This short time span leaves us with a history that is largely biographical and informal. Excellent inside sources are Fretwell (1975), Golley (1993), and Schoener (1987). By contrast, Kingsland (1995) and Hagen (1992) write as professional historians of science. Because models are pervasive in science, a history of their use is potentially as complex as the intellectual and social histories of disciplines themselves. Nonetheless, in ecology, anthropology, and archaeology, modeling has followed largely dichotomous routes.

Tansley, Lindeman, Odum, and colleagues began the development of what have become ecosystem **simulation models**. These efforts drew on concepts from information theory, operations research, and cybernetics which flourished during and immediately after World War II. They initiated the work of giving empirical substance and conceptual form to Tansley's 1935 definition of the ecosystem concept. Ecosystem approaches adopted the premise that biotic communities and their physical substrates were organized according to system-level properties such as homeostasis. The goal was a structural-functional model that mimicked the processes observed, in particular, natural systems (typically biomes, such as temperate grasslands). Complex box-and-arrow flow diagrams were the visual expression of these models.

The second track developed somewhat later, in the 1960s. Ecologists led by Robert McArthur, Eric Pianka, and John Emlen challenged the reigning descriptive naturalism. They parted ways with ecosystem efforts by developing simple, frankly speculative, predictive models addressing such questions as feeding behavior, population regulation, and species diversity. This **evolutionary ecology** track used hypothetico-deductive methods, and problem-oriented fieldwork focused on adaptive design. It adopted the premise that natural selection would optimize or stabilize some ecological property such as feeding efficiency, clutch size, or niche breadth, at the level of individuals. While the intent of many evolutionary ecology pioneers was understanding community structure, what they in fact created was the field of behavioral ecology. Behavioral ecology has since flourished despite routine rejection of early papers by major ecological journals (Schoener 1987).

Self-conscious attention to the use of models in archaeology lagged that in biology but has followed similarly divergent tracks. Clarke (1972) gives a thorough discussion of the kinds of archaeological models spawned by the "New Archaeology," categorized according to their alliance with morphological, anthropological, ecological, and geographical "paradigms." Three brief examples will establish the flavor of the early work with models. Using demographic and other assumptions, some drawn from ethnographic studies of extant foragers, as well as Monte Carlo techniques, Wobst (1974) simulated the MES (Minimal Equilibrium Size) of the social unit that would consistently provide suitable mates to maturing adults living in the low-density conditions assumed for the Pleistocene. He was then able to show how the size of this social unit, which varied between 175 and 475 persons, was affected by such factors as minimum band size (no effect), increased life expectancy (MES declines), or polygyny (MES increases).

Thomas (1972) used Steward's ethnographic reconstruction of Reese River (Great Basin) Shoshone life as the basis for a season-by-season simulation model of their subsistence-settlement system. His "systems analytic" (p. 691) model is represented as a multicomponent flow chart of male and female activities, lifezone locations, and branching points (pp. 679–680; Thomas, Figure 17.3). It draws on estimates of the productivity, localized year-to-year reliability, and spatial distribution of key resources (piñon nuts, Indian rice grass seed, and antelope). It has the objective of recreating the seasonal round in order to predict artifact distributions, and from that the goal of testing Steward's reconstruction against the archaeological record (Thomas 1973). Flannery (1968) developed an ecosystem approach based on cybernetic arguments to explore how seasonality and scheduling of an annual round might, when subject to small deviations such as fortuitous mutations in resource species, develop into early systems of plant cultivation in Mesoamerica.

Archaeologists and their anthropological colleagues in cultural ecology identified most readily with the system-simulation approach of biologists. However, the simulation approach did not flourish as Thomas (1972: 701) predicted. By contrast, use of evolutionary or behavioral ecology models of the type described more fully below appears to be growing (Winterhalder and Smith 2000). Bettinger (1991) gives the history for hunter-gatherer studies. Advocates of evolutionary ecology models in anthropology and archaeology generally followed a modeling strategy like that of their biological colleagues on the evolutionary ecology track (see O'Connell 1995; Smith and Winterhalder 1992; Winterhalder and Smith 1981).

A third and much newer development affecting archaeology, as well as other social sciences and the study of animal behavior, is agent-based modeling (Kohler 1999). These models typically simulate the outcome of interactions among a population of individuals who act on information collected from a particular environmental context. "Research using these models emphasizes dynamics rather than equilibria, distributed processes rather than systems-level phenomena, and patterns of relationships among agents rather than relationships among variables" (Kohler 1999: 2). An early example is the marvelously detailed and creative model by Flannery and Reynolds (Flannery 1986), analyzing the resource scheduling decisions of bands of foragers living in the prehistoric Oaxaca Valley. Similar applications can be found in Kohler and Gumerman (1999). In several respects—the scale of analysis, conceptual commitments, and degree of complexity—the agent-based approach is a potential bridge in archaeology between behavioral ecology and systems-level models.

CONTEMPORARY USES

Kinds of Models

A useful taxonomy separates scale models from heuristic models, and within the latter category distinguishes among theoretical, analogic, and empirical models. Brief descriptions follow.

A topographic map or architectural miniature is a very basic form of **scale model**. Both omit detail and reduce size but maintain fidelity of relative position and distance among selected features such as rivers and towns, or walls and windows. Some virtual (computerized) models are a variant, but are designed to give the perceptual illusion of realistic scales. An example is the house plan or archaeological site that one can "enter" visually in three dimensions on a computer screen. Geographic information systems (GIS) combine a scale model with visualization and advanced (database) abilities to analyze the elements that scale models best preserve: spatial correspondences based on relative position and distance.

Scale models represent relationships known to their makers. By contrast, **heuristic models** are problem-solving devices. Their usefulness lies in furthering the analysis of untested but hypothesized relationships. Heuristic models come in several forms, given further variety by the assumptions they make and the techniques used to solve them. In one basic form, heuristic models explore the implications of general theory. Such **theoretical models** serve as an operational bridge between abstract beliefs and concrete manifestations that are more directly amenable to observation and experimentation. Evolutionary ecology models, for instance, facilitate investigation of the observable consequences of natural selection for the physiology and behavior of organisms.

Analogic models derive their heuristic power from comparison with phenomena believed to share one or more essential features but to differ in others. Paleontological reconstruction of hominid locomotion or diet based on the structural-functional anatomy of living species is a classic example. Another is the claim that we can learn about the behavior of Pleistocene hominids by thinking of them as if they were social carnivores, or a particular species of primate. Analogic models depend on a justification for the choice of referent, and in this they usually are implicitly theoretical. In the instances cited, evolutionary theory warrants the claim that the comparisons are meaningful. But theory seldom is prominent. Instead, the referent itself, social carnivores, serves as a source of ideas for postulating generalized features of the analog hominids. Tooby and DeVore (1987; see also Clarke 1972: 40–42) list reasons to prefer theoretical over analogic, or in their terms "conceptual" over "referential," models, especially for behavioral studies.

Empirical models are derived from the referent phenomenon itself. Thus, an empirical model of an ecosystem might represent its constituent species as trophic components in order to replicate and analyze nutrient or hydrological flows. Empirical models simplify by collapsing detail into conceptual categories. In ecological studies these are usually structural or functional features. Successful empirical models attempt to generalize beyond the observed features of the system: What will happen to nutrient dynamics and runoff if forest cover in this ecosystem is reduced by 40%? Empirical models do not require a strong theoretical association. Consequently, they are most valuable and apt to be used when appropriate theory is lacking or is only weakly developed.

The three types of heuristic models differ primarily in the referent that serves as their creative starting point. They move from the theoretical, to the comparative, to the empirical. The categories partition a gradient of analytical inspiration, but the boundaries between them are not sharp. The theoretical, comparative, and empirical can mingle to varying degrees in specific applications. Likewise, the categories are not of equal status. Theory is implicit in analog models and theory building is presumably a desired outcome of empirical models.

A large number of dichotomies are used to characterize specific modeling techniques. For instance, models can be **static**, without an inherent temporal component or **dynamic** and thus time-dependent. They can be **deterministic**, using fixed or average expected values for parameters and input variables, or stochastic. In a **stochastic model** one or more parameters is characterized by a distribution for which individual values are unpredictable. Variance itself becomes an important part of the analysis. Solutions to a model may be **mathematical** (also called **analytical**), either in the form

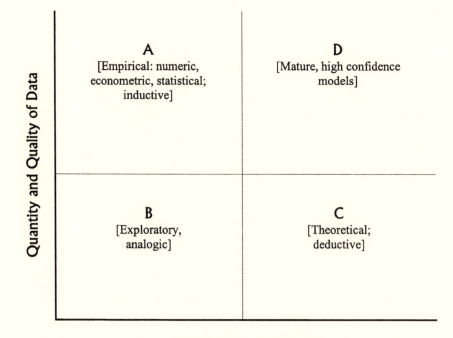

Understanding of Problem

Figure 12.1. A model for classifying types and uses of models. This model emphasizes generality over realism and sacrifices precision to both (modified from Holling 1978: 67–69).

of equations or graphs; or they may be achieved indirectly through simulation, in which the model takes the form of computational rules executed with software. Many further distinctions can be found in the literature.

Uses, Usefulness, and Shortcomings of Models

Models can be used at all stages of scientific investigation. They can help to (1) define and isolate a problem, (2) organize thought, (3) advance understanding of data or direct attention to relevant data yet to be gathered, (4) communicate ideas, (5) devise hypotheses and tests, and (6) make predictions (Starfield and Bleloch 1986: 1). Ideally, they reveal emergent or novel phenomena not anticipated in their design, a quality Thomas (1972: 690) calls "serendipity," but which is a predictable benefit when models are used with skill.

Figure 12.1 (adapted from Holling 1978: 67–69) organizes uses and types of models according to the state of knowledge in a subject. The quantity and quality of data available on a problem are depicted on the *y*-axis;

the degree of understanding in conceptual or theoretical terms is measured on the x-axis.

Statistical or other forms of empirical or numerical models are most useful if data are plentiful but theoretical understanding limited (cell A; Figure 12.1). Here analysis is exploratory. It is intended to reveal regularities, order data, and organize thought. Much of human demography and econometrics operates in this realm. By contrast, in cell D we have plentiful data and understanding to match. Here models take up the job of representing and applying relatively mature scientific knowledge. Models are used primarily to communicate and generate predictions. Some population genetic models and many models of engineering and physics have these qualities. Maps, of course, excel in them. Simplifying models can provide relief from the paralyzing effects of having too much knowledge to fully comprehend, that is, to keep usefully "in mind." Simplification can be important because overly complex models have a suite of liabilities (Richerson and Boyd 1987: 33–34): they can be difficult to understand and analyze, and they may offer few advantages in predictive ability. The importance of simple models in this cell reminds us that models are not the temporary tools of nascent or emerging knowledge, dispensable as a science matures. Their forms and uses may shift even as their usefulness endures.

Many models concerned with either human behavior or the historical (evolutionary) sciences operate in the cells B and C. With limited data and understanding (cell B), models necessarily are speculative and provisional. Here models help to define and isolate problems. They facilitate preliminary analyses. Evolutionary archaeology and some life history and behavioral ecology models sit here. As theoretical understanding increases (cell C), models can be used in an interpretive or inferential fashion, even if data are limited (cell C). Models in cells B and C commonly direct attention to novel data, facilitating efforts to advance empirically, in a positive direction along the y-axis.

Models in cell A commonly are inductive; those in cell C are deductive. Analogic models usually are confined to cell B. While scientific advance consists most obviously in moving from cells A, B, and C as far as possible into cell D, this most desirable of outcomes may not be feasible, especially in the short term. Game managers face population-ecology decisions that cannot wait decades for data collection. For many subjects of high interest, archaeology and related historical sciences will always operate with much less data than we would like. Extraordinarily creative and time-consuming effort may be required of prehistorians hoping to nudge their subjects of investigation from cells B or C small distances toward A and D. Taphonomic studies are an example.

However, even if data are constrained, there are potential gains to knowledge in striving to move from cell B toward C. Interpretive models well verified in other contexts may be used to make sound inferences about phenomena only incompletely substantiated with data (viz., ethnoarchaeological studies; see O'Connell 1995). When insufficient time or empirical hurdles are a problem, theoretical models advance the pragmatic aim of working as effectively as we can with limited information. By specifying and narrowing the analytical quest, they help to identify what kinds of data are needed in order to perform a compelling test, a special advantage when data are difficult to come by.

In practice, a model might be applied in three different modes: the evaluative, interpretive, and normative. The evaluative mode is focused on testing the model against observations. Evaluative statements commonly take the form: *If* the assumptions of the model accurately reflect the referent situation, *then* we expect the following observations. Here models provide provisional hypotheses and the analytical work lies in testing those hypotheses (see "Testing," below). The model is made subordinate to the empirical evidence.

The evaluative mode grades into the interpretive mode. In this mode one offers a plausible covering argument that the model applies to a situation; its congruence is accepted on this argument rather than by direct test. The consistency of the model with available observations is then used to interpret or extend them. Statements take the form: Because of its theoretical generality for social foragers, the producer-scrounger game likely characterized hominid hunter-gatherers, with the consequences x, y, and z for subsistence and social behavior. Interpretive use implies a model that is only weakly validated in either the theoretical or the empirical sense in that situation. Our willingness to engage in the interpretive use of a model depends on: (1) general confidence that the model captures the relationships it claims to represent, that is, on prior testing in related contexts; (2) on the covering argument for suitability in this context; and (3) on inability to make a more direct, evaluative use of the model in this context. The first two criteria recognize that models might be quite useful in a provisional way, even in situations in which they may eventually be tested directly. The third criterion recognizes their utility for the historical sciences (archaeology, history, geology, evolutionary biology) in which direct testing may not be feasible for any of a variety of reasons.

Purely evaluative use of social science models is rare because they are difficult to test thoroughly. An analyst willing to pursue evaluation is seldom so disinterested as to eschew completely extrapolating to interpretive uses. It likewise is the case that interpretive uses gain their plausibility by appealing to various indirect sources of evaluation. As a consequence it can be difficult to discern the relative balance of evaluation and interpretation in a particular application. Judgments are further complicated if authors are not explicit. It is tempting for the advocates of a model to slip unintentionally from evaluative to interpretive modes with few discernable signals that they have done so. Critics, on the other hand, are tempted to misread interpretive claims as evaluative. By associating the interpretive mode with the harder, scientific claims of the evaluative, they make their critical task easier.

The normative mode of applying models is more easily recognized. Here a model becomes the basis for a recommendation. The normative mode expresses confidence in the merit and applicability of the model, whether or not it conforms to empirical observations in the particular case. If the model has been tested and found to fit the case, it can serve its normative role, mainly that of reassurance, with high confidence: not only is behavior x observed when predicted, it is the behavior that *should* be observed. However, even if x is not observed, there may remain reason to assign a model a normative role. Although individuals are doing otherwise, x is what they should do if they are to most effectively realize their goals. The normative stance has an applied or practical flavor evident in microeconomic models. Normative use of models comes to the fore when pragmatic decisions must be made in the absence of exhaustive data, in fields such as conservation biology (Starfield and Bleloch 1986), economic development (Krugman 1995), or environmental assessment (Holling 1978).

The most immediate costs or dangers of modeling are simplification and reification. Models do simplify, selectively. In this, their most attractive feature (Boyer 1995) is also, for some, their greatest liability, lack of "realism." No one will easily confuse a map for a landscape. But many other models are less clearly distinguishable from the phenomena they represent, making it easy to mistake the model for the phenomena (reification). The selectivity accompanying the construction of a model means that information has been discarded, perhaps at a high cost. Models impose certain kinds of blindness. Problems may also arise if the potential arbitrariness of the selectivity is neglected. A model may neglect essential features of the problem or grant undue importance to features of little consequence. A more remote danger is the possibility that insistence on modeling will lead to the neglect or disparaging of subjects not, or not yet, amenable to formal treatment (Krugman 1995). Two preventative measures address these problems. First, users of models need to remind themselves periodically that models are instruments; they are the tools, not the object, of scientific workmanship. Second is thorough testing (see below).

[We] . . . build models to *explore the consequences* of what we believe to be true. . . . Because we have so little data . . . we learn by living with our models, by exercising them, manipulating them, questioning their relevance, and comparing their behavior with what we know (or think we know) about the real world. (Starfield and Bleloch 1986: 3) (emphasis in original)

Testing

However models are applied, their ultimate scientific value depends on the skill and thoroughness with which they have been tested. Appraisal is a significantly more general process than assessing the empirical fit of hypotheses with observations (Maynard Smith 1978). Four general classes of tests can be recognized:

(1) Is a model strictly faithful to its antecedent theory, and is that theory sound? These are not the straightforward questions they may seem. Some theories can be accepted with greater confidence than others. No theory, or more than one theory, may be perceived as applicable to the problem. And, even if a single choice is obvious, broad and compelling theories sometimes generate multiple, competing mandates concerning their most appropriate uses. The "pluralism" debates within neo-Darwinism attest to this (Ayala 1982; Gould 1983), as do debates over the best way to do ecology (Kingsland 1995) or evolutionary archaeology. Different schools of thought may make conflicting and hard-to-assess claims about which is the more legitimate heir to a particular theory.

(2) Does the model display internal logical consistency? There are two conditions here: (a) the conclusions should follow from the stated assumptions, and (b) they should follow from *only* those assumptions. Errors affecting the first condition are relatively uncommon. Deficiencies pertaining to the second condition are, unfortunately, a routine affliction of modeling. It commonly happens that the predictions of a model may depend on unrecognized assumptions, with the consequence that assessments about applicability and generality are misled. Relethford (1999) gives an example from models of hominid paleontology. A model may unwittingly assume what properly should be the object of inquiry. Krugman (1995: 53) states that von Thünen's central place model "assumes the [very] thing you want to understand: the existence of a central urban market."

In pursuit of logical consistency, good models bare their features forthrightly. Even good modelers sometimes neglect this transparency obligation, perhaps because the generality of a model is enhanced if it appears to depend on fewer rather than more assumptions. Nonetheless, those who use models regularly testify that the act of converting intuition or verbal reasoning into numerical, graphical, or mathematical form reveals assumptions, logical connections, and outcomes that otherwise would have been missed.

(3) Empirical evaluation of a model may entail direct testing of its assumptions. For instance, the encounter-contingent, resource selection model of foraging theory assumes that resource types are encountered randomly, according to a Poisson distribution. Although the model is used widely, to my knowledge this assumption has never been field tested. Direct testing of assumptions is important because assumptions may in part be dictated

by the availability of techniques rather than suitability to problem. For instance, early foraging theory models assumed deterministic input variables because stochastic or risk-sensitive techniques were not yet available.

(4) The final way of testing a model is a direct comparison of predictions with observations. Fit constitutes an indirect test of the model's assumptions and, working backward through this list of assessments, its internal consistency and antecedent theory. This is true *provided that* the predictions are unique to the model, the model unique to the theory, and the theory uniquely applicable to the problem. If we can derive the same predictions from theory or a model with different and incompatible assumptions, as happens with some frequency, then we are handicapped in choosing between them. In practice, when the predicted result is observed, it typically is taken as conferring a limited, favorable appraisal on higher levels of testing even when uniqueness is not assured. When fit is not observed, a search for the reason is initiated at those same levels. Was there an error in the derivation of the hypothesis from the model? Were the assumptions misplaced? Was the theory inappropriate? Hypotheses fail for distinctive and, when they can be discovered, usually informative reasons.

The most basic form of empirical test is a single circumstance or noncomparative hypothesis, as in the following example: Its socioecological conditions are such that we would predict polygyny in species (or society) *x*. More satisfying are multicircumstance, or comparative, tests of the form: given their different socioecological conditions, we would predict that species (or society) *x* is polygynous and related species or society *y* is monogamous. Or, given seasonal changes in the density, costs, and benefits of the available resources, we can predict that the forager's resource selection will show pattern *z* through the year. Multicircumstance tests require that we find natural or experimental situations that exhibit the required variability of input conditions. This can be difficult, even though the opportunities for comparative testing are diverse (Maynard Smith 1978: 43). One can make comparisons among entities (species, societies or populations, individuals), or track comparative differences as any of these entities experiences changing conditions (seasonal, migratory, life cycle, etc.). Simulation can be used to replicate natural or experimental tests that cannot be conducted in actuality. If simulation increases the predictive range and specificity of models, it may thereby make them easier to test against the limited data sets available (Kohler 1999).

Few are free of the temptation to base allegiance to a model on the creative effort that went into its making, rather than the skeptical effort that may go into its evaluation. Nonetheless, confidence in a model grows as the number and detail of its tested linkages with the phenomena increase. Confidence is enhanced if the parameter values in the model are estimated independently of the observations that are used to assess hypotheses. It always is worthwhile to push as far in the direction of quantitative tests as is possible. Qualitative tests can establish the necessity of an adaptive explanation, but not its sufficiency (Orzack and Sober 1993). Noting that hypothesis testing can only *in*validate a model, Holling (1978: 95) argues that we are seeking *degree of belief* in the efficacy of a model. The more ways in which the credibility of a model survives being put at risk, the greater our justification for confidence in it.

Analytic Compromises

Levins (1966) argued that models can be classified according to three independent and sometimes competing qualities: generality, realism, and precision. Good maps have virtually no generality, but score well on precision and to a lesser extent on realism. The Hardy-Weinberg law has a high degree of generality, low realism, and moderate precision. Ecosystem models give priority to realism; precision is secondary and generality of lesser concern. Evolutionary ecology models, by contrast, emphasize generality; realism and precision are secondary objectives. Agent-based models tilt that configuration of qualities toward realism.

Levins states that because it is impossible to maximize all three of these qualities at once, trade-offs are central to effective model-building. He also argues that it takes a family of interrelated and partially overlapping models to address any particular subject, such as population biology. The simplifications necessary to make models analytically tractable mean that each can represent only a partial view of the whole. A family of models is bound together by their antecedent theory, and by the ways in which they overlap in addressing the phenomena. Thus, the evolution of life history characteristics cites neo-Darwinian theory and involves models of clutch size, parental investment, altruism and helping behavior, senescence, and so on. Finally, Levins suggests that individual models could be assessed by a desirable quality, their *robustness*. Robustness appraises the degree to which the predictions of a model are independent of the details of its construction (e.g., its assumptions). In practice, it means achieving the same result from partially independent starting points. For instance, it is said that the encounter-contingent model for resource selection has six separate derivations (Schoener 1987).

Levins' views on modeling have been extraordinarily influential, despite some deficiencies. He was not specific about the meanings of generality, realism, and precision. He did not provide explicit arguments that this was an exhaustive list of desirable model qualities, or that an increase in one or two of them by necessity comes at the expense of another. He did not provide a specific protocol for assessing robustness. Nonetheless, these shortcomings appear not to have diminished widespread citation and use of Levins' analysis, perhaps because his description resonates so well with the experience of those who create and use models.

The disparity between the substance and the influence of Levins' brief for modeling tempts philosophizing, and Orzack and Sober (1993) have taken up the shortcomings listed in the previous paragraph. They try to sharpen Levins' terminology, for instance, by defining generality and realism as relative or comparative terms, applicable only within the context of models addressing like phenomena. They use examples to show that generality, realism, and precision are not independent of one another and do not always combine to generate a stable taxonomy of models. For example, the same model can be classified differently depending on the degree to which its parameter values are made quantitatively specific, or "instantiated," in their terminology. They reject as vague the argument that models can be appraised by their robustness.

In response, Levins (1993) states that the formal analytic methods used by Orzack and Sober have little or no bearing on the practice of model-building, or indeed, on science more generally. Orzack and Sober set out detailed examples to show that Levins' analysis is afflicted by ambiguous definitions and permeable, shifting categories. Levins embraces many of their examples and adds some of his own, but he rejects the larger lesson. In his view, it is entirely appropriate that the terms of his characterization are relative and that useful taxonomies of models are situational. That they can be confounded by formal logic and carefully chosen cases does not make them less reasonable as guides to the practice of constructing and using evolutionary models. Levins notes that philosophy is not evolutionary biology, and a too-tidy or strict sense of formalization does not necessarily advance creative or sound scientific practice. While the Orzack and Sober (1993) critique introduces some laudable caution, it seems unlikely that it will reduce the intuitive appeal of Levins' description of the trade-offs entailed in model-building.

General terms of approbation, like robustness, are common in the literature on modeling. Starfield and Bleloch (1986: 6–8) use the term *resolution* to describe a model's scope, what is or is not included, and the detail of its components. Models with too fine a resolution can become burdened with distracting detail; those with too coarse a resolution will yield inadequate understanding. Aris and Penn (1980: 9–11) speak of *craft*, to emphasize that a well-constructed model requires the triumph of judgment and skill over the uncertainty of incomplete knowledge. Clarke (1972: 4) speaks of *power*, a composite judgment made up of the comprehensiveness, predictiveness, efficiency, and accuracy of a model. Richerson and Boyd (1987: 43–46) use the term *plausibility argument* to summarize the degree to which a family of models is (1) theoretically and logically sound, (2) consistent with data, and (3) separable from competing approaches to the same subject. The variety of these terms for assessing model validity presumably arises from the multiple kinds of compromise that accompany the use of models. The diverse ways in which models can be used productively may also mean that any one-dimensional scale for judging their utility is necessarily somewhat ambiguous.

Metaphors, Narratives, and Reductionism

Several issues of a more philosophical nature might benefit from brief comment. First, how do models differ from metaphors and narrative? And second, what is the relationship between models and reductionism?

Metaphors amend a definition or image, usually by shifting its context. The metaphor, "love is a prickly rose," communicates the bittersweet quality of close personal relationships. Like models, metaphors represent one thing in terms of another in order to reveal properties not otherwise apparent. Like models, they are meant to add to understanding. Their qualities, such as precision, realism, or generality, are balanced according to the goal in using them. Metaphors may trade on suggestive ambiguity, whereas most models seek clarity and discipline, but even in these features there may be overlap. In search of a distinction, it will not do simply to claim that metaphors belong in the realm of literature and models in science. Science, like literature, depends on expressiveness and metaphors excel at facilitating communication. Nonetheless, there is a difference worth noting. In using a heuristic model we ask that it reveal not just the existence of a relationship in the referent—love is associated with troublesome as well as positive emotions, as roses come with thorns—but something about the causal basis for the relationship. Love may occasionally suffer emotional turmoil, but not for the reason that roses have thorns. Even in the case of analogy, a kind of model only slightly removed from metaphor, this causal likeness is implied, if not stated (Hesse 1966). To the extent that a metaphor has scientific aspirations, it is properly viewed as an analogy in disguise.

Terrell (1990) explores how the study of prehistory can take another literary form, that of **narrative** or story-telling. His examples come from archaeological accounts of the successive waves of migrants that settled the dispersed Pacific Islands. Terrell argues that such narratives have a number of liabilities as science, but are only one step removed from models, and can be valuable when formalized sufficiently that they can be compared and tested, used evaluatively.

It is also important to distinguish between simplification and reductionism. Both sometimes invite hostility. If they are confounded such criticism will be inappropriately magnified. "The complexity of real social and biological phenomena is compared to the toylike quality of the simple models used to analyze them, and their users charged with unwarranted reductionism or plain simplemindedness" (Richerson and Boyd 1987: 27). Models do simplify by selective neglect, but they are not thereby reductionist in ways that should invite automatic skepticism. Following Mayr (1988), simplification, or what he calls **constitutive reductionism**, is both appropriate and perhaps necessary for scientific analysis. Richerson and Boyd (1987: 40) call this **tactical reductionism**. By contrast, **explanatory reductionism** (the claim that higher-level phenomena are fully explained by sub-component properties) and **theory reductionism** (the claim that any theory applied to a higher level is only a special case of theory appropriate for lower levels) are more problematic. Models usually practice constitutive reductionism, but they need not entail either of the second two types. In fact, by fostering explicit simplification by parts, models may help us to avoid explanatory or theory reductionism, even as they give us entry to complex phenomena like cultural evolution (Richerson and Boyd 1987). The facile objection that models threaten human dignity by their simplification or reductionism is not creditable.

CASE STUDIES

Three examples will illustrate the utility of modeling in archaeology. These are drawn mainly from behavioral ecology, for the simple personal reason that I know this literature best. However, they might as easily have come from new archaeology (Binford's forager-collector model [1980], or Gould's [1980] analogic models of hunter-gatherer adaptations), from evolutionary archaeology (Rindos' [1984] co-evolutionary model of plant domestication), or other archaeological approaches. Modeling is one of the most ecumenical of scientific commitments; it transcends even sharp rivalries of method, interpretation, school, and totemic theorist.

Residential and Field Processing

Interpretations of prehistory depend on knowing if there are patterned relationships among the procurement and transport of resources, residential geography, and the discard of archaeologically visible materials. An important aspect of this problem arises when resources have high and low utility components. Because low utility parts (e.g., husks, shell, bone) are more likely to preserve, it is useful to know if processing and discard occur in the field where the resource is first located or at the camp where it may be transported for consumption. Bettinger et al. (1997) take up this question with a model first used in this context by Metcalfe and Barlow (1992).

The central place foraging model assumes that (1) humans will optimize their delivery of useful material to a central place; (2) procurement occurs in a locale some distance from the residential site, imposing outward travel and return transport costs; and (3) the resource can be separated into high and low value components. The essential trade-off is represented in Figure 12.2. Field processing increases transport efficiency because loads are made up of high utility parts only. But it reduces harvesting efficiency by taking

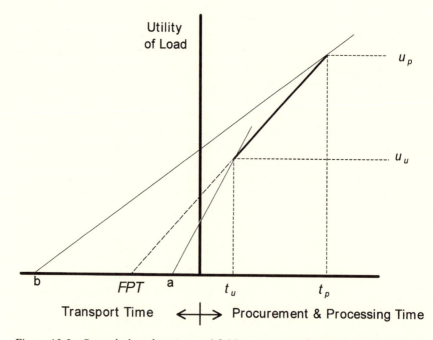

Figure 12.2. Central place foraging and field processing (after Metcalfe and Barlow 1992). This model applies to resources that can be processed to remove a bulky but low utility component (such as the shell of acorns or mussels), and that must be transported to a central place for consumption. The foraging costs and benefits of an *un*processed load of the resource (subscript u) are given by the procurement time (t_u) and resource utility (U_u). A load that has been field processed requires more work (t_p) to obtain and process, but has a higher utility (U_p). FPT is the Field Processing Threshold. If transport time is less than the FPT (point a), then hauling the resource unprocessed is the higher efficiency option. If transport time is greater than FPT (point b), then field processing before transport is a more efficient choice. Note that overall efficiency is given by utility divided by the time required for procurement, processing, and transport (or, the slope of the line segments drawn from "a" and "b"). A behavioral ecology model like this can be used to generate either qualitative or quantitative predictions by examining how changes in any of the input variables affect the relative efficiency of the two options.

field time that could be spent procuring more of the resource. Given measurement or estimates of activity costs and resource utility, processed and unprocessed, the model can be used to determine the travel costs (time or distance) at which field processing becomes more efficient; or, given a certain travel distance, it will show how much change in utility is required to shift from residential to field processing.

Bettinger and colleagues measure the volume of "burden baskets" used by California Native American groups to estimate transport parameters (e.g., volume, weight). They survey ethnographic observations which allow them to estimate the costs and benefits of processing black oak acorns (*Quercus kelloggii*) and big mussel (*Mytilus californianus*) to various stages. The results show that even short travel times (45 minutes) make it advantageous to dry acorns in the field. However, subsequent stages of acorn processing (shucking, cleaning, pounding, etc.) almost certainly occurred residentially, as the minimum travel time associated with field processing is prohibitively long (25 hours, or a distance of about 80 miles). In the case of plucking big mussel from productive habitats, the travel threshold for switching between field and residential processing is well within a daily foraging radius of two hours. In this circumstance, model predictions may allow for more accurate interpretation of the archaeological record, even though they are highly dependent on local environmental details (Bettinger et al. 1997: 897).

The model employed by Bettinger et al. gives them a means of identifying "distinctive archaeological signatures of specific human behaviours with reference to the general principles that organize those behaviours" (1997: 887; see O'Connell 1995). It stimulated experimental and ethnoarchaeological collection of novel data. The model would be interesting enough for its qualitative applications (e.g., increased travel time makes field processing more likely). But even in prehistoric settings, it can be applied quantitatively (e.g., travel times greater than 25 hours are required to make field processing and discard of acorn shells effective).

Production Risk and Social Integration

Four hundred years of northern Anasazi prehistory is the setting for a model-based study of relationships between agricultural production and social adaptation. Kohler and Van West (1996) develop a model in which the sufficiency and variability of maize yields predict periods of social integration and disintegration. They test these predictions against markers of social structure at village and supra-village levels in a 1,500-square-kilometer region of southwest Colorado.

Utility theory and risk-sensitive techniques developed in economics and behavioral ecology make up the theoretical and conceptual basis of their model. The model assumes that: (1) the utility function relating the quantity of production and its value is sigmoidal; (2) households have the goal of optimizing utility; and (3), intra-annual (spatial) and interannual (temporal) correlation among household maize yields are < 1. A simple graphical formulation shows that in years of high yield a household does best by avoiding production variance. Household members would prefer to consume the average yield available if households pool and evenly redistribute their production. Further, the advantage of pooling mechanisms such as village-level exchange and regional sociopolitical integration increases with production variance. By contrast, high variance and low average yields should lead to defection from such arrangements. Households can do best by "going it alone," and should withdraw from social interactions entailing food transfers. Through a stretch of variable but generally poor years, a household gives up more utility in its net donations to a pooling arrangement than it gets back, even if the quantities of maize given and received balance.

Empirical assessment of these predictions requires environmental measures of relative production level and variance, and archaeological measures of social integration. For the first, Kohler and Van West estimate relative corn yields for the A.D. 901–1300 period using paleoecological assessments of soil depth, elevation, soil moisture, and drought severity indices. Close dating is possible through tree-ring studies. They identify five unusually high, and an equal number of unusually low, production intervals, each lasting on the order of 10 to 50 years. This duration is presumed long enough for environmental conditions to have an impact on archaelogically visible social arrangements. The same data are used to calculate interannual and spatial variability of yields during each of the recognized intervals. The ten intervals are then rank-ordered from high production/high variance (greatest pressure for exchange) through low production/high variance (greatest pressure for defection), a deft translation of archaeological data into the input variables required by the model. For the second data set required, Kohler and Van West aggregate information from nine types of archaeological observation, each of which should correlate with increasing social integration (e.g., site size increase, roads). They use the break-up of aggregate sites as a measure of social disintegration.

An interval-by-interval comparison shows that "The general pattern of the [archaeological] record is strongly in the directions anticipated by the model" (1996: 183). For instance, the Chacoan build-up (A.D. 1100–1129) coincides with the highest period of expected cooperation, whereas the Chacoan break-up (A.D. 1130–1179) and regional abandonment (1270s–1280s) coincide with low yield/high variance situations, when defection from social integration is expected. This success is somewhat tempered by the observation that predictions based on yield alone, and on variability alone, perform as well as the risk-sensitive model which combines these two variables. This occurs because of a particular limitation in the data set: level of production and production variability are highly correlated. In principle, with less covariant data it would be possible to distinguish among these alternatives.

The Kohler and Van West model produces an important counterintuitive prediction: a modest quantitative increase in environmental variance, or a modest drop in yield, could select for a qualitative reversal in the adaptive trend: village-level and regional social integration will switch to *dis*integration. A single model shows how household self-interest can move social structure in either direction, and exactly what environmental conditions make the critical difference.

Paleolithic Population Ecology

Stiner et al. (2000) take up the implications of resource selection for human population dynamics in the Upper Paleolithic of southern Europe and western Asia. Their study gives an old idea (the Broad Spectrum Revolution, or BSR) a new and more powerful analytic purchase by allying it with models in population ecology and foraging theory. As developed by Lewis Binford and Kent Flannery, the BSR states that a combination of late Paleolithic population growth and/or habitat shifts led to intensified exploitation of a wide range of resources, especially small game and low value, difficult-to-process plant foods, thereby setting the stage for domestication and the origins of agriculture.

Stiner and colleagues document the pattern of small-game use in northern Israel and western Italy during the early Middle Paleolithic through Epi-Paleolithic periods—roughly 200,000 to 9,000 years B.P., with more precise dating varying by site—using archaeofaunal data. The percentage of small game in the overall diet and the variety of species taken are steady through this interval, but there are clear shifts in the type of organism that predominates in the small-game portion of the harvest. Relatively sessile, easy-to-capture and easily depleted species predominate early, but decline in importance late in the sequence. Edible shellfish and tortoises are key examples in Italy; tortoises, ostrich eggs, and slow-moving reptiles in Israel. In complementary fashion, relatively mobile, hard-to-capture and difficult-to-overexploit organisms increase in importance late in the period under scrutiny. Italian instances are birds of several types, hare, and rabbits; in Israel, instances are birds, hare, and squirrels. Some of the less mobile and more vulnerable species such as limpet and tortoise also decrease in size in the latter half of this period, an indicator of heavy exploitation.

Easily captured, small-game species do not go unused in the Upper and Epi-Paleolithic periods, but they are supplanted in importance by species more difficult to capture. Because these changes occur against a background of stable biotic communities, an environmental explanation for the shift is unlikely. Rather, Stiner et al. (2000) suggest that human foragers met subsistence needs from highly ranked (easily caught) species in the Middle Paleolithic. Because these hunter-gatherers were low-density, dispersed, and perhaps highly mobile predators, they did not seriously deplete these readily captured species, despite their vulnerability to overexploitation. The Upper Paleolithic shift of the small-game component of the diet to low ranked and hard-to-catch species shows that exploitation pressure had grown. High ranked small game continued to be captured on encounter, but their diminished numbers and size also reflect more intense harvesting. This interpretation is consistent with predictions of the diet breadth model of foraging theory, given an increase in human population density and greater economic pressure on faunal resources.

This explanatory scenario depends on a clear economic separation between small game that are easy to catch and easy to overexploit, and those that are more difficult to catch but also more resistant to exploitation. To test their idea, Stiner and colleagues develop a population ecology model which simulates the effect of different exploitation levels on species like those in their scenario. They draw life history parameters such as age at first reproduction, litter size, life span, and so on, from wildlife biology studies of modern analog species. To assess the sensitivity of their approach to the obvious approximations of this procedure, they calculate the results for one standard deviation above and below mean values. The desired analytic output is assessments of potential yield and resilience to exploitation; the calculations are done by a computer spreadsheet. The results show that hare and partridge will sustain harvests of 7 to 10 times those of tortoises before exploitation results in local extinction. This difference is of a magnitude sufficient to account for the archaeological pattern.

In their conclusions, Stiner et al. (2000) argue that foraging theory and population ecology models reveal, better than simple diversity measures, the subsistence "signature" that should be associated with intensification like that envisioned in the BSR. The life history variability of small game, and the scatter of small-game species across the lower end of the resource ranking scale, make them sensitive indicators of prehistoric human demography and subsistence stress.

Summary

Each of these studies is packed with archaeological data and each draws on models from economics and behavioral ecology. None of these studies sets out to directly test the model it employs. Rather they attempt to make interpretive sense of the archaeological record in terms of the model. Inasmuch as the empirical record or theory behind the models have independent credibility, and the archaeological record is subject to no competing and superior explanatory contenders, the consistency of model and data lends sound inferential substance to explanation.

FUTURE IMPORTANCE

The explicit use of models is an act of cognitive humility, admission that raw intuition—which usually means the implicit, unexamined use of models—is quite often a fallible guide to causal relationships in complex systems. Models bring discipline to private comprehension by fusing creativity with formal procedures. They facilitate clear and accurate communication. They advance efforts to identify and make use of critical data and to assess provocative ideas. It is hard to imagine a science without models of some form. Krugman (1995: 5) states that an idea will not be taken seriously in economics *unless* it can take the form of a simple model. It is a defensible claim that a science matures in parallel with its ability to develop the use of models.

An archaeologist attempting to assess progress in that respect might well watch the course of four efforts. First, to what extent can prehistorians recover data in forms that allow direct testing or evaluative use of models, or failing that, increasingly sound interpretive use of them? This is a y-axis question (Figure 12.1). Second, to what extent will simple, uni-topical models in fact coalesce into families predicted by Levins (1966), creating theory that is more synthetic in scope? This is an x-axis question. Third, will it be possible to reconcile use of optimization and equilibrium models with the role of agency and historical contingency in evolutionary processes? Ross (1999) discusses parallel issues between optimizing and historical approaches to adaptation. Broughton and O'Connell (1998) draw attention to the distinction in their review of evolutionary approaches in archaeology. Fourth, will it be possible to productively reconcile different schools of modeling (e.g., simple evolutionary ecology models based on individual-level, optimization assumptions and analytic solutions, with system-level approaches based in equilibrium assumptions and simulation solutions, with dynamic, agent-based simulations)? Said differently, will the generality of marginal value theorem (Charnov 1976) and the realistic intricacies of Guilá Naquitz (Flannery 1986) ever come to rest in the same analytical effort, and will the result be enlightening?

ACKNOWLEDGMENTS

For encouragement, ideas, and useful, critical comments, I would like to thank Robert Bettinger, Tim Earle, Sheryl Gerety, Tim Kohler, Paul Leslie, Hector Neff, Mitch Renkow, John Speth, Mary Stiner, and Bram Tucker.

REFERENCES

Aris, R., and M. Penn. (1980). The mere notion of a model. *Mathematical Modeling* 1: 1–12.

Ayala, F. J. (1982). Beyond Darwinism? The challenge of macroevolution to the synthetic theory of evolution. *Philosophy of Science Association* 2: 275–291.

Bettinger, R. L. (1991). *Hunter-Gatherers: Archaeological and Evolutionary Theory*. New York: Plenum.

Bettinger, R. L., R. Malhi, and H. McCarthy. (1997). Central place models of acorn and mussel processing. *Journal of Archaeological Science* 24: 887–899.

Binford, L. R. (1980). Willow smoke and dogs' tails: Hunter-gatherer settlement systems and archaeological site formation. *American Antiquity* 45: 4–20.

Boyer, P. (1995). *Ceteris paribus* (All else being equal). In J. Brockman and K. Matson (eds.), *How Things Are: A Science Tool-Kit for the Mind*. New York: William Morrow and Co., pp. 169–175.

Broughton, J. M., and J. F. O'Connell. (1998). On evolutionary ecology, selectionist archaeology, and behavioral archaeology. *American Antiquity* 64: 153–165.

Charnov, E. L. (1976). Optimal foraging, the marginal value theorem. *Theoretical Population Biology* 9: 129–136.

Clarke, D. L. (1972). Models and paradigms in contemporary archaeology. In D. L. Clarke (ed.), *Models in Archaeology*. London: Methuen & Co., pp. 1–60.

Flannery, K. V. (1968). Archeological systems theory and early Mesoamerica. In B. J. Meggers (ed.), *Anthropological Archeology in the Americas*. Washington, DC: Anthropological Society of Washington, pp. 67–87.

Flannery, K. V. (ed.). (1986). *Guilá Naquitz: Archaic Foraging and Early Agriculture in Oaxaca, Mexico*. Orlando, FL: Academic Press.

Fretwell, S. D. (1975). The impact of Robert MacArthur on ecology. *Annual Review of Ecology and Systematics* 6: 1–13.

Golley, F. B. (1993). *A History of the Ecosystem Concept in Ecology: More Than the Sum of the Parts*. New Haven, CT: Yale University Press.

Gould, R. A. (1980). *Living Archaeology*. Cambridge: Cambridge University Press.

Gould, S. J. (1983). The hardening of the modern synthesis. In M. Grene (ed.), *Dimensions of Darwinism: Themes and Counterthemes in Twentieth-Century Evolutionary Theory*. Cambridge: Cambridge University Press, pp. 71–93.

Hagen, J. B. (1992). *An Entangled Bank: The Origins of Ecosystem Ecology*. New Brunswick, NJ: Rutgers University Press.

Hesse, M. B. (1966). *Models and Analogies in Science*. Notre Dame, IN: University of Notre Dame Press.

Holling, C. S. (1978). *Adaptive Environmental Assessment and Management*. Chichester: John Wiley & Sons.

Kingsland, S. E. (1995). *Modeling Nature: Episodes in the History of Population Ecology*, 2nd ed. Chicago: University of Chicago Press.

Kohler, T. A. (1999). Putting social sciences together again: An introduction to the volume. In T. Kohler and G. Gumerman (eds.), *Dynamics in Human and Primate Societies*. Oxford: Oxford University Press, pp. 1–18.

Kohler, T., and G. Gumerman (eds.). (1999). *Dynamics in Human and Primate Societies*. Oxford: Oxford University Press.

Kohler, T. A., and C. R. Van West. (1996). The calculus of self-interest in the development of cooperation: Sociopolitical development and risk among the Northern Anasazi. In J. A. Tainter and B. B. Tainter (eds.), *Evolving Complexity and Environmental Risk in the Prehistoric Southwest*. Reading, MA: Addison-Wesley, pp. 169–196.

Krugman, Paul. (1995). *Development, Geography, and Economic Theory*. Cambridge, MA: MIT Press.

Levins, R. (1966). The strategy of model building in population biology. *American Scientist* 54: 421–431.

Levins, R. (1993). A response to Orzack and Sober: Formal analysis and the fluidity of science. *The Quarterly Review of Biology* 68: 547–555.

Maynard Smith, J. (1978). Optimization theory in evolution. *Annual Review of Ecology and Systematics* 9: 31–56.

Mayr, E. (1988). Is biology an autonomous science? In E. Mayr (ed.), *Toward a New Philosophy of Biology: Observations of an Evolutionist*. Cambridge, MA: Harvard University Press, pp. 8–23.

Metcalfe, D., and K. R. Barlow. (1992). A model for exploring the optimal trade-off between field processing and transport. *American Anthropologist* 94: 340–356.

O'Connell, J. F. (1995). Ethnoarchaeology needs a general theory of behavior. *Journal of Archaeological Research* 3: 205–255.

Orzack, S. H., and E. Sober. (1993). A critical assessment of Levins's *The Strategy of Model Building in Population Biology* (1966). *The Quarterly Review of Biology* 68: 533–546.

Relethford, J. H. (1999). Models, predictions, and the fossil record of modern human origins. *Evolutionary Anthropology* 8: 7–10.

Richerson, P. J., and R. Boyd. (1987). Simple models of complex phenomena: The case of cultural evolution. In J. Dupré (ed.), *The Latest on the Best: Essays on Evolution and Optimality*. Cambridge, MA: MIT Press, pp. 27–52.

Rindos, D. (1984). *The Origins of Agriculture: An Evolutionary Perspective*. Orlando, FL: Academic Press.

Ross, C. F. (1999). How to carry out functional morphology. *Evolutionary Anthropology* 7: 217–222.

Schoener, T. W. (1987). A brief history of optimal foraging ecology. In A. C. Kamil, J. R. Krebs, and H. R. Pulliam (eds.), *Foraging Behavior*. New York: Plenum, pp. 5–67.

Smith, E. A., and B. Winterhalder (eds.). (1992). *Evolutionary Ecology and Human Behavior*. New York: Aldine de Gruyter.

Starfield, A. M., and A. L. Bleloch. (1986). *Building Models for Conservation and Wildlife Management*. New York: Macmillan.

Stiner, M. C., N. D. Munro, and T. A. Surovell. (2000). The tortoise and the hare: Small game use, the broad spectrum revolution, and paleolithic demography. *Current Anthropology* 41: 39–73.

Terrell, J. (1990). Storytelling and prehistory. *Archaeological Method and Theory* 2: 1–29.

Thomas, D. H. (1972). A computer simulation model of Great Basin Shoshonean subsistence and settlement patterns. In D. L. Clarke (ed.), *Models in Archaeology*. London: Methuen & Co., pp. 671–704.

Thomas, D. H. (1973). An empirical test for Steward's model of Great Basin settlement patterns. *American Antiquity* 38: 155–176.

Tooby, J., and I. DeVore. (1987). The reconstruction of hominid behavioral evolution through strategic modeling. In W. G. Kinzey (ed.), *The Evolution of Human Behavior: Primate Models*. Albany: State University of New York Press, pp. 183–237.

Winterhalder, B., and E. A. Smith. (2000). Analyzing adaptive processes: Human behavioral ecology at twenty-five. *Evolutionary Anthropology* 9: 51–72.

Winterhalder, B., and E. A. Smith (eds.). (1981). *Hunter-Gatherer Foraging Strategies*. Chicago: University of Chicago Press.

Wobst, H. Martin. (1974). Boundary conditions for Paleolithic social systems: A simulation approach. *American Antiquity* 39: 147–178.

Chapter 13

Natural Selection

Robert D. Leonard and George T. Jones

INTRODUCTION

Perhaps no idea provided by Darwin is more significant than the concept of **natural selection**. Darwin (1959) defines it as follows: "[the] preservation of favourable variations, and the rejection of injurious variations, I call Natural Selection."

While reproduction is implied in Darwin's definition, the biologist Ernst Mayr makes the role of reproduction clear by stating that natural selection is "the differential reproduction of individuals that differ uniquely in their adaptive superiority" (1982: 57). Here Darwin's "favorable variations" are Mayr's reason for "adaptive superiority."

E. O. Wilson, perhaps the greatest evolutionary thinker of the latter quarter of the twentieth century, adds the concepts of genes and populations to his definition: "The differential contribution of offspring to the next generation by individuals of different genetic types but belonging to the same population" (Wilson 1975).

Hodge (1992) makes the point that natural selection is best conceptualized as an analog of **artificial selection** (human manipulation of animal and plant varieties), as was Darwin's intent when he coined the term "natural selection." The difference between artificial selection and natural selection is that while people select the favorable characteristics in the former, nature does so in the latter. Darwin (1998: 108) himself compared the respective efficacy of the two processes:

How fleeting are the wishes and efforts of man! how short his time! and consequently how poor will his products be, compared with those accumulated by nature during whole geological periods. Can we wonder, then, that nature's productions should be far "truer" in character than man's productions; that they should be infinitely better adapted to the most complex conditions of life, and should plainly bear the stamp of far higher workmanship?

Some researchers believe that it is best to refer to artificial selection as **cultural selection,** and see it as analogous to the operation of natural selection (Boyd and Richerson 1985; Cavalli-Sforza and Feldman 1981; Durham 1991; Richerson and Boyd 1992). That humans (and other animals) select favorable variants by managing reproduction in populations of other species (or themselves) itself is an evolved capacity favored by natural selection. Thus, logically, artificial selection may be considered a subset of the broader process of natural selection.

It is useful therefore to develop a definition of natural selection that is not reproductively based. Endler (1992) gives us perhaps the most workable view of natural selection (p. 221):

"Natural Selection" can be defined as a *process* that occurs if and only if these three conditions are present: the population has (a) variation among individuals in some attribute or trait (phenotypic variation); (b) a consistent relationship between that trait and mating ability, fertilizing ability, fertility, fecundity, and/or survivorship (fitness variation); and (c) a consistent relationship, for that trait, between parents and their offspring, which is at least partially independent of common environment effects (inheritance).

Endler's definition of natural selection also provides a definition of **drift,** a process meeting conditions (a) and (c) but not (b).

So, in a biological population, we may have variation among organisms in a trait—say, speed (condition a: phenotypic variation)—where some individuals are faster than others. If speed influences mating ability, fertilizing ability, fertility, and/or survivorship (condition b: fitness variation), and if offspring inherit a capacity to move swiftly, in whole or in part, from their parents (condition c: inheritance), then natural selection has occurred. The trait is then, by definition, an **adaptation.** If (b) does not hold, that is, if there is no impact on fitness, then the character state "speed" is not subject to selection, and is contrastingly subject to the process of drift.

One group of archaeologists who use Endler's definition of selection in their work sometimes call themselves Evolutionary Archaeologists or Selectionists. Evolutionary Archaeologists work from the position that technology is part of the human phenotype. This perspective is held in common in evolutionary biology, as the **phenotype** is often defined as the totality of the characteristics of an individual that is the product of the interaction of the genotype and the environment. This definition includes behavior and, when that behavior involves modifying material objects to supplement our interaction with our environment, it includes technology. Therefore, knowing (a) that there is variation in human technology, (b) that some of this variation affects fitness, and (c) that a form of inheritance occurs when we learn how to use technology, a number of archaeologists have used Darwinian theory to build evolutionary explanations of technological change. This admittedly inclusive concept of natural selection is a basic theoretical principle of Evolutionary Archaeology (EA).

To consider a technological example, let us state that (a) we have variation in cooking technology, and that some variants impact fitness (b). For example, if stronger ceramic walls allowed for more efficient processing, where more individuals could be fed with less, there would be fitness effects. In order to operationalize condition (c), however, archaeologists and many others (Boyd and Richerson 1985; Cavalli-Sforza and Feldman 1981; Dennett 1990; Durham 1991, 1992; Hull 1982) have recognized that inheritance here is of course not genetic, but learned, and the product of **cultural transmission**—the social acquisition of knowledge. As we all know, unlike genetic transmission, cultural transmission is not only passed from parent to offspring, but can come about through many kinds of human interaction. So, as in our earlier example, if conditions (a), (b), and (c) are present, natural selection has occurred, and the variant under study is, by definition, an adaptation. Where condition (b) is lacking, the technological trait is not the product of selection, is not an adaptation, but is subject to the process of drift. By definition, artifacts or attributes of artifacts that meet conditions (a), (b), and (c) are **functional** (under the operation of natural selection), those that lack condition (b) are termed **stylistic** (are subject to drift) (Dunnell 1978a, 1978b).

Evolutionary Archaeologists believe that by so extending the concept of the trait of individuals to include technological traits of organisms, and that by recognizing cultural transmission as a form of inheritance, we can bring the powerful Darwinian model to bear in our attempts to understand human evolution. One additional concept must be introduced here. Unlike people, who have reproductive success, artifacts have alternatively **replicative success**, or differential persistence through time and across space (Leonard and Jones 1987). The concept of replicative success is important because it allows us to bring an important empirical component to archaeology, that of the relative abundance of technologies in the archaeological record. Information about abundance, and the causes of varying abundance, allows us to operationalize the concept of natural selection in archaeology.

But how do we determine whether or not natural selection has worked to shape technology? Put another way, is a particular technology functional or stylistic? While we address this subject in more detail below, let us make some preliminary statements here. Making the determination as to whether or not a technology, or aspect of a technology, is functional or stylistic is most often a difficult task. First, Evolutionary Archaeologists make no a priori assumptions regarding whether or not a technology is either stylistic or functional. Most often, engineering studies that test the efficacy or performance of alternate designs provide the first line of evidence regarding function. In our cooking technology example above, engineering studies would evaluate the respective thermal properties of the different ceramic technologies. If our engineering studies suggest that under certain environmental conditions one technology offers an advantage over another in a specific context (e.g., one is less likely to break when heated at high temperatures), these are likely to be functional alternatives and thus their frequency is influenced by natural selection. If there is no such advantage, style and neutrality are indicated.

While engineering studies are an important beginning point, we may also examine the relative replicative success of the technologies over time and/ or across space. Stylistic and functional traits tend to behave differently across those two variables. Functional traits tend to spread rapidly, because they confer an immediate advantage to recipients. Although relatively long-lived, functional traits tend to be rapidly replaced when something better comes along. In contrast, stylistic traits appear, reach a point of popularity, then fade at about the same rate they become popular. Examples of the former include the internal combustion engine and the incandescent light bulb. Examples of the later include tail fins on U.S. automobiles in the 1950s and "lava lamps." Finally, functional traits tend to correlate with other traits we would consider adaptive. For example, the internal combustion engine found its way into many different settings, powering many kinds of machines. Moreover, like other adaptive traits, it moved across spatial or cultural boundaries with relative ease. Stylistic traits are more strongly circumscribed spatially. Indeed, like tail fins, they tend to be "defined with" a particular era and demographic group.

Once a case has been made that natural selection has occurred, the process of natural selection itself can be interpreted as to its form. There is **directional selection,** where selection favors one end of the normal distribution of a trait, which results in a shift of the normal distribution itself. An example of directional selection may have been the decrease in size of projectile points from Clovis to Folsom when the early inhabitants of the Western Hemisphere shifted from hunting elephants to bison. Or consider the shift in the memory function of computer chips, which appears to be under strong selective pressures to increase the number of instructions per unit time. **Stabilizing selection** holds the mode of the distribution relatively constant. Fishing technologies in general, specifically fishhooks and nets, seem to have been under stabilizing selection for thousands of years, perhaps because the stability of the mode is tied to the sizes and types of fish being caught. **Disruptive selection** selects against the most common variants, leading to divergence. We may be seeing disruptive selection in action with respect to the contemporary distribution of the written word. E-books, palm pilots, and the Internet are currently at the tails of the distribution, and the standard book (the mode) will never be the same. **Catastrophic selection** is strong selection where there are population crashes in harsh times, followed by growth and divergence when strong selection relaxes. This certainly happened in many parts of the world with colonization and the spread of diseases of European origin. This catastrophic selection affected not only human population numbers, but technology and behavior as well.

While the former types of selection describe shapes of distribution, two other "types" of selection refer to process. **Sexual selection** operates on traits related to obtaining mates. Although not fully explored in archaeology, sexual selection plays a role in costly signaling (Neiman 1997), and may play a role in explaining many stylistic traits as well as traits that are considered waste (Dunnell 1989). **Group selection** is a controversial idea where it is argued that selection operates on social groups as well as on individuals. Group selection has a long history in evolutionary biology, and has long been rejected for the most part. However, recent work by Sober and Wilson (1998) argues that group selection is a major force of evolution, and their mathematical proof is most convincing. The role of group selection may be a new hotbed of inquiry in the coming years in archaeology.

HISTORY IN ARCHAEOLOGY

The concept of natural selection has little history in archaeology prior to 1978. Dunnell (1980: 1950) argues that the concept is virtually absent in a non-Darwinian school of evolutionary thought called Cultural Evolution (CE), noting that it appears but twice in the influential book *Evolution and Culture* (Sahlins and Service 1960) as "an uncomfortable synonym of adaptation in an innocuous context." CE preferred the word "adaptation" instead.

The CE use of "adaptation" permeates the New and Processual Archaeology because of the influence of the work of the great Cultural Evolutionist Leslie White on his student Lewis Binford, one of the founders of Processual Archaeology. Adaptation is not presented as if to refer to a product of the process of natural selection, as we have used it above, but as a process unto itself (Kirch 1980). In effect, this view of adaptation—as process—is substituted for natural selection, perhaps because of a desire of anthropologists to maintain the distinction between humans and other organisms, which is done by interjecting the notion that humans intentionally adapt to improve their fit with the environment. As a result, neither the concept of natural selection nor adaptation in its biological usage has yet to be rigorously applied by Processual Archaeologists.

In the 1980s, however, two strong groups of evolutionary theorists emerged who sought to bring a Darwinian vision to archaeology. This presumably means bringing the concept of natural selection to archaeology as well. As noted above, one of these groups is Evolutionary Archaeology (EA). The second strong group is Evolutionary Ecology (EE). These approaches will be contrasted below, primarily with respect to how they view the concept of natural selection.

CONTEMPORARY USES

The last 20 years have generated hundreds of references to theoretical and empirical work of evolutionary archaeologists and evolutionary ecologists. While the vast majority of work in EE is with contemporary peoples and not the archaeological record, EA applications are almost exclusively archaeological. Fortunately, for the purposes of this review, two recent publications (Boone and Smith 1998; Lyman and O'Brien 1998) have managed to isolate the differences between the two perspectives on the conceptual importance of natural selection (and other evolutionary forces). This focus comes in large part because of the commentary generated and published in the same journal—*Current Anthropology.*

Proponents of both EA and EE regard their respective frameworks as Darwinian, and yet they differ in regard to which forces of evolutionary change are held as most important in the human cultural record. First and foremost, they differ in terms of whether or not the changes that we see in the archaeological record are directly the product of the operation of evolutionary processes such as natural selection and drift (the EA perspective), or alternatively, that the archaeological record represents phenotypic plasticity (the EE perspective). In other words, technology and human behavior evolve via selection and drift (EA), or have evolutionary processes shaped the human brain to make rational decisions, and technological change is not evolution at all, but merely reflective of our evolved capacities (EE)?

One EE researcher puts his perspective forth clearly. Mithen (1998) states: "In my 1990 book I put forward the argument that natural selection is relevant in our discipline only with regard to how it has shaped the human mind/brain—our means of making decisions" (p. S163). From Mithen's perspective, natural selection "has shaped" but no longer does so, and, importantly, probably has not shaped the behaviors that created the archaeological record since some time during the late Pleistocene when, presumably, the mind/brain achieved its modern aspect.

Most, if not all Evolutionary Archaeologists would disagree with Mithen. They might ask, for example, if evolution isn't still occurring, when did it "stop?" If it has stopped, will future generations of researchers influenced by EE recognize when it starts again, should it do so? On the other hand, perhaps Mithen's perspective is overstated, and other EE researchers might say that the point isn't that natural selection has stopped, but simply that natural selection is no longer the major operative process shaping evolutionary change. Indeed, along with selection and drift, EE regards our evolved cognitive capacities as generating a third key process in humans—that is, directed innovation. This suggests a second major difference between EE and EA. While EE sees directed innovation as allowing humanity to largely transcend the operation of natural selection, EA recognizes directed innovation, but sees the products as simply a source of variation upon which natural selection acts.

To EA, technologies have fitness consequences, and many are the product of natural selection. As such, technologies are not just the products of genotypes; they influence the success of those very genotypes. To EA, this is evolution. We read the historical record of artifacts and technologies as one of replicative success, but it is not difficult to see, even in the broadest demographic patterns, that these changes also altered reproductive success and the structure of genetic populations. To EA, behavioral plasticity is simply a proximate description of the present at any one point of time that ineffectively describes behavioral and technological change that are shaped by evolutionary processes that continue. Indeed, contra many who hold the EE perspective that natural selection has not been a major evolutionary force since the Pleistocene, there is reason to believe that evolution has accelerated at a pace never seen before (Wills 1998). With our ever-increasing population numbers, gene pool, changing environments, and technological change, never has there been so much grist for the evolutionary mill.

In considering the concept of natural selection—the task of this chapter—in Darwinian frameworks in archaeology, we are left in an odd position. If we assume the EE position that selection stopped sometime in the Pleistocene (and we know not where), or has ceased to be an important force in evolution, the concept has little theoretical value in archaeology. As a consequence, by their own criteria, there can be no EE examples in this chapter. We find this unfortunate, and unnecessary, and anxiously await the recognition in EE that evolution shaped not just our mind in the Pleistocene, but shapes our behavior and technology then and today.

Before we turn to examples, let us first state that we believe that the EE program has much to offer archaeology, and that assuming plasticity is not necessary for that program to continue to make worthwhile contributions. We also believe that the success of EE being almost exclusively in the modern realm of contemporary peoples instead of the archaeological record of past peoples has led to an unfortunate and unnecessary position amid their considerable successes. Many of the EE statements regarding plasticity are clearly **presentist**, that is, they are interpreting the past in terms of the present, rather than seeing the past and the present as the product of the same ongoing evolutionary processes.

We now turn to some examples of how natural selection is used in EA.

CASE STUDIES

When Evolutionary Archaeologists construct arguments about the nature and cause of a cultural pattern, or a change in that pattern they are developing historical explanations. It may be an obvious point, but the certainty with which we offer explanations relies not on any capacity to prove our arguments, but on the plausibility of those explanations, judged by their logic, sufficiency, and consistency with multiple lines of evidence. When we argue, for instance, that the frequency of an artifact trait increased because it was favored by natural selection (rather than increased by virtue of drift), we do so not because we know this for a fact, but because we find this to be the most plausible explanation, which we judge on several dimensions. These dimensions, or lines of argument, include the performance characteristics of the trait in relation to a selection context, the frequency distribution of the trait over time, and sometimes how that trait behaves spatially—its manner of diffusion. Ultimately, what we would like to demonstrate in every instance where natural selection is invoked to explain the differential persistence of a trait is whether that trait has measurably altered the fitness of the bearers possessing the trait. But that criterion is very difficult to assess with certainty.

We present below two examples in which researchers have attempted to evaluate whether archaeological traits are under the influence of natural selection. We have selected these examples to illustrate how arguments variously rely on performance criteria, historical trajectories, and fitness criteria to build cases for the operation of natural selection on behavioral and artifactual components of the human phenotype. In the first example, selection is shown to be operating on particular traits or trait complexes that form projectile point types. We conclude this example by examining the competition between two attribute variants and the consequences for chronological patterns among Great Basin projectile points. In the second example, selection is suggested to favor wasteful behaviors of individuals and/or groups, thereby enhancing fitness by limiting reproduction while ensuring survival of existing offspring.

Textbook examples of the workings of natural selection often focus on a single trait, that is, beak forms among finches or coloring among moths, which appear to differentially influence the survival of phenotypes that vary with respect to the trait. In these examples the fitness consequences of alternative variants of the trait are quite substantial. Moths with the "wrong" coloring, for example, are easily seen and much more likely to be preyed upon than moths exhibiting more "adaptive" coloration. Hence, the likelihood of survival of the first moth, and thus its fitness, is much lower than the better-adapted moth. But many traits are not so likely in isolation to determine the survival of their bearers. Rather, they contribute in subtle and complex ways to fitness. This makes evaluating the influences of a particular trait within a matrix of fitness-enhancing and fitness-detracting traits all but immeasurable experimentally or in a historical record. As in the case of somatic traits, this is probably the case for behavioral and technological components of the human phenotype as well.

With this proviso in mind we turn our attention to our first example, asking why trait variants in a simple technological system exhibit differential persistence. Just this kind of question frames Braun's classic study of Middle Woodland ceramic vessel technology (Braun 1987). He found that an evolving subsistence pattern that involved an increasing utilization of seeds introduced strong selective pressures for capable cooking vessels. The basis for judging which competing variants—ceramic vessel wall thickness—were more capable (gave a mechanical advantage in the selection context) was based on performance or engineering analyses. In such circumstances, when significant cost differentials exist among alternative variants it can be argued plausibly that there should be a straightforward relationship between artifact fitness and the fitness of the human phenotype.

Our example considers another class of artifacts, the stone tips of projectiles. Like ceramics, projectile points long have held the interest of archaeologists because of their value as index fossils, and for seriation-based chronological inference. Unlike ceramic attributes, which have been used to create chronological types, however, the attributes defining projectile types have more often been treated as if they were functional rather than stylistic. In evolutionary terms this would mean they were under selection rather than being selectively neutral (Leonard and Jones 1987; Neiman 1995). Which of these alternative views is correct is difficult to resolve.

From an engineering or performance standpoint, a number of attributes of projectile points would appear to influence their mechanical efficiency and cost (e.g., time and energy involved in production and repair). In addition to symmetry and sharpness, which relate to flight and penetration, hafting attributes can be differentiated on the basis of how effectively they mechanically bond the elements of the projectile. We can also imagine that the resistance of a projectile point to damage or its capacity to be resharpened also influence cost. For each goal, one variant will enhance the performance of the projectile over other variants. Thus, where selection forces are strong, and one or more of these traits are affected, there should be trends toward character fixation or narrower tolerances of metrical traits (stabilizing selection).

Beck (1995, 1998) has examined this issue with respect to projectile points in the Great Basin. Rather than examining the issue from the standpoint of projectile point types, the unit traditionally used for chronological studies, Beck examines nine traits that are used in the definitions of these types. Just as some physical traits of an organism and not others will be under selection at a particular point in time, the traits that archaeologists combine to create units (i.e., types) will be affected by selection forces to different degrees. Thus, a trait complex—a type—may be *primarily* under selection or *primarily* neutral at any one point in time, but this situation may change as context changes. By examining the behavior of attributes instead, it should be possible to detect which are responding to selection forces.

On the basis of performance characteristics of projectile points, it is fairly clear that each of the measured attributes that Beck considers—attributes relating to mass and hafting—potentially can influence the effectiveness of the projectile system. From this standpoint, then, performance analysis is one step in establishing the sufficiency of a selection argument. To differentiate the forces of natural selection and drift on these attributes, Beck focuses on their behavior through time.

For a quantitative trait like length, temporal patterns in the mean and variation about that mean should differ under various types of selection forces. In the case of directional selection, the mean will shift over time in a particular direction, while in the case of stabilizing selection, the mean will remain effectively the same. In the case of disruptive selection, the mean will fluctuate, but the emergence of additional modes should be evident (Beck 1998: 23).

The behavior of stylistic or neutral traits is different from that of traits under selection (Neiman 1995). The effects of drift give rise to frequency distributions over time that "despite short-term fluctuations, tend to be unimodal with the mode occurring near the center of the distribution" (Neiman 1995: 23).

Using the projectile points from Gatecliff Shelter (Thomas and Bierwirth 1983), which contains a well-dated 4,500-year occupational record, Beck examines nine attributes in order to discern if any show directional trends through time. Two attributes, neck width and proximal shoulder angle (PSA—relates to the shape of the haft element), exhibit such trends. Before taking this analysis further, however, it is important to recognize that this record represents two weaponry systems, the spearthrower and the bow and arrow. The directionality seen in neck width, which is linked to the shaft diameter of the projectile, certainly was imparted by rapid replacement throughout the Great Basin of the atlatl and dart by the bow and arrow.

Beck suggests that the point tips in these two technologies were not necessarily under the same selection constraints and thus should be considered separately. Indeed, when large and small points are separated (on the basis of neck width), different traits show directional trends. Among large points, two length measurements and PSA exhibit directional trends, while the thickness and PSA of small points are distributed in time as if under selection.

The temporal patterns of the remaining traits are less distinctive. In all cases the mean fluctuates back and forth from horizon to horizon at Gatecliff, a pattern suggesting drift (Beck 1998: 28). Beck argues, however, that such fluctuation can be misleading because most functional traits operate within tolerance limits and thus can fluctuate randomly within those limits. Selection operates on the tolerance limits, while drift controls the patterns within those limits. If we look once again at neck width, a trait already determined to be functional, we see that this trait varies widely among dart points but much less so among arrow points; the limits of the two, however, are different. Bettinger and Eerkens (1997) contend that the smaller variation in arrow points relates to the greater complexity of the technology generally and more critical tolerances for effective performance. Beck shows a similar behavior to that of neck width among all of the other traits, suggesting they, too, are functional.

One final analysis involves a closer examination of PSA. This variable actually conflates two nominal traits used in Great Basin projectile point classification. The first is the type of haft, that is, whether the point is side-notched (PSA > 150 degrees) or corner-notched (PSA < 150 degrees); and second, if the point is corner-notched, whether the stem is expanding (150 > PSA > 110) or parallel/contracting (PSA < 110). Beck shows that when partitioned according to these two variables, a monotonic pattern through time is obtained, and thus she concludes that it is this combination of type of haft and shape of stem into PSA that is largely responsible for the historical behavior of Great Basin projectile point types, a trait that she has shown to be under selection and thus functional.

In a different discussion, Beck (1995) shows that the two haft types—side-notching and corner-notching—actually were in competition during the period about 8500 to 8000 B.P. when she believes the spearthrower first was introduced. Side-notching wanes by about 5000 B.P. while corner-notching increases. She suggests that the latter out-competed the former because corner-notching, in the long run, was a more efficient hafting technology. Her argument turns on the fact that, of the two notching variants, side-notching weakens the projectile point near its center. As a result, if a side-notched point breaks at the haft it cannot be easily resharpened because there is little remaining mass. A less vulnerable and more easily retooled corner-notched point appears to have been a more efficient use of tool stone. Hence, Beck suggests, selection for corner-notching reflected its lower cost. The broader selection context is simply one in which one form of notching—side-notching—entails greater risk, that is, a somewhat lower probability of successful prey capture and corresponding higher subsistence costs.

Writing about a decade after the publication of his seminal review of evolutionary theory in archaeology, Robert Dunnell offered a glimpse of how evolutionary theory might offer a new perspective on the reason for the construction of mounds by Middle Woodland cultures of the eastern

United States (Dunnell 1989, 1999). Although admittedly an explanatory sketch, Dunnell's conception of the problem has led to several other studies (e.g., Madsen et al. 1999) seeking explanations of public or monumental architecture, or, to characterize these phenomena more in line with Dunnell's thinking, wasteful behavior.

The question as Dunnell poses it was what selective advantage accrued to individuals or groups who participated in the construction of burial mounds during Middle Woodland times (and what change in selection forces in the Late Woodland ended these practices)? In framing a theoretical approach to this question, Dunnell takes the position that artifacts "are the hard parts of the behavioral segment of phenotypes" (Dunnell 1989: 40).

Dunnell likens the question of why humans participate in wasteful expenditures of energy in mound construction to any organism's "decision" to delay reproductive opportunities in order to store energy against the risk of future perturbations that might reduce fitness. By not converting energy to offspring, an organism reduces its rate of reproduction, but may enhance the likelihood of survival of offspring. Thus, a lower rate of reproduction is offset by an increased rate of survival. In conceptualizing mound construction in this way, Dunnell recognizes wasteful behavior as a capacity to, in a sense, store energy or human effort. In this view Dunnell sees selection as relating rather directly to reproductive success. In particular, natural selection favors energy conservation strategies that reduce risk in settings of severe and unpredictable subsistence shortfalls.

But certainly, by constructing mounds great supplies of energy are expended that cannot obviously later be extracted from these earthworks. Of course, we could move conceptually to ideas about the symbolic storage of energy in such public edifices, but Dunnell's argument stays close to the material arena. He sees wasteful behavior as an evolutionary response to severe environmental perturbations, which is selected for because it both diverts energy from reproduction and establishes a reservoir of time that a person or group can devote to subsistence and/or reproduction when difficult conditions arise.

Dunnell's ideas oppose the conventional notion that mound construction was only possible once the enhanced productivity of agriculture had become available. He claims just the opposite, that Middle Woodland populations were still generalist foragers who faced periodic subsistence shortfalls. By reducing the rate of reproduction, Middle Woodland population size was kept well below carrying capacity. With the development of intensive agriculture in the Late Woodland, mound construction ended and the energy released was diverted to adapting to agricultural production. In essence, Late Woodland populations contributed the time that had been "stored" in mound building to making their new subsistence activity work.

Wasteful displays are a widespread phenomenon in the archaeological record. Several other studies have built on Dunnell's thesis, offering up additional functional arguments for the expression of waste. In effect, these analyses have explored some of the proximate causes that might support the selection for wasteful behavior. In their analysis of ceremonial architecture in Polynesia, Graves and Ladefoged (1995) express another selective advantage to what they prefer to term "superfluous" behavior. They argue that this class of behavior "may establish a social context for resource and labor pooling" (1995: 162). Along with Dunnell, they imagine the selective advantages of superfluous behavior will be strongest where risks of environmental perturbations affecting subsistence are greatest. But they argue further that suprapolity integration provides the context in which labor pooling is possible, enabling sharing of risk over large geographic territories in which perturbations may be differentially felt.

In support of their model, Graves and Ladefoged cite the fact that ceremonial architecture developed first and tended to persist in those Polynesian localities that experience the greatest perturbations. Moreover, they find these behaviors were most strongly manifested in marginal districts where labor and resource pooling would achieve the largest benefits for individuals or groups. In the case of Easter Island, in particular, they suggest that superfluous behavior had the effect of stabilizing population size at low levels (Graves and Ladefoged 1995: 165). Where ceremonial architecture persisted for some time, Graves and Ladefoged suggest the disappearance of these behaviors matches trends of increasing agricultural intensification in some cases and, in others, corresponds to the drop in population sizes following the introduction of European diseases. In both instances diminished superfluous behavior is tied to commission of greater effort toward subsistence pursuits.

Like Dunnell's argument, Grave and Ladefoged's treatment is not a full-scale test of the waste or superfluous behavior hypothesis. Their sketch does, however, reconceptualize a problem in such a way as to better accord with the archaeological record. For our interests here, natural selection is conceptualized similarly in both studies, that is, in terms of how these behaviors achieve enhanced reproduction and survival for individuals or groups. But it is not clear at which scale, the individual or group, selection is thought to act most strongly. Insofar as the record represents small communities of cooperating individuals, kin or group selection might be counted as a dominant mechanism. Yet this idea is not spelled out clearly in either study (see Dunnell 1999 for a discussion of this issue).

In another consideration of wasteful behavior, Neiman (1997) more clearly takes the view that such behaviors confer advantages to individuals, not groups. That many individuals, both kin and unrelated people, may cooperate in these behaviors suggests only that a set of different survival strategies are under selection. The empirical focus of Neiman's study is the manufacture and construction of dated Mayan monuments. Elaborately carved and costly to manufacture, these monuments represent, for Neiman's purposes, examples of wasteful advertising. Neiman observes that monument construction is wasteful "because it represents fitness costs that, unlike the time and energy expended foraging, have no apparent compensatory fitness benefit" (Neiman 1997: 269). Huge investments in the procurement of monument stone and in the maintenance of individuals "skilled in the use of a complex system of hieroglyphic writing, the accompanying iconographic repertoire, and in carving and painting" (Neiman 1997: 269) diverted resources away from other, more direct, fitness-enhancing behaviors.

In Neiman's view, selection will favor conspicuous consumption when that behavior faithfully conveys information between sender and receiver. More specifically, waste advertises in a novel manner some kinds of information about the sender that are not easily conveyed by more direct means. The advantage to the sender comes if the signal results in the receiver acting in ways that benefit the sender. But as Neiman points out, there must be a compensatory advantage for the receiver to correctly interpret the signal. Wasteful advertising, then, "is engineered by natural selection so that the sender's and receiver's strategies enhance their fitness, relative to alternative strategies, thus driving the signaling system to fixation" (Neiman 1997: 270).

In the example that Neiman develops, the signal reflected by Mayan monuments is the competitive abilities of the sender. To keep the system "honest," there should be a tendency for more effective competitors to invest in wasteful signals that exceed the level that can be afforded by their competitors. Similarly, there should be pressures favoring the proper interpretation of this information by receivers. The end result of this co-evolutionary relationship, Neiman argues, is the fixation of rules for sending and decoding wasteful signals. He goes further to suggest that, in any particular cultural context, variation in such a system will reflect the competitive abilities of the poorest advertisers, the variance of competitive ability among competitors, and the payoff accruing investments in advertising.

The examples of wasteful behavior treat archaeological patterns of a different scale than our example of projectile point morphology. Experimental performance evaluations, which are critical in judging if projectile point attributes are functional, cannot be used to judge if mound building suppressed birth rates and yet still enhanced the reproductive fitness of Middle Woodland populations. What we need to be more certain of the veracity of this claim about wasteful behavior, whatever form it takes, is a means to show that it can have the stipulated effects on reproduction; that is, by lowering reproduction rates, fitness is enhanced.

Madsen et al. (1999) have tackled this issue. Building a simulation model, they show how different reproductive strategies or mixes of strategies might evolve in environments that are highly variable, as contrasted with those that are stable. Their analysis is developed to determine if reproductive behaviors emphasizing low fecundity can be selected for under any circumstance (and yield higher fitness levels), or if high-fecundity strategies are always favored. What the simulations demonstrate is that wasteful behaviors, which result in lower fecundity, indeed are capable of achieving higher reproductive success than high-fecundity strategies in resource settings with low predictability. Moreover, the simulation results also indicate frequency of wasteful behavior should be negatively correlated with mobility. That is, groups with fewer prospects of moving from low energy settings to higher energy ones should invest more effort in waste than more mobile groups.

CONCLUSIONS

Many archaeologists dispute the claim that natural selection plays a role in the success or failure of artifactual and behavioral traits. In short, they argue that behavioral variation and fitness have no necessary relationship. But based on the examples we have looked at, the opposite seems to be the case. While it is quite true that measuring the fitness effects of trait variants—here artifacts—is difficult, this problem is little different from establishing how allelic variation influences fitness in populations. At the scale in which waste was considered, the fitness consequences seem more obvious since the commitment of energy to mound building is so considerable. At much finer scales, when we consider something like the relative advantages of a hafting attribute, we must imagine how significant are the effects when the infinitesimally small advantages of one technology over another are summed over the long term.

These examples indicate that the same kinds of arguments that are used to establish the effects of selection on biological systems can be applied to the behaviors and technologies of humans. These arguments rest on the same kinds of evaluations: how traits function, how trait variants may perform more or less effectively in differing contexts, and what consequences those differentials may have for the fitness of individuals, kin groups, or more inclusive groups. When such arguments concern features of the historical record, whether about anatomy or artifacts, they are at best plausible and sufficient claims, not proofs of the working of selection. "Proof" comes only with general acceptance of the proposed explanation in the absence of a better one. This is but one strength of evolutionary studies, along with a general appreciation that an even better argument may well come along in the future.

REFERENCES

Beck, C. (1995). Functional attributes and the differential persistence of Great Basin dart forms. *Journal of California and Great Basin Anthropology* 17: 222–243.

Beck, C. (1998). Projectile point types as valid chronological units. In A. F. Ramenofsky and A. Steffen (eds.), *Unit Issues in Archaeology: Measuring Time, Space, and Material*. Salt Lake City: University of Utah Press, pp. 21–40.

Bettinger, R., and J. Earkens. (1997). Evolutionary implications of metrical variation in Great Basin projectile points. In C. M. Barton and G. A. Clark (eds.), *Rediscovering Darwin: Evolutionary Theory and Archaeological Explanation*. Archeolgical Papers No. 7. Arlington, VA: American Anthropological Association, pp. 177–191.

Boone, J. L., and E. A. Smith. (1998). Is it evolution yet? A critique of evolutionary archeology. *Current Anthropology* 39: S141–S173.

Boyd, R., and P. J. Richerson. (1985). *Culture and the Evolutionary Process*. Chicago: University of Chicago Press.

Braun, D. P. (1987). Coevolution of sedentism, pottery technology, and horticulture in the central Midwest, 200 B.C.–A.D. 600. In W. F. Keegan (ed.), *Emergent Horticultural Economies of the Eastern Woodlands*. Occasional Paper No. 7, Center for Archaeological Investigations. Carbondale: Southern Illinois University, pp. 153–181.

Cavalli-Sforza, L. L., and M. W. Feldman. (1981). *Cultural Transmission and Evolution*. Princeton, NJ: Princeton University Press.

Darwin, C. (1859). *On the Origin of Species By Means of Natural Selection, or the Preservation of Favoured Races in the Struggle for Life*. London: John Murray.

Darwin, C. (1998). *The Origin of Species*. New York: The Modern Library.

Dennett, D. C. (1990). Memes and the exploitation of imagination. *The Journal of Aesthetics and Art Criticism* 48(2): 127–135.

Dunnell, R. C. (1978a). Style and function: A fundamental dichotomy. *American Antiquity* 43(2): 192–202.

Dunnell, R. C. (1978b). Archaeological potential of anthropological and scientific models of function. In R. C. Dunnel and E. S. Hall (eds.), *Archaeological Essays in Honor of Irving B. Rouse*. The Hague: Mouton, pp. 41–73.

Dunnell, R. C. (1980). Evolutionary theory and archaeology. In M. B. Schiffer (ed.), *Advances in Archaeological Method and Theory*, vol. 3. New York: Academic Press, pp. 35–99.

Dunnell, R. C. (1989). Aspects of the application of evolutionary theory in archaeology. In C. C. Lamberg-Karlovsky (ed.), *Archaeological Thought in America*. Cambridge: Cambridge University Press, pp. 35–49.

Dunnell, R. C., and. D. M. Greenlee. (1999). Late Woodland period "waste" reduction in the Ohio River valley. *Journal of Anthropological Archaeology* 18: 376–395.

Durham, W. H. (1991). *Coevolution: Genes, Culture, and Human Diversity*. Stanford, CA: Stanford University Press.

Durham, W. H. (1992). Applications of evolutionary culture theory. *Annual Review of Anthropology* 21: 331–355.

Endler, J. A. (1992). Natural selection: Current usages. In E. F. Keller and E. A. Lloyd (eds.), *Keywords in Evolutionary Biology*. Cambridge, MA: Harvard University Press, pp. 220–224.

Graves, M. W., and T. N. Ladefoged. (1995). The evolutionary significance of ceremonial architecture in Polynesia. In P. A. Teltser (ed.), *Evolutionary Ar-

chaeology: Methodological Issues. Tuscon: University of Arizona Press, pp. 149–174.

Hodge, M.J.S. (1992). Natural selection: Historical perspectives. In E. F. Keller and E. A. Lloyd (eds.), *Keywords in Evolutionary Biology.* Cambridge, MA: Harvard University Press, pp. 212–219.

Hull, D. L. (1982). The naked meme. In H. C. Plotkin (ed.), *Learning, Development, and Culture.* New York: John Wiley & Sons, pp. 273–327.

Kirch, P. V. (1980). The archaeological study of adaptation: Theoretical and methodological issues. In M. B. Schiffer (ed.), *Advances in Archaeological Method and Theory,* vol. 3. New York: Academic Press, pp. 101–156.

Leonard, R. D., and G. T. Jones. (1987). Elements of an inclusive evolutionary model for archaeology. *Journal of Anthropological Archaeology* 6: 199–219.

Lyman, R. L., and M. J. O'Brien. (1998). The goals of evolutionary archaeology. *Current Anthropology* 39: 615–652.

Madsen, M., C. Lipo, and M. Cannon. (1999). Fitness and reproductive trade-offs in uncertain environments: Explaining the evolution of cultural elaboration. *Journal of Anthropological Archaeology* 18: 251–281.

Mayr, E. (1982). *The Growth of Biological Thought: Diversity, Evolution, and Inheritance.* Cambridge, MA: Harvard University Press.

Mithen, S. (1998). Comment on Boone and Smith. *Current Anthropology* 39: S163–S164.

Neiman, F. D. (1995). Stylistic variation in evolutionary perspective: Inferences from decorative diversity and interassemblage distance in Illinois woodland ceramic assemblages. *American Antiquity* 60: 7–36.

Neiman, F. D. (1997). Conspicuous consumption as wasteful advertising: A Darwinian perspective on spatial patterns in classic Maya terminal monument dates. In C. M. Barton and G. A. Clark (eds.), *Rediscovering Darwin: Evolutionary Theory and Archaeological Explanation.* Archeological Papers No. 7. Arlington, VA: American Anthropological Association, pp. 267–290.

Richerson, P. J., and R. Boyd. (1992). Cultural inheritance and evolutionary ecology. In E. A. Smith and B. Winterhalder (eds.), *Evolutionary Ecology and Human Behavior.* New York: Aldine de Gruyter, pp. 61–94.

Sahlins, M., and E. S. Service. (1960). *Evolution and Culture.* Ann Arbor: University of Michigan Press.

Sober, E., and D. S. Wilson. (1998). *Unto Others: The Evolution and Psychology of Unselfish Behavior.* Cambridge, MA: Harvard University Press.

Thomas, D. H., and S. L. Bierwirth. (1983). Material culture of Gatecliff Shelter: Projectile points. In D. H. Thomas (ed.), *The Archaeology of Monitor Valley 2: Gatecliff Shelter.* Anthropological Papers No. 59. New York: American Museum of Natural History, pp. 177–211.

Wills, C. (1998). *Children of Prometheus: The Accelerating Pace of Human Evolution.* Reading, MA: Perseus Books.

Wilson, E. O. (1975). *Sociobiology.* Cambridge, MA: Harvard University Press.

Chapter 14

Population

Kevin M. Kelly

INTRODUCTION

Like other concepts encountered in this volume, **population** has a variety of meanings (e.g., demographic, Malthusian, ecological, genetic, statistical, evolutionary, Darwinian). For example, statisticians define a population as the entire set of items or measures of interest. Demographic uses of the term focus on individuals circumscribed by geopolitical boundaries (Howell 1975: 17–18; Kertzer and Fricke 1997; Levy and Lemeshow 1999). Similarly, population ecologists use the term to describe the aggregated members of a species within some defined area (e.g., Andrewartha 1971: 10; Sutherland 1996: 1–4). Population biologists (e.g., Hastings 1997: 1) define a population as "a group of individuals of the same species that have a high probability of interacting with each other." Population geneticists restrict the definition further, identifying a population as a group of interbreeding organisms of the same species (Futuyma 1997; Hanski 1999).

Underlying all of these manifestations is the fundamental notion of the population as a "defined collection." Grouped as populations, individuals (and items) exhibit collective properties (e.g., density, size, age structure, a life history, a distribution in time and space, gene frequencies). Populations can be of any size and although the elements need not be identical, they must share at least one measurable attribute. The presence (or absence) of a single attribute is the simplest form of specification. The variables used to identify population membership may be interval (e.g., weight, birth order, antiquity), categorical (e.g., gender, location, language, presence/absence), ordinal (e.g., more/less, older/younger) or ratio (e.g, age, length) (see LeCompte and Schensul, 1999a: 115–119; Sokal and Rohlf 1981: 10–

11, for brief discussions of variable types). These attributes identify who or what are the designated members of the population in question and should, by inference, also indicate the features of the population that are of particulate interest.

In anthropology and archaeology, for example, populations of interest have been defined as the individuals living in a particular village (e.g., Durham 1991; Neel and Weiss 1975; Welsch et al. 1992); the speakers of a particular language (e.g., Howell 1979; Kelly 1990); the members of a specific religious sect (e.g., Glass 1953); the members of a socially recognized ethnic minority (e.g., Madrigal et al. 2001); and the skeletal remains from certain sites or locales (e.g., Weiss 1973). In addition, populations have been inferred from the distributions of certain kinds of artifacts (e.g., Bar-Yosef and Kuhn 1999; Kirch 1997); the genes of living people (e.g., Kayser et al. 2000); ancient DNA (e.g., Kolman and Tuross 2000); ecosystems having certain definable characteristics (e.g., Clark and Kelly 1993); and even on the basis of single fossil skulls (e.g., Leakey 1959). Each of these examples is a "defined collection." However, none of these designated populations is inherently or necessarily a Darwinian population.

HISTORY

As we consider what it means to say that a "population" is a Darwinian population, it is important to remember that evolution—what Darwin called "descent with modification"—had been recognized as a historical process long before Darwin. More than a century earlier, Buffon (1749) argued that species change in response to their environment and he suggested that such change comes about as a consequence of natural processes rather than by divine intervention. Similarly, Charles Darwin's grandfather, Erasmus Darwin (1794–1796), was aware that members of a species both change through time and compete for resources. Still better known are the writings of Jean-Baptiste Lamarck (1809, 1815), who suggested that species adapt to changing environments by use and disuse of organs. According to Lamarck, organ systems develop in response to wants and needs of the organism. Thus, in Lamarck's view, evolution occurs because attributes acquired by parents are passed on to their offspring.

Before the works of these philosopher naturalists, species were not only thought to be immutable, but it was also believed that every organism possesses all of the qualities and conditions necessary to be a member of its species. Mayr (1991) has labeled this extreme position **typological essentialism**, since according to this view, every species—seen in an Aristotelian manner—has its own "essence," and how far the individuals in any given species may have deviated from this defining essence is seen as unimportant (see, e.g., Sober 1992: 247–278).

Nonetheless, the writings of the later explorers/naturalists Charles Darwin and Alfred Russel Wallace (1855, 1864) were predicated on this earlier recognition that intraspecific variation exists and change occurs. Lamarck and his contemporaries, for example, had correctly perceived the role of the environment in evolutionary change. However, they failed to produce a satisfactory explanation for how evolutionary change takes place. What Darwin (and Wallace) contributed was a convincing evolutionary mechanism, natural selection.

Darwin's notion of population as well as his inspiration for the idea of natural selection came from Malthus (1798). In *An Essay on the Principle of Population*, Malthus (1798) explains why the size of an animal population may remain stable over time. In nature, individuals tend to aggregate with other members of their species in order to exploit resources and to procreate. Malthus, an economist, observed that although the numbers of adult animals may remain more or less constant, many more offspring are born to these animals than reach maturity. He concluded that high infant mortality prevents most of their offspring from reaching adulthood. Malthus suggested that humans, like animals, are capable of overproducing, and he observed that poverty and famine are natural outcomes of unchecked population growth.

Charles Darwin saw the implications of Malthus' observations for his own work. Darwin knew from Malthus (1798) that under favorable environmental conditions, most offspring will survive, and consequently, the number of individuals in a population tends to increase geometrically. Also drawing from Malthus, Darwin recognized that anything in the natural environment that works to check population growth thus limits the biological variability of populations. From these observations, Darwin concluded that most offspring die as a result of a "struggle for survival."

At the same time, Darwin recognized from his own careful and extensive observations that individual physical variations can be observed within virtually every plant and animal species. These differences—however minor they may seem to be—are real. Moreover, although Darwin was uncertain how the environment could influence the development of biological variation, he judged that such variation must be inherited.

Darwin understood that inherited variation was critically important to his theory. Expanding on Malthus' environmental checks on population size, Darwin suggested that the environment favors organisms whose "individual differences" make them better able to survive and pass on their own characteristics to the next generation. In contrast, physical variations that are not as adaptive tend to be eliminated—not simply by the bearer's own death but also due to the bearer's diminished capacity to produce offspring. This is the process that Darwin called **natural selection**.

Key here is the idea that natural selection happens because some individuals, being better adapted to their environment, give rise to more progeny than others. Darwin understood, in other words, that an individual's evolutionary success cannot be measured only in terms of survival; it must be measured in terms of the capacity to leave offspring.

Thus the concept of a **Darwinian population** is intrinsically tied to the idea of "the environment" and to the fact of biological procreation. By positing the heritability of physical variation and by incorporating the environment as a driving force of change, Darwin defined populations as collections of individuals created by the act of procreation and maintained over time by the biological fact of descent.

In his day, Darwin's concept of evolution was widely accepted. However, the theory of natural selection was also widely criticized because Darwin knew little of the basic principles of heredity (Bowler 1997: 316; Eiseley 1961: 233–253). Although he was certain that individual difference could be inherited, he was decidedly unclear about the mechanics inheritance involved. The fundamentals of genetics were discovered by a Moravian monk, Gregor Mendel [1822–1884]. Mendel's research (1866), however, received little attention until its rediscovery in 1900 and thus had no effect on evolutionary theory until it was championed by William Bateson (1909) and Thomas Hunt Morgan (1915) in the early 1900s (Marks 1997: 418–419). In the twentieth century, the work of Sewall Wright (1921, 1922, 1933, 1968, 1969, 1977, 1978), R. A. Fisher (1930), J.B.S. Haldane (1932), Theodosius Dobzhansky (1970), and others established that the forces of evolution act not on individual genes as such but instead through the survival and reproductive success of individuals. But by the same token, as Darwin saw, individuals in our species can be thought of as being clustered together into small, local populations within which matings are most likely to occur. Nonetheless, matings also happen *between* such local populations, and in the case of Homo sapiens, they happen often enough to keep our kind of animal intact as a single, widely dispersed species.

Using our own species as an example, therefore, we can see that the size of a Darwinian population can be defined by a probability distribution, and local populations by this definition do not have discrete boundaries. Population geneticists refer to the subdividing of a species in this way as its **population structure**, and today it is becoming increasingly common to refer to the aggregate of such locally recognizable grouping of individuals as a **metapopulation** (Hanksi 1999; Hanski and Gilpin 1991; Hanski and Simberloff 1997; Levins 1970). From this perspective, a species can be thought of as a "highest order" metapopulation, and its component local populations are generally referred to as local populations, subpopulations, breeding populations, or demes.

CONTEMPORARY USES

Although the Darwinian meaning of the word "population" can be seen when this concept is looked at in historic context, one issue in particular clouds its contemporary use as an analytical tool. In its most common and familiar usage, a population is defined simply as (or is assumed to be) a group of individuals living in some more or less well-defined area. Thus anthropologists and archaeologists routinely write about populations identified as the current or former members of various socially recognized ethnic or linguistic groupings (e.g., Durham 1991; Howell 1979; Kelly 1990; Madrigal et al. 2001; Neel and Weiss 1975; Weiss 1973; Welsch et al. 1992), or as the makers of particular kinds of artifacts or archaeological features found in some more or less well-specified locale or region (e.g., Braun 1996 [1987]; Kirch 1997; Minnis 1985: 50–54; Spriggs 1997). However, it is not self-evident how "populations" defined in these ways non-biological correspond to Darwinian populations, even when investigators then go on to invoke certain evolutionary principles (e.g., Braun 1996 [1987]; Johnson and Earle 1987; Pearsall 1995). Despite its importance as an evolutionary concept—or perhaps because of its status as a familiar demographic category—when the term "population" is used by archaeologists and anthropologists, precisely what kind of population is intended is often left unspecified. Indeed, it seems to be routinely taken for granted by many authors that every reader knows how "populations" are *always* defined.

That this was not always the case is illustrated by Howell (1979). Writing soon after anthropologists had begun to embrace the union of demographic methods and evolutionary models (e.g., Swedlund 1975; Ward and Weiss 1976), Howell (1979) demonstrates an understanding of the importance of population both as a demographic and as an evolutionary concept. In particular, she took great care to provide definitions for demographic (Howell 1979: 17–18) as well as genetic usages of the term (pp. 355–358).

CASE STUDIES

Two examples illustrate the varied manner in which the population concept has been applied to archaeological phenomena within a Darwinian framework. At issue in the first case is how well archaeological evidence can be used to define Darwinian populations. The example I use is the spatio-temporal distribution of a particular kind of artifact found in the southwest Pacific called "Lapita" pottery. Skeletal remains associated with this pottery exist; however, the human remains are fragmentary, and the sample sizes are statistically quite small. Thus, as is often the case in archaeology, the population affinities of the long-dead peoples associated with this archaeological phenomenon must be inferred from non-biological traits.

Lapita's importance in the archaeological record arises from several features, not the least of which is the fact that the people currently occupying Lapita site localities in the Fiji-West Polynesia region are arguably the descendants of the ancestral Polynesian population (Green 1992; Kirch and

Green 1987). In addition, the peoples of Polynesia, in common with numerous populations of island and coastal Melanesia as well as populations of Southeast and East Asia, speak one of the languages assigned to the linguistic taxon known as Austronesian. In fact, many Pacific archaeologists and prehistorians believe the people who made Lapita ceramics were Austronesian-speakers (e.g., Bellwood 1979, 1991; Kirch 1997; Shutler and Marck 1975; Spriggs 1997). Due in large part to these geographic and linguistic associations, the term "Lapita," although technically a ceramic style, is commonly applied to the people who made those pots (e.g., Kirch 1997).

Ceramics are the product of human action and in that sense are associated with a human population. However, the ceramics themselves are a collect (i.e., a population) whose elements are defined by the presence of certain geometric designs and the manner of creation. What is often forgotten is that this population (i.e., Lapita ceramics) is defined by specific attributes that are relevant within a particular paradigm or model. Whether the populations relevant to one realm of inquiry (e.g., ceramics) are equivalent or comparable to others (e.g., humans) will be discussed below.

The second example concerns recent attempts to apply Darwinian principles to the evolution of cultural attributes (e.g., Dunnell 1980, 1985, 1995; Jones et al. 1995; Teltser 1995). Although its relevance may not be readily apparent, it provides another study of the fit of the Darwinian concept of population to archaeological inquiry. In particular, Dunnell (1980: 63) has argued that

[i]*f a given trait is heritable to a measurable degree* (the mechanism need not be known) *and if it also affects the fitness of organisms possessing the trait to some measurable degree* (recognizing the possibility of neutral or stylistic traits), *then the trait must be subject to natural selection* and will be fixed in populations. (emphasis in original)

In that sense, culture attributes might be analyzed as traits (memes) that spread through social units like the alleles of a gene spread through the population (Dawkins 1976).

In defense of this application, Teltser (1995: 4), citing Dunnell (1980) and Lewontin (1970), notes that "[e]volutionary theory is a framework for understanding the differential persistence of variation." Indeed, although there is a general sense in which memes are analogous to genes, the genetic metaphor for cultural transmission quickly breaks down. Whereas genes can only be transmitted from parent to child (**vertical transmission**), memes can be transmitted between any two individuals (**horizontal transmission**). Since one can acquire and transmit cultural attributes at any point in life, cultural evolution is, at best, Lamarckian and decidedly non-Darwinian.

Moreover, I hasten to note that variation exists only with reference to differences between comparable, definable units. In the Darwinian paradigm, that unit is the population. The vertical transmission of genetic information makes it possible for us to identify (or to model) the members of the initial and the subsequent generations (i.e., the Darwinian populations) and therefore makes it possible for us to talk about variation and evolution.

Two recent publications (Boone and Smith 1998; Dunnell 1995) reveal something of archaeology's inattention to the Darwinian population concept, and more generally, how the evolutionary archaeology versus evolutionary ecology debate has focused almost exclusively on the "role of natural selection," to the detriment of discussions of other important Darwinian principles and concepts. In a chapter curiously titled "What Is It that Actually Evolves?", Dunnell (1995) makes what is ostensibly the benign argument that artifacts are evolutionary units subject to variation and selection. Boone and Smith (1998: S142–S144) soundly criticize this notion, arguing—under the unfortunate heading "What is evolving? Replicators and phenotypes"—that Dunnell's (1995) thesis ignores the replicator-phenotype distinction and the problems with the transmission of cultural traits briefly described above. Specifically, Boone and Smith (1998: S143) note that "selection can act on phenotypic variation . . . only to the extent that it is heritable."

Although I concur with this critique, I am troubled by the fact that Boone and Smith (1998), like Dunnell (1995), blur the distinction between the units of selection (phenotypes) and the unit of evolution (the population). While it is true that artifactual characteristics vary over time (and space) and that artifacts are subject to selection, there is no Darwinian sense in which artifacts (or for that matter, phenotypes) should be thought to evolve. Darwinian evolution occurs within populations. Although characteristics of cultural attributes clearly change over time and in that sense evolve, we can only know whether the frequencies of these attributes change with reference to a population. Does a comparable evolutionary unit exist for cultural attributes? How does one discern a population of memes? What is the appropriate population within which to study the evolution of cultural phenomena? Answers to these questions will clearly have to wait for another discussion. However, as Dunnell (1995: 44) cautions, "until the matter of units is taken more seriously . . . there is no reason to expect that evolutionary accounts will be anything more than just another story."

FUTURE IMPORTANCE

It is impossible to write about evolution or diversity without reference to the concept of population. The population (however defined) is the group that one wishes to describe and about which one wishes to draw conclusions. Unfortunately, although the population is the primary focus, investigators are often forced to study a sample. Samples are used because the population is either too large to conveniently study or simply unavailable to study in its entirety. In fact, archaeologists and other evolutionary scientists are often forced to employ a kind of reverse sampling strategy, aggregating the elements in order to infer the existence of a population. The question is often not how to choose a sample to represent our population but rather, what population does our "sample" represent? (I have placed the term sample in quotes because a sample properly only exists in relation to a population.) Collections of discovered items (e.g., artifacts) only become samples when one relates them to a population. Over time, these relationships often change as the investigator's and the discipline's focus of interest evolves. For example, consider the changing relationships among fossil hominids as new discoveries lead to the lumping and splitting of taxa. In other words, the population is often abstracted from the sample rather than the sample having been drawn from the population.

The difference between a population and a sample is that with a population our interest is in defining the population's characteristics, whereas with a sample our interest is in making inferences about the characteristics of the population from which that sample was drawn. A critical feature of any scientific investigation is the testing of hypotheses by statistical criteria. By studying a sample, the investigator hopes to reach valid conclusions about the population.

However, in order to draw inferences from the sample, the investigator must make certain assumptions about both the population which the investigator is generalizing and the sample being used. The process of using a sample to make inferences about a population is called a **sampling strategy** (see LeCompte and Schensul 1999b; Pelto and Pelto 1978; Weir 1990). Those assumptions convenient by divide into two categories: (1) those with which the investigator is fairly confident and is willing to accept and (2) those about which the investigator is somewhat doubtful and is therefore interested in testing. The assumptions with which the investigator is confident are the basis for the model, while those about which the investigator is interested in testing are the **hypotheses**. Examples of model assumptions include the use of linguistic reconstruction as standard for ordering and interpreting genetic and archaeological data (e.g., Kirch 1997; Spriggs, 1997); and the premise that natural selection operates on cultural phenomena (e.g., Dunnell 1980) as well as the investigator's acceptance of the study sample as adequate representation of the population. Examples of hypotheses include the suggestion that the dispersal of Lapita ceramics is associated with spread of Austronesian languages (e.g., Clark and Kelly 1993) as well as the assertion that post-contact artifact change reflects natural selection as opposed to acculturation (e.g., Ramenofsky 1995).

In order for the investigator to accept a conclusion with any certainty, it is important that only one of the assumptions (preferably the hypotheses) is in doubt. However, all of the assumptions made by the investigator (model and hypotheses) have the same logical status (i.e., they are unproven). Indeed, one can easily imagine a time or place where the investigator may choose to the test the assumptions of the model. Given their indeterminate status, erroneous model assumptions (e.g., a biased sample) may lead the investigator to accept false hypotheses. At the same time, any test that rejects the hypotheses also calls into question the assumptions of the model.

In order to understand evolutionary relationships within a Darwinian paradigm, one must remain keenly aware of the assumptions of the model, for as with any model, to failure to attend these assumptions may lead to erroneous conclusions. Of particular concern to this discussion is the fact that one's ability to draw valid inferences is predicated on the assumption that the sample is representative of the population.

As we have seen, populations are collections defined by selected attributes for specific reasons. Thus, a Darwinian population is a collection of individuals defined by procreation and common descent for the purposes of understanding variations in the spatial and temporal distributions of physical variations. Whether populations defined on the basis of archaeological attributes are comparable to Darwinian populations remains open to debate. However, the reality is that the comparability of populations defined using different attributes can rarely, if ever, be demonstrated and thus must always be treated as an assumption. For this reason, it is important that the researcher carefully and completely defines the population. Without a clear definition of the population, it is impossible to know what the sample represents. For example, some of the issues and consequences of relying on historic names and categories to identify genetic populations are discussed by MacEachern (2000) and Terrell (2001; Terrell et al. 2001). At the same time, without a clear definition of the population how does one judge what is relevant? How is one to know what one means? How does one know what one is interpreting? How does one know whose history one is writing?

REFERENCES

Andrewartha, H. G. (1971). *Introduction to the Study of Animal Populations*, 2nd ed. Chicago: University of Chicago Press.

Bar-Yosef, O., and S. L. Kuhn. (1999). The big deal about blades: Laminar technologies and human evolution. *American Anthropologist* 101: 322–338.

Bateson, W. (1909). *Mendel's Principles of Heredity*. Cambridge.

Bellwood, P. (1979). *Man's Conquest of the Pacific*. New York: Oxford University Press.

Bellwood. P. (1991). The Austronesian dispersal and the origin of languages. *Scientific American* 265: 88–93.

Boone, J. L., and E. A. Smith. (1998). Is it evolution yet? A critique of evolutionary archaeology. *Current Anthropology* 39: S141–S173.

Bowler, P. J. (1997). Darwin, Charles Robert. In F. Spencer (ed.), *History of Physical Anthropology: An Encyclopedia*, vol. 1. New York: Garland Publishing, pp. 316–318.

Boyce, A. J., C. F. Küchemann, and G. A. Harrison. (1967). Neighboring knowledge and the distribution of marriage distances. *Annals of Human Genetics* 30: 335–338.

Braun, D. P. (1996) [1987]. Coevolution of sedentism, pottery technology, and horticulture in the central Midwest, 200 B.C.–A.D. 600. In M. J. O'Brien (ed.), *Evolutionary Archaeology: Theory and Application*. Salt Lake City: University of Utah Press, pp. 270–283.

Buffon, G.L.L., Comte de. (1749). *Histoire Naturalle*. Paris.

Cavalli-Sforza, L. L., P. Menozzi, and A. Piazza. (1994). *The History and Geography of Human Genes*. Princeton, NJ: Princeton University Press.

Clark, J. T., and K. M. Kelly. (1993). Human genetics, paleoenvironments, and malaria: Relationships and implications for the settlement of Oceania. *American Anthropologist* 95: 613–631.

Crow, J. F. (2001). The beanbag lives on. *Nature* 409: 771.

Darwin, E. (1794–1796). *Zoonomia*. 2 vols. London: J. Johnson.

Dawkins, R. (1976). *The Selfish Gene*. Oxford: Oxford University Press.

Dobzhansky, T. (1970). *Genetics and the Evolutionary Process*. New York: Columbia University Press.

Dunnell, R. C. (1980). Evolutionary theory and archaeology. In M. B. Schiffer (ed.), *Advances in Archaeological Method and Theory*, vol. 3. New York: Academic Press, pp. 55–99.

Dunnell, R. C. (1985). Methodological issues in contemporary Americanist archaeology. In P. D. Asquith and P. Kitcher (eds.), *Proceedings of the 1984 Biennial Meetings of the Philosophy of Science Association*, vol. 2. East Lansing, MI: Philosophy of Science Association, pp. 717–744.

Dunnell, R. C. (1995). What is it that actually evolves? In P. A. Teltser (ed.), *Evolutionary Archaeology: Methodological Issues*. Tucson: University of Arizona Press, pp. 33–50.

Durham, W. H. (1991). *Coevolution: Genes, Culture and Human Diversity*. Stanford, CA: Stanford University Press.

Eiseley, Loren. (1961) [1958]. *Darwin's Century: Evolution and the Men Who Discovered It*. Garden City, NY: Anchor Books.

Ereshefsky, M. (ed.). (1992). *The Units of Evolution: Essays on the Nature of Species*. Cambridge, MA: MIT Press.

Fisher, R. A. (1930). *The Genetical Theory of Natural Selection*. Oxford: Clarendon Press.

Futuyma, D. J. (1997). *Evolutionary Biology*, 3rd ed. Sunderland, MA: Sinauer Associates.

Gage, T. B. (1997). Demography. In E. Spencer (ed.), *History of Physical Anthropology: An Encyclopedia*, vol. 1. New York: Garland Publishing, pp. 323–330.

Glass, H. B. (1953). The genetics of the Dunkers. *Scientific American* 189: 76–81.

Golson, J. (1971). Lapita ware and its transformations. In R. C. Green and M.

Kelly (eds.), *Studies in Oceanic Culture History*, vol. 2. Pacific Anthropological Records, No. 12. Honolulu: Bernice P. Bishop Museum, pp. 67–76.

Green, R. C. (1992). Linguistic, biological, and cultural origins of the initial inhabitants of Remote Oceania. Prehistoric Mongoloid Dispersals Symposium 1992. Tokyo: University of Tokyo.

Haldane, J.B.S. (1932). *The Causes of Evolution*. London: Harper.

Hanksi, I. (1999). *Metapopulation Ecology*. New York: Oxford University Press.

Hanski, I., and M. E. Gilpin. (1991). Metapopulation dynamics: Brief history and conceptual domain. *Biological Journal of the Linnean Society* 42: 3–16.

Hanski, I., and D. Simberloff. (1997). The metapopulation approach, its history, conceptual domain, and application to conservation. In I. A. Hanski and M. E. Gilpin (eds.), *Metapopulation Biology*. San Diego, CA: Academic Press, pp. 5–26.

Hastings, A. (1997). *Population Biology: Concepts and Models*. New York: Springer.

Howell, N. (1979). *Demography of the Dobe !Kung*. New York: Academic Press.

Johnson, A. W., and T. Earle. (1987). *The Evolution of Human Societies: From Foraging Group to Agrarian State*. Stanford, CA: Stanford University Press.

Jones, G. T., R. D. Leonard, and A. L. Abbott. (1995). The structure of selectionist explanation in archaeology. In P. A. Teltser (ed.), *Evolutionary Archaeology: Methodological Issues*. Tucson: University of Arizona Press, pp. 13–32.

Jorde, L. (1980). The genetic structure of subdivided populations. In M. Crawford and P. Workman (eds.), *Methods and Theory in Anthropological Genetics*. Albuquerque: University of New Mexico Press, pp. 177–199.

Kayser, M., S. Brauer, G. Weiss, P. A. Underhill, L. Roewer, W. Schiefenhövel, and M. Stoneking. (2000). Melanesian origin of Polynesian Y chromosomes. *Current Biology* 10: 1237–1246.

Kelly, K. M. (1990). Gm polymorphisms, linguistic affinities, and natural selection in Melanesia. *Current Anthropology* 31: 201–219.

Kertzer, D. I,. and T. E. Fricke. (1997). *Anthropological Demography: Toward a New Synthesis*. Chicago: University of Chicago Press.

Kirch, P. V. (1997). *The Lapita Peoples: Ancestors of the Oceanic World*. Oxford: Blackwell Publishers.

Kirch, P. V., and R. C. Green. (1987). History, phylogeny, and evolution in Polynesia. *Current Anthropology* 28: 431–436.

Kolman, C. J., and N. Tuross. (2000). Ancient DNA analysis of human populations. *American Journal of Physical Anthropology* 111: 5–24.

Küchermann, C. F., A. J. Boyce, and G. A. Harrison. (1967). A demographic and genetic study of a group of Oxfordshire villages. *Human Biology* 39: 251–283.

Lamarck, J. (1809). *Philosophie Zoologique*. Paris: Dentu.

Lamarck, J. (1815). *Historie Naturelle des Animaux sans Vertèbre*. Paris: Verdière.

Leakey, L.S.B. (1959). A new fossil skull from Olduvai. *Nature* 129: 721–722.

LeCompte, M. D., and J. J. Schensul. (1999a). *Analyzing and interpreting ethnographic data*. Ethnographer's Toolkit, vol. 5. Walnut Creek, CA: Alta Mira Press.

LeCompte, M. D., and J. J. Schensul. (1999b). *Designing and conducting ethno-*

graphic research. Ethnographer's Toolkit, vol. 1. Walnut Creek, CA: Alta Mira Press.

Levins, R. (1970). Extinction. In M. Gerstenhaber, *Some Mathematical Problems in Biology*. Providence, RI: American Mathematical Society, pp. 77–107.

Levy, P. S., and S. Lemeshow. (1999). *Sampling of Populations: Methods and Applications*. New York: John Wiley & Sons.

Lewontin, R. (1970). The units of selection. *Annual Reviews of Ecology and Systematics*, 1: 1–17.

MacEachern, S. (2000). Genes, tribes, and African history. *Current Anthropology* 41: 357–384.

Madrigal, L., B. Ware, R. Miller, G. Saenz, M. Chavez, and D. Dykes. (2001). Ethnicity, gene flow and population subdivision in Limón, Costa Rica. *American Journal of Physical Anthropology* 114: 99–108.

Malthus, T. R. (1798). *An Essay on the Principle of Population; as it Affects the Future Improvement of Society; with Remarks on the Speculation of Mr. Godwin, M. Condercet, and Other Writers*. London: Johnson.

Marks, J. (1997). Genetics (Mendelian). In F. Spencer (ed.), *History of Physical Anthropology: An Encyclopedia*, vol. 1. New York: Garland Publishing, pp. 418–421.

Mayr, E. (1991). What is a species and what is not? *Philosophy of Science* 63: 262–277.

Mendel G. (1866). Versuche über Pflanzenhybriden. *Verhandlugen des Naturforschended Vereines in Brünn* 4: 3–47.

Minnis, P. E. (1985). *Social Adaptation to Food Stress: A Prehistoric Southwestern Example*. Chicago: University of Chicago Press.

Molnar, S. (1983). *Human Variation. Races, Types, and Ethnic Groups*, 2nd ed. Englewood Cliffs, NJ: Prentice Hall.

Morgan, T. H. (1915). *The Mechanism of Mendelian Heredity*. New York: Holt, Rinehart & Winston.

Neel, J. V., and K. M. Weiss. (1975). The genetic structure of a tribal population, the Yanamama Indians. XII. Biodemographic studies. *American Journal of Physical Anthropology* 42: 25–52.

Pearsall, D. M. (1995). Domestication and agriculture in the New World Tropics. In T. D. Price and A. B. Gebaur (eds.), *Last Hunters, First Farmers: New Perspectives on the Prehistoric Transition to Agriculture*. Santa Fe, NM: School of American Research Press, pp 157–192.

Pelto P. J., and G. H. Pelto. (1978). *Anthropological Research: The Structure of Inquiry*, 2nd ed. Cambridge: Cambridge University Press.

Ramenofsky, A. F. (1995). Evolutionary theory and Native American artifact change in the postcontact period. In P. A. Teltser (ed.), *Evolutionary Archaeology: Methodological Issues*. Tucson: University of Arizona Press, pp. 129–147.

Relethford, J. H., and M. H. Crawford. (1998). Influence of religion and birthplace on the genetic structure of Northern Ireland. *Annals of Human Biology* 25: 117–125.

Roberts, D. F. (1956). A demographic study of a Dinka village. *Human Biology* 28: 323–349.

Romney, A. K. (1999). Culture consensus as a statistical model. *Current Anthropology* 40: S104–S115.

Shutler, R., Jr., and J. C. Marck. (1975). On the dispersal of the Austronesian horticulturalists. *Archaeology and Physical Anthropology in Oceania* 10: 81–113.

Sober, E. (1992). Evolution, population thinking, and essentialism. In M. Ereshefsky (ed.), *The Units of Evolution: Essays on the Nature of Species*. Cambridge, MA: MIT Press, pp. 247–278.

Sokal, R. R., and F. J. Rohlf. (1981). *Biometry*, 2nd ed. San Francisco: W. H. Freeman.

Spriggs, M. (1997). *The Island Melanesians*. Oxford: Blackwell Publishers.

Sutherland, W. J. (1996). *From Individual Behaviour to Population Ecology*. New York: Oxford University Press.

Swedlund, A. C. (ed.). 1975. *Population Studies in Archaeology and Biological Anthropology: A Symposium*. Washington, DC: Society for American Archaeology.

Teltser, P. A. (1995). The methodological challenge of evolutionary theory in archaeology. In P. A. Teltser (ed.), *Evolutionary Archaeology: Methodological Issues*. Tucson: University of Arizona Press, pp. 1–11.

Terrell, J. E. (2001). The uncommon sense of race, language, and culture. In J. E. Terrell (ed.), *Archaeology, Language, and History: Essays on Culture and Ethnicity*. Westport, CT: Bergin and Garvey, pp. 11–30.

Terrell, J. E., K. M. Kelly, and P. Rainbird. (2001). Foregone conclusions? In search of "Papuans" and "Austronesians." *Current Anthropology* 42: 97–124.

Theime, F. P. (1954). The population as a unit of study. *American Anthropologist* 54: 504–509.

Wallace, A. R. (1855). On the law which has regulated the introduction of new species. *Annals and Magazine of Natural History* 16: 184–196.

Wallace, A. R. (1864). The origin of human races and the antiquity of man deduced from the "theory of natural selection." *Journal of the Anthropological Society of London* 2: clvii–clxxxvii.

Ward, R. H., and K. M. Weiss (eds.). (1976). *The Demographic Evolution of Human Populations*. London: Academic Press.

Weir, B. S. (1990). *Genetic Data Analysis*. Sunderland, MA: Sinauer Associates.

Weiss, K. M. (1973). Demographic models for anthropology. *American Antiquity Memoir* 27.

Welsch, R. L., J. Terrell, and J. A. Nodalski. (1992). Language and culture on the north coast of New Guinea. *American Anthropologist* 94: 568–600.

Wilson, R. A. (ed.). (1998). *Species: New Interdisciplinary Papers*. Cambridge, MA: MIT Press.

Wright, S. (1921). Systems of mating: General considerations. *Genetics* 6: 167–178.

Wright, S. (1922). Coefficients of inbreeding and relationship. *American Naturalist* 56: 330–338.

Wright, S. (1933). Inbreeding and homozygosis. *Proceedings of the National Academy of Sciences* 19: 411–420.

Wright, S. (1943). Isolation by distance. *Genetics* 28: 114–138.

Wright, S. (1946). Isolation by distance under diverse systems of mating. *Genetics* 31: 39–59.

Wright, S. (1968). *Evolution and the Genetics of Populations, vol. 1: Genetic and Biometric Foundations*. Chicago: University of Chicago Press.

Wright, S. (1969). *Evolution and the Genetics of Populations, vol. 2: Theory of Gene Frequencies*. Chicago: University of Chicago Press.

Wright, S. (1977). *Evolution and the Genetics of Populations, vol. 3: Experimental Results and Evolutionary Deductions*. Chicago: University of Chicago Press.

Wright, S. (1978). *Evolution and the Genetics of Populations, vol. 4: Variability Within and Among Natural Populations*. Chicago: University of Chicago Press.

About the Contributors

GARY M. FEINMAN is Chair and Curator of Mesoamerican Anthropology and Archaeology at The Field Museum. He has conducted regional surveys, intensive site surveys, and excavations in the Valley of Oaxaca, Mexico, for over 20 years. For the past seven years, he also has been a member of a collaborative archaeological team that is carrying out systematic regional survey and excavation in eastern Shandong Province, China.

JOHN P. HART is Director of Research and Collections at the New York State Museum. His research has recently focused on the history and evolution of maize-beans-squash agriculture in the northern Eastern Woodlands of North America.

GEORGE T. JONES is the Leonard C. Ferguson Professor of Archaeology at Hamilton College. For the past fifteen years he has investigated Paleoindian mobility and settlement patterns in the Great Basin of the western United States.

JOHN KANTNER is an Assistant Professor of Anthropology at Georgia State University. His research concentrates on the development of prehistoric societies in the American Southwest, with an emphasis on the application of evolutionary theory and the analysis of settlement patterns and ceramics.

KEVIN M. KELLY is an Associate Research Scientist in the University of Iowa College of Public Health and Adjunct Associate Professor in the Department of Anthropology and the Department of Community and Behavioral Health. His current research focuses on community-based health initiatives and on the cultural and biological identification and adaptation of populations.

CHAPURUKHA M. KUSIMBA is an Associate Curator of African Archaeology and Ethnology at the Field Museum of Natural History, Chicago, and Adjunct Associate Professor of Anthropology at the University of Illinois, Chicago. His research has focused on East African archaeology, history, and ethnology. He is the author of *The Rise and Fall of Swahili States* (1997).

SIBEL BARUT KUSIMBA is an Assistant Professor of Anthropology at Lawrence University in Appleton, Wisconsin. She has carried out research on Paleolithic and historic hunter-gatherers in Kenya.

ROBERT D. LEONARD is an Associate Professor of Anthropology at the University of New Mexico. His research focuses on the prehistory of the American Southwest and Northern Mexico.

R. LEE LYMAN is Professor of Anthropology and Chairman of the Department of Anthropology at the University of Missouri-Columbia. His research interests include zooarchaeology and taphonomy, evolutionary theory, and the history of Americanist archaeological method and theory.

SCOTT MACEACHERN is Associate Professor of Anthropology at Bowdoin College. His research is particularly focused on processes of ethnic group definition and state formation during the later Iron Age in northern Cameroon and Nigeria.

MICHAEL J. O'BRIEN is Professor of Anthropology and Associate Dean in the College of Arts and Science at the University of Missouri-Columbia. His research interests include evolutionary theory, especially with respect to phylogenetic reconstruction, and its application to the analysis of the archaeological record.

PAUL ROSCOE is Professor of Anthropology at the University of Maine. His current research involves comparative projects on the societies of contact-era New Guinea, including the emergence of political complexity, warfare, and the hunters and gatherers of New Guinea.

STEPHEN J. SHENNAN is Professor of Theoretical Archaeology at the Institute of Archaeology, University College London, and Director of the AHRB Centre for the Evolutionary Analysis of Cultural Behaviour, an interdisciplinary research center linking Archaeology and Anthropology at

University College London and Archaeology at the University of Southampton. His research is focused on the application of evolutionary method and theory to archaeological problems, especially in the prehistory of Europe.

DEAN R. SNOW is Professor and Head of the Department of Anthropology at the Pennsylvania State University. He is best known for his past work in Iroquoian archaeology, but his recent work has come to focus on broader demographic issues relating population size and ecological constraints in the Eastern Woodlands and elsewhere. His current work makes use of geographic information systems (GIS) technology.

JAMES STEELE is a Lecturer in Archaeology at the University of Southampton, in England. His current research interests include the evolution of the human brain and language capacity, and demographic models of human dispersals.

JOHN EDWARD TERRELL is Curator of Oceanic Archaeology and Ethnology at Field Museum of Natural History and Adjunct Professor of Anthropology, University of Illinois, Chicago. Since the late 1980s, his research has focused on the anthropology, geomorphology, biodiversity, and prehistory of the Sepik coast of northern New Guinea. He has been writing about ecological, biogeographical, and Darwinian research strategies and models in archaeology and anthropology since the mid-1960s.

TODD L. VANPOOL is a Doctoral Candidate at the University of New Mexico. His research has focused on the archaeology of northwestern Mexico and southern New Mexico, and evolutionary approaches to archaeology.

BRUCE WINTERHALDER is Professor of Anthropology and Chair of the Curriculum in Ecology at the University of North Carolina, Chapel Hill. When not analyzing the foraging mode of production with behavioral ecology models, he conducts research on agro-ecology in the Andes of southern Peru. He currently is working on a book-length analysis of hunter-gatherer ecology and economy.